GILBERT & GEORGE

A PORTRAIT

GILBERT & GEORGE

A PORTRAIT

DANIEL FARSON

HarperCollins*Publishers*

HarperCollins*Publishers*
77–85 Fulham Palace Road,
Hammersmith, London W6 8JB

Published by HarperCollins*Publishers* 1999

9 8 7 6 5 4 3 2 1

A catalogue record for this book is
available from the British Library

ISBN 0 00 255857 2

Set in Postscript Joanna with Frutiger Light display by
Rowland Phototypesetting Ltd,
Bury St Edmunds, Suffolk

Printed and bound in Great Britain by
Caledonian International Book Manufacturing Ltd, Glasgow

CONTENTS

(All photographs of works by Gilbert & George: Prudence Cuming Associates)

BLACK AND WHITE

Between pages 48 and 49

George's mother, Hermione Ernestine

Gilbert's mother, Cecilia

Gilbert carving Madonnas in his father's workshop

Gilbert in San Martino, the village in the Dolomites where he grew up

George and friends on their way to the annual carnival in Totnes

Gilbert with other students at the Kunstakademie in Munich

George with other students at Dartington Hall School, photographed by Don McCullin for the *Observer*

George demonstrating his spinning painting at the art school of Oxford Technical College

A moment of relaxation on the roof of St Martin's School of Art, London, spring 1968

With *Design for Foreheads*, worn during 1969 and 1970

Off to send Charcoal Sculptures to a Paris group exhibition, outside the artists' home and studio in Fournier Street, 1970

With Anthony d'Offay, c.1972

With Illeana Sonnabend at the Musée nationale d'art moderne, Centre Georges Pompidou, Paris, 1981

In the Market Café, Fournier Street, December 1991 (photo: *Vincent Knapp*)

In Moscow with Daniel Farson, 1990

Between pages 80 and 81

David Robilliard (photo: Gilbert & George)
Stainton Forrest (photo: Daniel Farson)
In Tiananmen Square, Beijing, September 1993 (photo: Bernhard Widmann)
Outside the National Art Gallery, Beijing (photo: Keith Davey)
Beijing
On the Great Wall
In a Beijing restaurant with Raymond O'Daly, Yu Yi-Gang and James Birch
Opening of The China Exhibition at The Art Museum, Shanghai, October 1993
Shitty Naked Human World, Kunstmuseum, Wolfsburg, Germany, 1994
In New York at the time of The Fundamental Pictures exhibition, 1997
In Stockholm for the exhibition at Magasin 3, 1997
Brick Lane, London, 1997
With Daniel Farson in Appledore, Devon, 1997

COLOUR

Between pages 144 and 145

Retrospective exhibition at the Solomon R. Guggenheim Museum, New York, 1985
The Sexual Pictures (1982–83), Kunsthalle, Basle, Switzerland, 1986
The Naked Shit Pictures, South London Gallery, 1995
The Fundamental Pictures, Sonnabend Gallery, New York, 1997
The Fundamental Pictures, Lehmann Maupin Gallery, New York, 1997
Retrospective exhibition at ARC Musée d'art moderne de la Ville de Paris, 1997
George the Cunt & Gilbert the Shit magazine sculpture (1969)
Charcoal on paper sculpture (1970)
Bloody Life No. 3 (1975)
Henry Ainley postcard sculpture (1970)
The Singing Sculpture (1991) (photo: Jon & Anne Abbott)

Cunt Scum (1977)
Fallen Leaves (1980)
Four Knights (1980)
Living with Madness (1980)
Stream (1980)

Between pages 176 and 177

Coming (1983)
Shitted (1983)
Death (1984)
Hope (1984)
Life (1984)
Fear (1984)
We (1983)
The Wall (1986)
Flow (1987)
Here (1987)
Tears (1987)
One World (1988)
Shag (1988)
Coloured People (1989)
Eight Shits (1994)
Human (1994)
Ill World (1994)
Naked Eye (1994)
Blood and Piss (1996)
Lavatory (1996)
Piss on Us (1996)

EDITOR'S NOTE

Gilbert & George were a logical choice of subject for Dan Farson as a follow-up to his acclaimed 1993 book *The Gilded Gutter Life of Francis Bacon*. Both Bacon and G&G are frequently identified by art writers as belonging to a line of British visionaries stretching back to William Blake. G&G's notoriety – like Bacon's, or even Jack the Ripper's (another of Farson's subjects) – seems particularly suited to his sometimes irreverent style of appraisal and description. Farson often reveals the prosaic reality behind myth; yet none of his biographical subjects was more severely scrutinised than himself in his 1997 autobiography *Never a Normal Man*, in which his revelations are both appalling and endearing. Similarly, Gilbert & George have said that they 'humiliate' themselves in their pictures (most recently by exhibiting works in which they appear naked with brightly coloured excrement, urine, blood and sperm) so that they can beat the critics to it. This common ground between biographer and subject was helped, no doubt, by their immediate camaraderie and mutual affection.

Gilbert & George: A Portrait was originally intended by Farson to be a full biography of the artists, whose qualification to be considered as one subject is sustained by their unique artistic partnership, singular in its purpose and direction. Challenging territory for any biographer. In the end, however, Farson was cheated not by his subject, but by time. The manuscript he completed shortly before his death in November 1997 is indeed the most comprehensive account to date of both Gilbert's and George's separate early years, largely the fruit of a visit by G&G to Farson's Devon home. But he never had the opportunity to discuss the artists' subsequent years with them in such detail. What remains is an entertaining and insightful portrait of Gilbert & George, based primarily on Farson's personal experiences with the artists since he met them in 1989.

In 1990 Farson accompanied Gilbert & George to their exhibition in Russia, and chronicled this experience in his book *With Gilbert & George in Moscow*. (At the time this was only the second ever exhibition in the Soviet Union by a living Western artist: the first was by Francis Bacon.) Moscow was the first of many travels Farson made with the artists between 1990 and 1997, visiting their exhibitions in Shanghai, New York, Paris and Stockholm. All of these excursions are recorded in detail in this book, as are the controversies surrounding The Naked Shit Pictures exhibition in London in 1996 and an assessment of the critical debate on G&G's work on both sides of the Atlantic.

Farson was meticulous, if old-school, in his research and note-taking, though he never used a tape recorder to interview those who have known or worked with Gilbert & George, including myself. During the summer of 1997 he and I had several meetings to discuss this book, as well as my own collaboration with G&G on a collection of their writings and interviews, which Thames & Hudson and I published later that year (*The Words of Gilbert & George*). Dan and I had been acquainted since the Moscow exhibition, but did not know each other well. I looked forward to this opportunity to know him better, which he made especially enjoyable by insisting we always meet in Soho over breakfast, the time of day at which he would be most alert. (Mischievously, Dan would empty nips of vodka into his orange juice from time to time, and at 11 a.m. would suggest a move to the Coach and Horses – an invitation not always declined.) During the months that followed, parcels flew back and forth between us. I last saw him in early October, for the opening of Gilbert & George's retrospective exhibition in Paris. He was not well, as was apparent in his growing impatience with the media circus and the large crowds which thronged the exhibition. Nevertheless, soon after he returned from Paris he finished his manuscript.

Following Dan's death, I was asked by his publishers to oversee the final preparation of the book for publication. In this I have been greatly assisted by Gilbert & George themselves, who have checked the accuracy of facts, names, dates and much more, in the most scrupulous fashion. They have also generously provided a selection of personal photographs, many of which are published here for the first time. Their cooperation and openness have been invaluable. Robert Lacey, who also worked with Dan on his autobiography, revised the manuscript with great care and sensitivity. Richard Johnson at HarperCollins, Bill Hamilton at the A.M. Heath Agency, and Karen Lamey, Dan's close friend and the executor of his estate, have been equally determined to see this book published, and I am grateful to them for the invitation to become involved.

Robert Violette
December 1998

WITH GILBERT & GEORGE

It's a tricky business writing about your friends. In the past, almost subconsciously, I have been so anxious to be impartial that I have often praised my enemies and denigrated those I like. This was misguided prejudice against the very people to whom I should be more than fair.

Determined to avoid that pitfall in this book, I should declare that I have grown to love the phenomenon that is Gilbert & George. They are the most unusual couple I know, and it would be all too easy to take advantage of their foibles. Though self-contained they are vulnerable. Like many who draw attention to themselves, they are sensitive to criticism. Like a few who try to be eccentric, they are genuinely so. They are the politest people I know, and I have witnessed this in Moscow, Shanghai and New York as they accept the compliments of strangers with infinite grace – 'How kind!' 'Extraordinary!' 'Very sweet!' – while I followed in their royal wake.

Few artists have backed into the limelight with such discretion, yet their skill in introducing their work to a large public is unequalled, and is largely based on their own calculation rather than that of a gallery. Indefatigable travellers – 'We don't care about such things,' said Gilbert when I sympathised about a punishing flight to Tokyo in 1997 – they have attended their exhibitions across the world, from Cracow to Shanghai, making them among the most internationally famous artists. It has cost them plenty: the exhibitions in Russia (1991) and China (1993) were sponsored by themselves and the Anthony d'Offay Gallery, and not a picture was for sale. 'We didn't want to sell,' said George. 'The pictures would have ended up destroyed.' Conversely, the Japanese are keen art collectors, and Gilbert told me with pride that their books are best-sellers in the art shops. What they are doing is simple and effective: by ploughing the profits back they are building for the future. With their special rapport with students, enhanced by their personal appearance, they have secured a future generation of admirers.

Do they set out to shock? They would deny it, but of course they do, starting as far back as their 1969 'magazine sculpture', which shows George with a sweep of hair while Gilbert's falls blackly over his forehead. The words 'GEORGE THE CUNT' and 'GILBERT THE SHIT' are pinned in paper letters to their suits. Both wear ties and have roses in their lapels, and are grinning happily. The words are instantly forgotten: the initial shock turns to an impression of disarming innocence.

I first saw an exhibition of Gilbert & George's pictures at the Anthony d'Offay Gallery in London in 1989, the For AIDS exhibition, when they and d'Offay donated the profits to charities connected with AIDS. I recoiled. I did not like the work, but its impact lived with me for days, and I went back to see it again. Having watched their progress over the years, I have seen them experimenting and exploring in many directions – from their Singing Sculpture in 1969, with themselves as the exhibit, up to the scandalous Naked Shit Pictures at the South London Gallery in Peckham in 1995 and The Fundamental Pictures in New York in 1997, when I spent most of the time in their company, one of the most stimulating experiences of my life.

Scandalous? Undoubtedly. In 1995 they tried to test the climate by putting two Naked Shit pictures into a group exhibition at London's Serpentine Gallery, a public space situated in Kensington Gardens. When one of the pictures was refused they wrote to the director, Julia Peyton-Jones, expressing their 'horror and deep distress'. They succeeded in partially reversing the ban, with the offending pictures (which included *Bum Holes*) replaced by two different Naked Shit pictures. I remember seeing them at the private view of this group show, Take Me I'm Yours, of which they were the stars, and the subject-matter of their work seemed entirely irrelevant. They were satisfied by the public's response, and went ahead with the show in Peckham, which was greeted with both reverence and fury – not a bad combination.

I am still smiling over a conversation which their German biographer Wolf Jahn overheard in a New York restaurant at the time of their Fundamental Pictures exhibition in 1997. Two collectors, probably a husband and wife, had just been to see the two exhibitions, and discussed which picture they wanted to buy, in rather loud voices.

'I like *Piss, Piss, Piss*,' declared the woman.

'So do I,' said the man, 'but I prefer *Spit on Shit*.'

Unaware that the couple were referring to pictures, I gather that the diners fell very quiet. On hearing this story, Gilbert & George were delighted.

CHAPTER ONE

GEORGE IN
THE WEST COUNTRY

George was born in Plymouth on 8 January 1942. As the city, which was an important naval base, was being targeted by the German bombers, a local aristocrat, Lord Mildmay, invited pregnant women to stay in the greater safety of his home on the outskirts called Flete. George's mother was suitably grateful, christening her son Flete George Charles. Each morning Lord Mildmay came round to see if the ladies were all right, and after the births he presented each of them with an engraving of Flete – George has his to this day.

He has a brother, Alec, two years older: 'A vicar, rather a cranky one, Evangelical, converted by Billy Graham in the 1950s.'

Were you converted?

'Not for a single second!'

The two shared a room until George was fifteen, and his brother was appalled by 'all the dirty stuff' he mumbled in his sleep.

What sort of dirty stuff?

'How should I know? I was asleep.'

George does not remember his father: 'Maybe he left us before

I was born. No memory. I was not allowed to say "Dad" or "Daddy" at home.' But at the age of twenty-one he tracked him down at an address in Devon, which he remembered seeing on an old postcard: Rose Cottage, Dulverton. Sure enough, it proved to be a cottage with roses round the door, which was opened by a woman who told him that her husband was in the pub down the road. 'I was shaking when I went into the crowded bar, and he was pointed out. "I have something to say. Please can we go into the other bar?"' The man told him impatiently to state what he wanted. After several unsuccessful attempts to persuade the man to see him on his own, George came out with it: 'My name is George, and I think I'm your son.' His father immediately put down his darts – 'Good God. Let's go to the other bar.'

This was traumatic for George, especially when he realised that his father had no wish to see him again, though he claimed to have sent money to the family until George was fifteen – 'I knew nothing about that.'

By an extraordinary coincidence, George's father was 'saved' two years later by an Evangelical vicar who turned out to be his first son.

'Jesus has brought the family together,' his brother informed George pontifically.

'I did that two years ago!'

When George revealed his secret mission, his brother told him he should never have done it. George has not seen his father since.

It sounds as if his father behaved badly in deserting the family, but there is another side to the story. 'He had come back from the trenches,' George explained, as if he were referring to the First rather than to the Second World War, 'and he was appalled to hear the enormous gossip surrounding his wife.' This was a time when gossip ruled a small West Country community. Hermione Ernestine was a free spirit, and her influence on George is invaluable – 'She's had three marriages and lots of gentlemen – and me!' She was hard-working, protective of her sons and determined that they should better themselves. She was determined to maintain standards, while dismaying the neighbours with the succession of gentleman admirers. This was regarded as outrageous at the time, particularly in the West County, which is renowned for petty intolerance. Like many of those who defy convention, she could be conventional in her wish to be thought puritanical, and was furious when the journalist Lynn Barber referred to her as 'tarty' in a 1991 profile, quoting Gilbert. George reassured her that this was a 'modern' compliment meaning 'youthful', which placated her. But when he brought Gilbert to stay in the 1960s, when he was twenty-six and Hermione in her early fifties, he would not allow him to stay under the same roof.

Whyever not? I asked.

'For obvious reasons,' said George.

'She was a very powerful lady,' Gilbert explained. 'She's very clever. Very interfering. A very big love-hate relationship.'

With you?

'Don't ask! I don't think she was very approving of me.'

George: 'It was difficult for her to explain to her friends and family that her son had brought a gentleman rather than a lady. But she's mellowed: every Christmas she sends me a shirt; for the last few years she's enclosed a tie for Gilbert.'

Gilbert: 'Suspicious of me? I don't know. Maybe it was because I was foreign.'

George: 'She was one of the first women locally to be divorced. She had to bring up two children on her own, and when she returned from the divorce court in Exeter and the neighbours came out to look, she cried out, "Chain them up, girls! I'm a free woman now." Very rare in those days, for that class.'

Ironically, she sounds as Italian as Gilbert – one can imagine her portrayed in a film by Anna Magnani.

Because of the Blitz the family – including George's maternal grandparents – were evacuated to Totnes, which George thinks of as his home town. 'Working as a waitress, and a dozen other jobs, my mother was absent for much of the time, and because there was no father I stayed with my grandmother. When my grandmother was ill, I worried, "What will happen to us if she dies?"'

Was it a poor childhood?

'I'd say so, but we thought we were better off than anyone else and they were worse off. Always brought up to be better. My mother wanted my brother and me to be different.'

She certainly succeeded in your case, I thought, as George told me this.

'It was not snobbery, but betterment. I wore white ankle-socks and shoes, while the other boys wore boots. If it wasn't for those conspicuous ankle-socks, I'd still be in Totnes!'

George and his brother were sent for elocution lessons with an elderly theatrical gentleman who told them: 'If you join the Navy they take your trousers down and paint your cock blue.' Presumably this gave the old boy some sexual gratification: 'He made advances, but they were not alarming, just friendly. There was always just one of us in the room.' As well as enunciating 'How now brown cow?', the theatrical gentleman was an amateur poet who printed his own verse in volumes such as *Dart, Loveliest of Rivers, and Other Poems*. The house was filled with dried beech leaves and peacock feathers.

If Magnani could have played George's mother, Tennessee Williams could have written much of the script. 'We had so many "uncles": Uncle Tom, Uncle Ben, Uncle Bob, and one of the Fathers from Buckfast Abbey. When a fun fair came to town, for example, mother would befriend one of the workers, who might come back to the house. Or if a man laid a carpet in a house where she was working, he might also become a friend.'

Was she notorious?

'She was well known for her admirers, including one of my schoolteachers.'

The setting for this hurly-burly, a flat right in the heart of Totnes, was suitably stark: one room with gas stove and sink, another where the three of them slept; a third, unfinished and damp, was only used for the chamber pot. The shared lavatory was a hundred yards down a passageway. 'We never had pets. As a working mother she couldn't have them.' I pointed out that George and his brother could have looked after one. Surprised, he replied, 'We never thought of that. It was rather a middle-class thing to have pets, and we knew we were lower-class. We could peer into other people's homes and see another way of life, with bookshelves.' Perhaps to compensate, George bought books from an early age – the usual boys' favourites, such as R. M. Ballantyne's *The Coral Island* ('I had a crush on Rolf, the effeminate one, but I never talked sex to my brother Alec') and *The Gorilla Hunters*.

George was anxious to get away. 'I wanted to escape from the poverty of the time,' he told Wolf Jahn. 'At home, everything was very run-down. There was never any money, nobody had a nice piece of furniture, nobody had a radio that worked. We had no bathrooms, there was no lavatory in the house, there was no hot water in the house, there was no heating, we had gas lighting. I always remember, when I first went to school, there was a horrible smell in the classrooms, and it was the boys shitting in their trousers. And that was because it was the first time the poor boys ever had a proper meal. They had school dinners, that big meal of stew and apple pie and custard and things they weren't used to. They didn't know how to leave the classroom, so they were shitting in their trousers. And that was the kind of immediate post-war poverty that I disliked so intensely.'

George enjoyed the local school, but he had to leave it at the age of fifteen: 'I didn't know I was leaving. I just didn't think like that. My mother's sister Barbara arranged a job for me in the best shop in town: a bookseller, stationer, various gifts. It was owned by Thomas Spink, who had bought two shops when he left the army, one in Kingsbridge, the other in Totnes, and fitted them out in the grand style.'

Was George's aunt perceptive in procuring him this 'superior' job?

'Yes, I think so. Barbara was superior. Her husband was a cattle auctioneer, quite grand, and when we stayed with her we had treats from the farmers, like Devonshire cream and fruit.'

He looked amazed when I asked if his mother ever made jam.

'Never, not at all! She wasn't a countrified person.'

Gilbert: 'She was bombastic and looked down on people who did something like that, thought it old-fashioned. She wanted to be modern.'

Was she a modern woman? It sounds like it.

George: 'Without a doubt. She wasn't interested in the church, whereas the rest of the family were.'

Gilbert: 'Unusual for the time.'

George: 'And then to be remarried. Bad enough to be divorced.'

They were on the bus from Paignton on the way home from their weekly outing – 'My mother always took us somewhere nice.'

Gilbert snorted with impatience: 'Had to dress up and be bloody different!'

Ignoring this, George continued: 'On this day a sailor appeared on the upper deck of the bus. He had boils on his neck, and a cap with the tally-badge "HMS *Minesweeper*". They got talking and he ended up in our house, and they got married.'

This was Uncle Bob, who would be a new influence: 'He was interested in drawing, model-making, writing short stories, one of which was published in *Esquire*.' As *Esquire* was a prestigious magazine, this was a considerable achievement. He also made garden ornaments with popular inscriptions like:

> A wise old owl sat in an oak
> The more he heard the less he spoke,
> The less he spoke the more he heard,
> Oh, why not follow that wise old bird?

George laughed as he remembered, for this is very much his sort of humour today. 'I was very fond of him.'

With the puritanical streak of the badly-behaved, George's

mother strongly disapproved of Uncle Bob's excessive drinking. 'One night there was an enormous row and they went to a pub, and I think they became tipsy. There was a lot of banging about, and an ambulance came to take her to hospital. No idea what happened. Never found out. Next day I saw her in hospital and she was very ill. All she could say was, "The fish, the fish." Perhaps that was it: Uncle Bob loved fish, but she'd never cook it for him because of the smell, but that night she had. Because of the row they never ate it, and she might have worried that the stove was still on.'

When she came out of hospital she threw all Uncle Bob's belongings into the front garden to be collected. George never saw him again. 'Aunt Barbara told us not to worry, but we were a little worried and sad, though quite prepared. It didn't come as the shock it might have been in a middle-class family.'

You took her side?

'No question of that. My brother and I had big arguments as to who was going to marry Mummy when we grew up. She had married very young, still a teenager when I was born and still *very glamorous* . . .'

Gilbert: 'I never looked that close!'

I asked if George loved her.

'Oh yes, we love Mother.'

'I think she was very protective then,' Gilbert conceded, though I sense he meant over-protective.

George was already painting when Uncle Bob was there, and after the night's battle he completed a picture showing the row, which he called *The Estrangement*. It was shown in a local annual art exhibition at Birdwood House in Totnes and favourably mentioned in the *Totnes Times*, a cutting which George has kept. In view of the fracas it depicted, was George embarrassed when his mother saw the painting on public display?

'Not that I remember.'

Despite the turbulence and comparative discomfort, George's was a happy childhood, thanks to his mother's resilience. 'Without doubt! We were very privileged. Granddad had a car, a fine Jowett, and none of the other boys had a car in the family. He'd been a drummer boy in the Boer War, lied about his age, worried at the medical because he had no pubic hair. We only knew what Granny told us about the war, and the First War too, for he never talked about it. A lot of that generation were so horrified by war they kept it private. In the First War he was on a ship as a marine bandsman which was torpedoed. When his best friend was rescued from drowning, his hair had turned white.' George's grandfather was Scottish, named Raeburn, and a book of Sir Henry Raeburn's pictures was kept in the house, with the implication that they might have been related, though George doubts this.

Gilbert frowned: 'Maybe it *is* true?'

George continued: 'Granddad was very old and very grumpy; he had an ulcer, we used to hide away from him.'

Were you close to your brother, frequently on your own?

'As small children, yes. Not after he was converted as a teenager.'

Gilbert: (contemptuously) 'Religion!'

George: 'He worked as an apprentice electrician, went round with glass accumulators to all the houses.'

At the age of sixteen George started night classes in painting and pottery at Dartington Hall – a turning point. It is characteristic of George's luck that Dartington Hall School, the one ideal place for him, was so close to his home that he could have walked there – and did, every evening, a distance of two miles to the adult education centre.

Founded in 1926 by Leonard and Dorothy Elmhirst, Dartington was a progressive co-educational school backed by considerable money. Elmhirst was a Yorkshireman who worked his way to America, where he studied agriculture at Cornell University and met his future wife, Dorothy Whitney Straight, a wealthy young widow with three children, which is one reason why Dartington was co-educational. Her father was a well-known financier, who had served as Secretary of the Navy under President Cleveland. She remembered: 'My father died in 1904, leaving me at the age of seventeen with an independent fortune. The fact that I inherited money at an early age led me to feel that I was economically privileged and that wealth entailed social responsibility.'

In due course the Elmhirsts created a community rather than just a school, but their dreams of an educational Utopia were ridiculed at the time as cranky and sexually abandoned – 'a sort of nudist colony, free love and all that', as one misguided critic described it. Despite the scandal it attracted, Dartington survived, and its reputation became legendary. By the 1930s, parents of its pupils included Bertrand and Dora Russell, Aldous Huxley, the architect Clough Williams-Ellis and the publisher Victor Gollancz. The setting was beautiful, standing beside the River Dart in a hall first mentioned in the registers of 833. The building was derelict when the Elmhirsts took it over, and they poured in their money to restore and expand it – a cause of grievance to the local farmers because of the better wages they paid their labourers. But the Elmhirsts' real offence was personal: they did not hunt or fish or pay social visits; their politics were 'leftish', and some of the staff were socialists, agnostics, even pacifists. Worst of all were the artists and foreigners the place attracted, who spoke strangely and struck unconventional attitudes.

Dartington Hall was perfect for George. 'One day my tutor, Ivor Weeks, said, "Why don't you become a full-time student?" It had never occurred to me that I could become a proper art student, because of the money, I suppose. "I'll talk to Leonard Elmhirst," he promised.'

George's own description of Dartington is of a Rural Redevelopment Movement devoted to cider-making, wood-carving and forestry, with a textile studio, model farm and school. The Elmhirsts' aim was to create a self-contained community which trained the young by giving them freedom of choice, an antidote to the rigid discipline of most English boarding schools.

Photographs in Victor Bonham-Carter's *Dartington Hall: The History of an Experiment* show the scale of the undertaking, made possible by Mrs Elmhirst's fortune: landscaped gardens with stone steps; a Poultry Service Building the size of a small mansion; large nursery gardens; and a magnificent farmstead with a pristine modern cowyard. All rural movements sound fey, but Dartington's worked, though Lucian Freud, an earlier student in 1937, exploited the permissiveness to skip classes and ride the school horses, a passion which led to the fantasy of becoming a jockey and the reality of his only known sculpture, a sandstone carving made when he was fourteen and revealing formidable strength. He was soon moved to the more conventional school Bryanston.

Luck is partly being in the right place at the right moment, and George realised this, seizing on the idea of becoming a full-time student: 'A college to remember – an idea of an ideal society. The model farm was hi-tech, there was also a theatre and a string quartet. In the art school there were probably only ten students, very select, and I was the only person with a grant.'

Revealing his knowledge of George's upbringing, Gilbert added: 'All the others were from well-off families, and paid. George was the exception, taken in as an outsider.' Speaking with fraternal pride, he mentioned that when Lynn Barber wrote her profile for the *Independent Magazine* in October 1991, she promised one of their works would appear on the cover; but when they saw it they thought, 'No. It's Morandi' (an Italian still-life painter, 1890–1964). But it was, as they quickly realised, an early George. 'And the stupid bastards at the *Independent* framed it in a fake cheap gilt frame,' said Gilbert, 'which of course no paintings had at the time.' As for the comparison with Morandi: 'He [George] did some beautiful paintings, some like William Scott, semi-abstract.'

Was George happy after he gave up his job at the shop and became a student at Dartington?

'Absolutely! An amazing time. Dartington was always in the newspapers due to scandals, but it was very positive also.' Older than the other students, George can be seen in a photograph by the young Don McCullin for a 1960 feature on the school in the *Observer*. It was assumed that the two years he spent there would lead to his acceptance by the Bath Academy of Art, a teacher training college in Corsham, where Howard Hodgkin was one of the tutors: 'Ivor Weeks, the one who believed in me when I did art-school classes, thought I should become an art school teacher myself.' Weeks assumed that teaching was George's vocation, and so did George, who took this step for granted. Everyone from the art class in Dartington who wanted to go to Corsham always got in. To everyone's amazement, especially George's, he was rejected. Mortified and bewildered, he thought bitterly of the less talented 'twerpy' girls who had sailed through, leaving him stranded. Had there been a mistake? What had gone wrong?

Ivor Weeks was also shocked that his best student had been rejected, and contacted Corsham, whose explanation was unequivocal: 'Maybe this person will be an artist, but certainly not a teacher.'

George was thrilled: 'I was extremely flattered, for this was a big moment for me. Ivor had believed in me, but I had never thought of myself as an artist until that moment. It was the most encouraging rejection I could have had.'

Ivor Weeks remembers George as a floppy-fair-haired boy: 'An amazing boy, remarkable in his work, still at secondary modern school, living in Totnes where his brother used to keep him awake at night by turning the pages of the Bible. Early in the 1960s he became a full-time student when we started our art department, one of the first students.'

Was he primarily a painter at this stage?

'Yes. When he left he gathered all the paintings together. He valued them greatly, but I believe most were destroyed in a fire. Dartington held a small exhibition of Gilbert & George photo-pieces in 1978, following a visit to them in Fournier Street which was absolutely empty except for two chairs.'

George used to babysit for Weeks's four children, whom he entertained with his fantasies of becoming a 'super tramp'. He once invited him to his home in the council house, where his mother served the food but did not eat with them.

Asking about George's rejection by Corsham, where Weeks had been a teacher, he explained: 'At that time they required a certain number of O-levels and A-levels, and George only had a couple. I had great faith in him; I thought he was remarkable. Partly due to my Corsham background, I recognised the naive quality of his work, which I admired.'

But Weeks admitted to Lynn Barber, 'To have demanded normal art student behaviour would have been disastrous – I protected him from the other students . . . There was a hint of strangeness, I didn't go into it. Everything he did was interesting, his special qualities had been ignored at school, full of intriguing stories. His art was so different and peculiar – it didn't seem to come from anywhere. It seemed naive or primitive, but incredibly detailed and well-observed. I remember one still life of jewellery – an unusual subject for the late fifties – and it had a feeling of loving care, a bit like Morandi.' Though Weeks doubted if George had even heard of Morandi. He regrets he did not buy any of his pupil's work, but the music teacher at Dartington, Heather Williams, bought the still life reproduced on the cover of the *Independent Magazine*, for £2.10s.

After George's failure to gain a place at Corsham, he felt there was only one course of action open to him: to leave Devon, to get out. With a small suitcase he hitch-hiked to London, where he had been only once before. 'The world I was brought up in was totally different from the world today – very isolated. I'd never left my home county until I was twenty.'

Adversity is the spur of life, and George's Corsham rejection was fortunate – indeed, I flinch at the thought of him as a schoolteacher. In London he got work immediately, serving behind the china counter at Selfridge's by day and as a barman at the popular Players Theatre in The Strand in the evening. He saw an advertisement in the *Evening Standard*, 'and a very nice queer head barman took me on'. In the raucous, mock music hall reconstruction, it was his job to enter the stage with a tankard of beer, which he placed on the rostrum to the cheers of the audience, who knew the show was about to start, with the moustachioed Master of Ceremonies making his entrance a few moments later. George became part of the troupe, and was in his element – though his mother was unenthusiastic, as she had been when he left the shop in Totnes to study at Dartington: 'She thought that art was not for me, because I wore glasses. Or maybe because it was less reliable.'

Gilbert: 'He was always a bit of a show-off, a bit of a dandy – you can see it in every photograph. In a school photograph there he was in the middle of the children, like a teacher. That was George. He became a Master of Ceremonies himself, drinking, smoking and misbehaving for the first time.' Belatedly, George was relishing the rebelliousness of youth. Though the exaggerated mannerisms of the MC with his gavel were a travesty of genuine music hall, where the turns were announced simply by a change of number on the side of the stage, the Players was fun, and the splendid old songs and lyrics attracted a fairly posh crowd. The theatre was plagued by spiders, which the bar staff did their best to eliminate. George was entranced one evening when a grand, bejewelled 'lady' sat down at the bar and one of her long false eyelashes fell off. 'Sorry about that, madam,' apologised the head barman, thinking it was another spider and sweeping it into the bin.

Then there was a change of direction which was so surprising that it seems as if someone else's chapter had been included by mistake: George became the nanny to a small boy whose mother had gone to Africa. This startling development began when he arranged to meet a girl he had studied with at Dartington, who was now at the Central School of Art in London. One of her friends was the wife of an anthropologist. She was about to go to Africa for a year, and was worried about their ten-year-old son, who would be staying at home in Oxford. These progressive parents did not want a conventional nanny, but someone more 'professional', and asked George if he would like to look after the boy. George accepted. His duties included cooking the boy's breakfast, taking him to school, collecting him in the afternoon and preparing dinner.

Gilbert: 'He thinks that was the best time of his life.'

George: 'It was a lovely time. They were well-off with a lovely house and garden.'

How close was he to the boy?

'Tremendous friends!' G&G laughed exuberantly. Tempted? (More laughter.)

'No, I don't think he was, but very close.'

Did he miss London?

'No, but I've just remembered that I came back one afternoon to find the school had broken up early. He'd drunk a quantity of cider, but in fact it was sherry and he and his friends were completely drunk, hitting the tame rabbits gently with golf clubs.'

The boy, Francis Barber, is married today, and still sees George occasionally.

When Francis's mother returned, George went to the art school of Oxford Technical College (which had nothing to do with the university). He still thought of himself as an artist, 'But never a normal student: the others at Dartington were middle-class girls; it was more of a finishing school for them. I doubt if I painted seriously that first year – just dabbling.'

He loved Oxford so much that he stayed on at the art school for a year. Then, in his mid-twenties, came another 'amazing piece of luck'. He was in London for the day, and was walking down Charing Cross Road when he bumped into a Portuguese teacher who had been at the art school in Oxford. He invited George to see the St Martin's School of Art.

'"Where is it?"'

'"Here! We're right outside." He took me to the top where the art school was and introduced me to the Principal, Frank Martin, the creator of the famous sculpture department. Amazing! I believe

I was highly regarded as a student at Oxford, so it is possible that the Portuguese, Waldemar D'Oray, thought it would be a feather in his cap and an asset to the course if I joined. When we left he turned to me in the lift and smiled: "That's fine! He's accepted you for the course." I had no idea.'

And that is how George arrived at St Martin's School of Art in 1965. Gilbert joined him there two years later, as if it were destined, the two moving irresistibly in the same direction.

CHAPTER TWO

GILBERT IN
THE DOLOMITES

G ilbert was born in the small village of San Martino in the Italian Dolomites on 17 September 1943. This area was alien to the rest of Italy. They even spoke a different language – Ladino: 'I don't feel Italian, but I love Italy.'

The family house was right in the village, and Gilbert's father was the fourth generation of shoemakers. 'My grandfather lived on the first floor and we were on the second floor, with the workshop on the ground floor. My father made very good shoes, lost all his money but very proud of his shoes. I have three sisters and one brother – I was the second. Mother was a cook for a big family who worked in Verona for a time and then in a German-speaking town very near us. I learnt German and Italian at school, but Ladino is my real language; not a dialect, but an extremely old language going back before the Romans. I had a very happy childhood, always extremely busy, more than now, doing everything, but all the time painting, wood-carving, making sculptures.'

Gilbert's early interest in wood-carving was true to the alpine traditions of the district, but he also had a love of science and an interest in electricity. Also, more surprisingly, singing: 'The vicar wanted me to be the organist; always after me. I had to sing soprano with all the women. Looking back, he was just a big queen!' But Gilbert was bad at languages: he had a problem visualising words, and a habit of forgetting numbers. 'There's always one missing or added,' George confirms.

Gilbert's passion for art started at an early age, when he was six or seven: 'For a time there was nothing else. My uncle was doing some small oil paintings, very artistic, very clever. He had some sort of bone cancer, three years in hospital at Venice and then Cortina near us, where he started to paint, but all that finished with the Second World War.'

His father was exasperated by Gilbert's constant changes of direction, berating his mother, who was highly ambitious for her son: 'What do you want to do with this boy? Every day it's something different.'

The rules and taboos were rigid in this remote community close to the Carnic Alps and the Austrian border. Gilbert's father had a sense of humour, but it was reserved for his friends rather than for his family. 'I was rather frightened of him, always hiding behind my mother.' As in most households, his father drank with his friends on Sundays while the women cooked.

Did you love him?

'No.'

Did you love her?

'Yes. Later we got on much better. He didn't have much money but she had some of her own, a woodland she was allowed to sell which she had inherited from her father. This meant that we were sent to special schools.'

As a child, Gilbert's mother suffered from heart trouble, and was often ill: 'When she was eighty-three the doctor said she had such a strong heart he was unable to kill her.'

George: 'I think I met her twice – very pleasant.'

Compared to the claustrophobic atmosphere of Totnes, Gilbert was surrounded by the inspiration of snow, mountains and swirling rivers. On Sundays he would accompany his father when he fished for trout. But art was the one thing that mattered to him – he always wanted to go to art school. When he was fourteen his mother took him over the mountains into the next valley, to Wolkenstein. The village had a wood-carving tradition that went back for hundreds of years, now devoted to Madonnas for American and German churches, and to cute little Bambis sold in shops all over the world. Its art school was entirely based on wood-carving.

Gilbert stayed with an old, childless couple, and became like their son – 'They were crying when I left after three years.' Self-supportive, he made Bambis, cribs, animals, sheep and small Madonnas in the evenings. His ideal was Michelangelo.

In 1959, at the age of seventeen, Gilbert experienced a twist of fate remarkably close to George's at Dartington: 'Normally if you do three years at art school, you went to a special school in Florence or Venice to become an art teacher. But that summer some Austrian professors stayed in our village and became friends with the new vicar, who was very artistic and had been to the Munich Academy. They decided together that I should not go south and instead arranged for me to go to art school in Hallein, near Salzburg. It was a difficult time for me, because I had to speak German for the first time. I'd learnt a little, but never spoken it before. I stayed in a Christian hostel run by nuns, part of the art school, and I accepted everything. I was alone quite a lot, the only person from a different place, and I must admit I was bullied, hanging me by my feet from a window on the fifth floor, a macho initiation.'

George: 'Tribal, sexual.'

Gilbert: 'They stripped me naked and put me in one of the metal trunks half-filled with clay.'

Why didn't he just get out?

'Not if they don't want me to.'

This was Gilbert's first unhappiness: 'I wouldn't tell anyone – not my parents – but it was difficult. I was very good at everything

I did, so the tormenting soon finished, and then the tormentor became my best friend.'

Otherwise Gilbert remembers Hallein as a pleasant medieval town, a city of salt mines. If he was lonely it is understandable, separated as he was from his family, and also because of his intrinsic nature: 'Friends? Not a lot. I never had a lot of friends. Even in the first art school, very few friends. I was always an outsider, always from another place, so there was prejudice.'

Back home there was trouble when he returned for a visit to hear his father drunkenly shouting from his room in the attic. The row was about money, and Gilbert remembers that one day there was absolutely nothing in the house, not a penny: 'My father couldn't make enough money making shoes, competing with factories.' Gilbert was glad to return to Hallein, and equally glad to leave after a year – 'I had sorted out what I wanted to do: to be loved by the nuns! I was their favourite.'

George remembers Gilbert's father admiringly: 'Very elegant, well-dressed, citified rather than countrified [he must have greeted George in his best Sunday clothes]. Very proud, a little vain, extremely nice. Gilbert's mother was much nicer to me than mine was to Gilbert.'

In spite of the problems with money there were always a lot of people in the house, and food was never a problem in the country, with a big garden. This was in the time before the onslaught of mass tourism, which Gilbert regrets, though the profits it could have brought the village would have been welcome then: 'The Dolomites are much too popular now, especially with Italians from Milano. Though I had an Italian passport, and still do, I thought of myself as Ladino.'

The way that fate reverses, Gilbert's bully at Hallein had a father in Munich with whom he would live while he studied for the Academy. 'I thought this would be very good for me, and went with him for one day to Munich and visited the Academy, and liked it. It was big enough for me! Enormous, impressive. By now bully-boy was my closest friend – very funny! He thought he was better than me at art, that's why he was a bully-boy, because he thought he was the best.'

But you were better?

'I had to send in my slides when you apply to join. A big joke – every artist sends in transparencies except for George and me. We made a point of never doing this, that's why it's a joke. I was accepted, the youngest person in the whole Academy: I wasn't even eighteen. Bully-boy was accepted as well. We had to work under a particular professor. Mine did painting and sculpture, and he took to me!' Gilbert's voice is suffused with merriment: 'I was the *superstar*, and this changed everything for the bully-boy, for I was the superior.'

How did he react?

'He became even closer. He had a girlfriend on the side, but we were always together. Heinrich *adored* me.'

Did you see him again when you left Germany?

'Once or twice. I never want to go back and keep up old friendships.'

Were you popular?

'Very! I *was*! One season I had a shaven head. As for the sculpture, it was very old-fashioned, not sensational, though we sculpted from naked models all the time.'

Was he happy?

Gilbert gave a sweeping gesture of contempt for such a compromise: 'YAH! I had my first drinking session – camaraderie. To start with I stayed yet again in a Christian hostel, then I had a room with a couple who had run away from Dresden after the bombing, with a queeny son with a high-pitched voice who danced alone in his room, and a neurotic daughter who couldn't get a man – I wasn't good enough. I was there for six years, getting an amazing grant from Germans who wanted to be friendly with Italians; I was suddenly a very rich boy. By now I spoke German. It was very nice, but at the end I felt I was not getting anywhere – the art school was too old-fashioned, too stuck in the past. I don't know of one student who emerged as an artist even though they had two thousand. So I listened to these rumours from England, that the most progressive was the St Martin's School of Art. A boy from Cardiff in one of the classes told me: "If you want to go there, I'm going to St Martin's and I'll ask for you to join." It's a very strange story – he came back and said they'd take me.'

Why?

'They were interested in foreign students. So I decided to go to England with Heinrich, who had a sister in London and a German student friend at the Camberwell School of Art. We came over in the summer, and I went to St Martin's and talked to some Jewish teachers from Russia who spoke German. Saw them on the top floor and said how excited I was. Totally mad, like a dream! I met Frank Martin, but I don't remember what he said because I couldn't speak English.' Gilbert returned to Germany for the whole summer to organise money by helping to restore churches, and moved to London in September 1967 with a big suitcase containing his life's belongings.

'"Here I am!" They didn't remember me and did not admit me at the beginning, so I just stuck there, camping out, showing my work to the professors. I think Philip King, then a very famous sculptor, got me in. Such a big problem for a foreign student with a £150 fee, and I only had £300 for the whole year. But I paid. Extraordinary that they took me up! They'd never do that in another art school.'

But Gilbert was lucky: St Martin's was different.

CHAPTER THREE

ST MARTIN'S
SCHOOL OF ART

I f Gilbert had never come to St Martin's he might
have had a distinguished career of his own, but
it would not have been comparable to the
phenomenon of Gilbert & George. The same applies to George,
who might have become a successful painter. But their lives would
have been thwarted. Their coming together proved that single stroke
of luck that everyone hopes for. It is impossible to conceive of their
future without it. They galvanised each other; they inspired each
other; they were meant for each other. That is not gush, but the
literal truth.

At first, Gilbert continued in a state of bafflement: 'It was all
amazing, coming from a small village in the Dolomites at that time.'

George: 'It was a very casual department, totally unofficial, no
filling in of forms.'

This meant that Gilbert was cast into limbo for the first two
weeks, sitting outside wondering what was going on: 'I was very
relieved when the waiting game finished – except for the £150.'

Asked about the uncharacteristic kindness of the fates in bringing
them together, George agrees that the similarities in their upbring-

ings were more interesting than the differences: both were from the country, had attended a series of art schools but been bypassed as teachers, and produced exceptional work but were undistinguished academically. George had failed his 11-plus, one of the few pupils at his school to do so: 'Thank God I didn't pass. The other boys went to grammar school and on to minor jobs. Nothing matters.'

I asked if he really meant that.

'Yes. No thing. Nothing much. Sometimes something goes completely crazy – after a year it's the right thing.'

As for Gilbert's Catholicism, when I asked if he was still a practising Roman Catholic he laughed: 'You must be joking!' Neither he nor George has gained succour from religion. 'But I went to church every Sunday until I was nineteen, and never committed a mortal sin.'

When was his last confession?

'When the vicar in Munich asked if I wanked.'

Gilbert's assimilation into St Martin's is all the more astonishing because he could not speak a single word of English, and had to communicate with George by sign language: 'There were students from many countries there, including some Germans whom we affectionately called "the Nazi bitches", and they translated for me. There were no other Italian students.'

It is hard to convey the *laissez-faire* attitude of the school at the time, with no control and certainly no discipline. Yet, as George asserts proudly: 'It was the finest art school in the world, with an international reputation for the sculpture department in particular, constantly featured in the Sunday supplements and on television, with students such as Barry Flanagan, Richard Long, Bruce McLean, and teachers like Jan Dibbets, Philip King, William Tucker and Anthony Caro. In Munich, Gilbert knew this was the place to aim for. Extremely avant-garde. 'You didn't have to do anything you didn't want to. Didn't need qualifications. Frank Martin loved the idea of students from all over the world – and that's how I ended up there!'

It seems that students could coast along without doing anything whatsoever, and this suited G&G, who were finding their way in a congenial atmosphere.

Barry Flanagan – the sculptor whose hares leap joyfully outside municipal buildings all over the world – talks of them with critical affection: 'I remember meeting George for the first time. He looked much the same: spectacles, well-dressed, slightly dandy, public school-boy erectness. Independent, but popular, in the sense of gregarious. I was impressed by a piece of plywood with his name in bright day-glo lettering. It struck me as significant, the address to the individual highly worked out. All of us were originals, with a sense of ourselves – G&G certainly had that. I never thought of them as naïve, nor as innocents. I thought of them as *studied*. I was on their original mailing list, which they compiled after their first year, interviewing everyone – teachers and students. The cards they sent out were not shit, but poetic and charming.'

Was there jealousy in the school?

'No, we were all our own people and managed well. A new generation of galleries were opening and welcomed us. It was a nice time.'

I asked Gilbert if there was an instant rapport with George.

'I'd say so. Love at first sight!'

Turning to George, I wondered if this was the sort of relationship so popular in the Royal Navy, with the older sailor taking the younger under his wing – hence the term 'winger'.

George looked startled, as well he might: 'No, it was not like that at all, but an immediate friendship.'

Even so, with Gilbert scarcely able to make himself understood, he was in need of a mentor.

'He wore a black suit,' Gilbert remembers, 'and white ankle-socks still, and always carried a book, like an intellectual. He used to behave like a doctor, arriving after everyone else, and then make a plaster cast of fried eggs on the floor.'

Showing off?

'No, just extreme. He smoked posh Gold-leaf cigarettes.'

George: 'The whole college meant nothing, except for the one unofficial course of Advanced Sculpture. We never once went into another department. People asked us about the painting department, but I never went there once, didn't even know where it was. We existed in isolation on the top floor, only a dozen of us, very select. County Hall didn't even know of the course, invented by Caro and Frank Martin.'

Did they get on with Caro?

'We didn't have to. We did what we liked.'

The teachers, including Philip King, who became head of the Royal College of Art, and William Tucker, who moved to America, believed in the new concept of abstract sculpture supported by Bryan Robertson, then director of the Whitechapel Art Gallery.

Were they an influence?

George laughed at such absurdity: 'What do you think? Only that we rejected their style. They didn't believe in content, only shape and colour. We realised that if we took this sculpture out into the street it would lose all meaning — an elitist art.'

G&G made sculptures you could hold in your hand: one was a stick, another a mask: 'At the end of our time there we found ourselves working together without realising it.'

Gilbert: 'The first work we did together was a human face. We had a mould and poured in liquid colour. I did this first, then George put in what he wanted — a combined effort — then more coloured resin [fibreglass], and when it was full we removed the mould.'

George: 'These were the first faltering steps to G&G.'

Gilbert: 'We arranged for photos to be taken of us with the sculptures, and that's when we realised we were the sculpture.'

That you were the sculpture?

George: 'Exactly. That course taught us to be artists, gave us the confidence and the arrogance to be superior with our vision. Some showed hostility to our work from the start, with Caro always pointing out "very good students who would go far" who have never been heard of since. They were always students working in his style – always a mistake in a teacher. All were interested in studying art; we were only interested in becoming baby artists.' But he conceded: 'There was a big revolt against the supremacy of formalistic sculpture, which never recovered.'

Gilbert is able to invest words with an enthusiasm tempered by his slight accent, which gives an additional sense of surprised humour, so it is not always easy to know if one should take him seriously. Sometimes, quoted in print, their jokes misfire. Asked recently what they intended to do with the house they have bought next door but one to their own in Spitalfields, George answered immediately: 'Turn it into a children's brothel,' the sort of hilarious, throwaway remark which can look damning on the page. Remembering St Martin's, Gilbert indulged in his favourite expletives: 'Extremely exciting – *unbelievable!* We felt we knew what had to be done. When we were on top of the building we felt on top of the world. That's why we went round the commercial galleries knowing we'd be turned down. That was amusing for us.'

George: 'We got a list of all the galleries and went to every one inviting them to show our work.'

'Where are your slides?' came the familiar response, which they ignored: '"If you'd like an exhibition, we'll make you one." They all said no, and we felt totally reassured, enormously proud.'

The refusals might have been disconcerting to an artist on his own, but jointly G&G were undaunted.

Presumably you were outsiders?

'Yes,' said George. 'Half of the students ingratiated themselves with the object of becoming teachers.'

Was there a camaraderie?

'Not many high-jinks, and though people said there were sex and drugs we didn't see that.'

Gilbert: '*We were so well-behaved!* In the afternoons we walked all over London, and I used to go to English classes in Soho, near

Berwick Street Market. But what impressed me most was looking through the windows on that top floor of St Martin's: crazy autumn sky colours – violet, orange and pink – all based on white like the Pre-Raphaelite pictures. Remarkable skies. I'd never seen that before, and it made an amazing impression. I loved London.'

George: 'I always wondered what would have happened if some of these things had not taken place. On the other hand I remembered that when I was twelve I heard about Van Gogh and bought a book of his letters, and realised you didn't have to be clever, you didn't have to be trained, didn't necessarily have to be educated or well-behaved. You could just be an artist. You could be a great artist without these things. You could be crazy and a great artist.'

Gilbert: 'Even to us today the idea of total freedom is inspiring.'

What incredible luck that G&G should have teamed up; who else could have coped with either? Or was it more than luck?

George: 'We felt years ago – even in the pictures we do – we feel there's a big hand moving us, that *something* is doing it to or for us.'

George stayed at St Martin's for three years, from autumn 1965 to spring 1968; Gilbert for one, from 1967 to 1968, after which he felt there was nothing more for him to do there. How did their relationship start?

Gilbert: 'He was always looking into this room where I was working, trying to impress everyone with my skills in order that I be allowed to stay there.'

George: 'Not speaking, for he wouldn't understand. Just *browsing!*'

Gilbert: 'He arranged a display and asked me if I wanted to join him and create it in the room downstairs. Something like the branch of a tree in multi-colours like the skies I saw through the window. When we left at the same time, without realising it we were already working together. It was not the result of a conscious decision. One of the most memorable experiences was when George invited me to see his place in the East End.'

Before that, Gilbert had returned to Germany and worked briefly for a firm restoring churches: 'It was very well paid, and English currency restrictions were very strict.'

George: 'I sent him a postcard, and as soon as he received it he came back at once.'

Gilbert: 'I was coming *anyway!*'

But I have heard of George's infinite delight as he saw Gilbert through his window in Wilkes Street, Spitalfields, and ran to meet him.

When Gilbert told me 'It was love at first sight!' I wondered if this was part of his dry, almost cynical humour. Plainly it has been an epic love affair, but what is the full truth of their relationship? I braced myself as I turned to George on the third morning of their visit to North Devon: 'Were you already married when you first met Gilbert?'

The shutters came down.

CHAPTER FOUR

SEX, SHAGGING AND G&G

George was indignant. I had never seen him lose his temper, but perhaps he was close to it now. But it was a question I had to ask, a subject I had to raise. While I respected his privacy, I felt his moral outrage was exaggerated. After all, his marriage had been revealed in the press, though George had seemed equally agitated when the interviewer tried to probe, though Gilbert laughed mischievously: 'Don't look at me!'

'We never go into details of actual sex,' he told her. 'I'm sure we have very elaborate and complicated love lives and sex lives behind us, but we never like to go into details about that. We're probably more frank in our pictures than any other artist alive, but our art is not personal in that way, not autobiographic.' Gilbert joined in: 'We eliminate personal lives.' When the interviewer persisted, George threw a tantrum like a child: 'Not telling! Not telling!' Gilbert glowered: 'It wouldn't be useful.'

With the usual absurdity of labels, they have been described as 'gay' artists, but this is largely due to the abundance of lithe young men in their pictures. There is no hint of it in their private lives.

In Totnes it never occurred to Ivor or Mrs Weeks that George might or might not be gay, and they refer to his girlfriends at Dartington – one of them a student at the school, who was reprimanded for going out with a town boy. The only time George has approached the subject was his admission to Ivor Weeks that at the age of twelve he had befriended another boy, and the teacher called him in to say: 'This friendship is unhealthy.' 'Don't you think that was a horrible thing to say to an innocent child? I took this "unhealthy" literally, and looked for physical effects for days.'

When I asked about sex at Dartington, George was vehement: 'That's part of a different story. Not part of the G&G story! Who would one leave out? List every shag? Who did what to whom is not important. If we compiled a list of whom we did and didn't shag, we would disappoint many and anger others.'

It is important to most people.

'Not to G&G. Most people can't even remember all the shags they've had.'

Explaining their reluctance to be candid (though they had suggested 'The Lowdown on Gilbert & George' as the title for this book), Gilbert said, 'It would take all the magic away – it would be boring. We believe we deal with sex in the gentle way we want to in our pictures. If sexual confession was a way of changing society we'd do it, but we believe in doing it through our pictures.'

George pounced on the advantages of not confessing: 'It's because they don't know, or think they don't know.'

'That's it!' Gilbert exclaimed – 'That's the best story!'

Carried away, George said: 'You can drag Victoria Station and find out what you want [presumably meaning nothing]. When Sarah Kent [of Time Out] interviews us we feel that somehow at the back of her mind she thinks we're evil. I've been tempted to tell her, "Sarah, here's a shovel, dig up the backyard and see if you find any teenage corpses – but don't dig in that corner!"'

'We've got to be so careful,' he admitted, 'because for a long time they started to analyse every word in order to discredit us.'

Gilbert agreed: 'We used to be very open, but it became very dangerous. "Beware of Strange Men who do Funny Things" – Brian Sewell [art critic for the London *Evening Standard*] was inciting lynch law.'

I attempted to return to the subject of marriage.

'That's going back,' said George severely. 'Not part of the G&G story. Every artist we know of has different partners, and I can think of very few artists who haven't had sex with both sexes. We always say to journalists, if you take a photo of us leaving a dodgy sauna bath, you wouldn't get a penny for it.'

'That isn't true,' said Gilbert blandly.

Ignoring this, George continued: 'Any good artist experiments sexually, I'm sure. Everybody's totally bored by that – shagging a boyfriend or a girlfriend.'

But it is relevant to ask if you were married when you met Gilbert.

'I don't think it is relevant,' he replied heatedly. 'No more important than anything else I was doing at the time. It was more important that I was studying at the St Martin's School of Art and Gilbert turned up there.'

Gilbert: (gleefully) 'There's so much speculation, and we like that!'

George: 'Whatever they imagine about G&G is right. They're all correct, because there's nothing we haven't done. None of their imaginings can compare to the elaborateness of sexual reality.'

Gilbert: 'Reality is much more complex.'

George: 'Than anything they can imagine.'

Gilbert: 'The supreme mystery surrounding us – they have me with girls going off to Italy, while George goes to his family home in Hampstead every evening.'

George: 'They even knew what type of car I drove – I've never been behind a steering wheel in my life!'

This referred to the amusing press 'innings' in 1996 as the antidote to the 'outings' of unfortunate clerics and film stars who were dragged reluctantly into the limelight and exposed as gay. A witty columnist had the idea of 'inning' G&G, claiming they were secretly heterosexual, going their separate ways after shutting up shop for the evening, as if they were haberdashers. In fact the 'inning' was so light-hearted that it drew attention away from the reality. George's marriage lasted long enough to produce two children, with a boy now in his early twenties, which suggests that he was still involved with his wife for at least three years after meeting Gilbert, though their contact must have been spasmodic, considering that G&G were seldom apart. The marriage seems to have taken place in 1966, and was known about in the West Country though, curiously, almost no one seems to have met George's wife. When the couple visited Ivor Weeks she stayed outside in the car – presumably she drove. Someone who did meet her told Weeks: 'I assure you she's not the sort of lady to be ashamed of.'

And that's about it. Why not acknowledge the marriage and move on? After all, it was a long time ago. Yet as George sat in my little courtyard in North Devon, it was as if I had accused him of something heinous. He is proud of his relationship with Gilbert, and would not wish to sully it in any way. 'Every marriage is more fucked up. Artists said our partnership wouldn't last; now every one of them has broken up.'

Is the sense of mystery deliberate?

'Unavoidable,' said George. 'It is mysterious even to us.'

'Amazing,' said Gilbert. 'Every time they see the two of us walking in the street they're amazed – what the hell is going on?'

George: 'In a back street in Barnstaple last night, a young couple gave us an odd look and then came back. "Are you the modern artists? We saw you on the telly. Carry on the good work." We did become a symbol to mixed couples, who admired the idea of two people and would like the same equality that we have, and would like that in their relationships.'

Do you ever quarrel?

'We don't believe in that.'

'At the beginning there was more tension,' Gilbert admitted, 'but less and less.'

George: 'Outside, life is such a big battle, everyone fighting like dogs, and we don't want to be like that.'

Gilbert: 'If we started to quarrel, everything would fall apart.'

I asked Barry Flanagan if the other students and teachers at St Martin's thought that G&G were having an affair: 'I never thought that. I couldn't speak for the others.'

You don't think it was a love affair?

'No. A partnership. I wouldn't be surprised if they'd never had sex.'

Ultimately, it is G&G's business and theirs alone. Like all of us, they should be allowed their secrets, increasingly hard though that is today. Why dissipate the sense of mystery which surrounds them? If George does have a family, it is plain that they respect his discretion and have not gone running to the newspapers. That in itself is a credit to all of them.

Perhaps I should try to track the family down, but that would be impolite to George. I believe the story of Gilbert & George is the stronger without 'telling all', without the shagging. Frankly, I have no idea what goes on, but of one thing I am absolutely certain – in whatever form, the love affair between Gilbert and George is one of the most enduring of this century.

CHAPTER FIVE

FOURNIER STREET

The idea of George having a respectable home in North London would be funnier if it were not so unimaginable. It seems inconceivable today that he could live anywhere but Fournier Street.

In writing this book I have been struck time and again by George's ability to be in the right place at the right moment, and he was irresistibly drawn to the East End of London. After the war the area was blisteringly poor yet gloriously alive. It reeked of the past, and absorbed George as just another outsider, indifferent to his peculiarities. This is the genius of the East End, even if the new-comers do not speak a word of English. In the nineteenth century the nearby docks with their forests of masts, beautifully conveyed in the engravings of Gustave Doré, had the vitality of Port Said – and the degradation too. Ironically, the two leading reformers were Jack the Ripper, whose murders focused attention on the appalling conditions, and Hitler, who bombed the slums in his effort to destroy the docks. Unfortunately, those slums had a jauntiness which has not been replaced – except, perhaps, in the streets surrounding Fournier Street, in Spitalfields.

With the trade pouring in from the East India and West India Docks, few parts of any town were busier, and it was all too easy to be submerged, as Joseph Conrad observed in *Chance*, with a sea captain staying at the Eastern Hotel on the junction of West India Dock Road and Commercial Road:

> the inhabitants of that end of town where life goes on unadorned by grace or splendour; they passed us in their shabby garments, with sallow faces, haggard, anxious or weary, or simply without expression, in an unsmiling sombre stream not made up of lives but of mere unconsidered existences whose joys, struggles, thoughts, sorrows and their very hopes were miserable, glamourless, and of no account in the world.

My respect for Conrad is unreserved, yet I dare to disagree: he understood the East better than the East End. He failed to appreciate that the East Enders had to rise above such conditions, and did so with the help of the wit of cockney rhyming slang (few people who use the word 'berk' today know what it means) and the gusto of music hall. It thrilled audiences when Marie Lloyd staggered on stage clutching her battered birdcage with the cock-linnet (I have seen the original, delightfully crude compared to the elegant pagodas used by artistes today), and confided:

> We had to move away, 'cos the rent we couldn't pay,
> The moving van came round just after dark;
> There was me and my old man
> Shoving things inside the van,
> Which we'd often done before, let me remark . . .

The East Enders roared – booze, bailiffs and the moonlight flit: they understood – and when Marie reappeared as the height of elegance in her Directoire dress they were proud and flattered that one of their own could rise so high.

That was the strength of the East End – resilience – and that at least was unchanged when George moved there in 1965. To start with he lived in Wilkes Street, named after the politician John Wilkes (1727–97), the champion of civil rights and the cause of the American colonists. Like Fournier Street around the corner, it was in the shadow of the splendid Christchurch Spitalfields, designed in the early eighteenth century by Wren's great pupil, Nicholas Hawksmoor, though in Peter Ackroyd's novel *Hawksmoor* (1985) it was built on strange foundations. George finds this a brilliant idea: 'Hawksmoor first built the foundations and then, finding an excuse to sack the builders, he secretly had seven horrors built into the foundations and cemented over: one a strangled prostitute, one baby cut into three pieces – magical horrors. When it was all covered up, he rehired the builders and the church rose on top of that evil. He said that to *defeat* evil you have to *do* evil, which in medical terms is of course perfectly reasonable. It is the vaccination theory, isn't it? They have to give you a little bit of the illness to make you immune to it.'

At this time Gilbert was living in rented rooms, first in Turnham Green and then in Tufnell Park, arranged for him by St Martin's. Almost inevitably, the latter was 'a weird place run by a gay couple who wanted to speak Italian to me all the time, when I wanted to learn English'. He paid just over three pounds in weekly rent.

I have referred to Gilbert's innocent excitement when George invited him to his home in Wilkes Street. The flat consisted of two rooms, with no kitchen or bathroom, only a lavatory in the back yard. George paid £16 a month for it, which he considered a bargain. Gilbert felt an immediate sympathy with the East End, which consolidated George's. He remembers the initial shock of walking down Brick Lane: 'It was like walking into a book in the nineteenth century: amazing light, and few people in the street, more like literature than reality. George had this big room on the third floor, always a big fire and a fork for frying bacon.'

George: 'A very camp fire!'

Gilbert: 'Everything disciplined, everything had its own place.

There was a Russian Jewish lady opposite and we used to shout across to tell her the time from the Christchurch clock, and she demanded to know why they didn't paint the church white as they would have done in her homeland. Her background had been tough: once, unchaperoned on a St Petersburg train, she was seen with a young man, and was forbidden to speak to any man afterwards. George took me once a week to Hoxton Music Hall, where he taught art to hooligans and police cadets twice a week to make money after his student grant ran out.'

'I got that job with some difficulty,' said George. 'A woman had given the go-ahead but said I needed a certificate from County Hall, where I was confronted by a man at a desk with a strong smell of peppermint from twelve feet away. I gave him a rough idea of what I had in mind for the class and he became totally enraged, red in the face, shouting "Leave now!" because he hated modern art. I was extremely unhappy and went to see Frank Martin, who gave me lunch and told me the man was a raving alcoholic, hence the peppermint, and his wife was divorcing him.'

George reapplied and got his certificate, and went to help with the classes, and they loved him; he taught them art. At Christmas he worked as a postman in order to raise money for a party for his hooligan pupils, and all their cockney friends came and got so drunk he had to pull them away from the windows in case they were seen. George startlingly explains that 'they were all fucking each other'.

The area was very run-down: 'There was a tramp who dashed in and seized a handful of our meal and ran out, that's how poor it was.' Another elderly tramp asked for directions to a hostel and burst into tears when George told him, most respectfully. 'It's so many years since someone called me "sir",' he said.

Ivor Weeks always had faith in George, but he believes that it was only when he met Gilbert that 'the George of now happened – the George I knew could be articulate, but he lacked the confidence to speak out. That came from Gilbert.' Yet he knew that the artistic drive had always been there, and a *precision* which he still sees in their work today: 'George was rather an awkward draughtsman, Gilbert far more fluent.' In the early days he thought he could identify their separate styles, before they eliminated drawing altogether. But George responded angrily to the suggestion that they lack the basic skill of drawing – 'I think we're the most trained artists we know. I did seven years studying painting, sculpture, graphics, pottery, and Gilbert did eleven years.'

Gilbert: 'This whole idea that you have to draw is nonsense, because in the nineteenth century everyone could draw, even Queen Victoria. Turner was accused of not being able to draw, but what was important was his vision.'

The next throw of the lucky dice was to move to a house in Fournier Street, where they rented the ground floor in 1968. The house, indeed the entire street, was 'totally wrecked', but had been so distinguished when it was occupied by Huguenots escaping religious persecution in France in the late seventeenth and early eighteenth centuries that a barrier was erected near Christchurch to prevent the *hoi-polloi* from trespassing. Today, with many houses restored like Gilbert & George's, it is regarded as one of the most important eighteenth-century streets in London. Gilbert says that many of the streets in the area are French; George adds: 'Constant change. The Huguenots had to leave here too because English law was against them.'

Gilbert: 'They were weavers, silk merchants, and became so rich they had to leave this part of London for tax reasons.'

George: 'Complicated reasons. Then this area was inhabited by Germans – there are still two German churches – then it became Russian, Jewish. It is constantly in flux. Even during our time, it has changed so many times: the Jewish people left and Maltese arrived, then people from Somaliland and then came the Bangladeshis, and now it's more mixed.'

'Eccentric people arrived,' said Gilbert, without a hint of irony.

In 1974 they were able to buy their house and studio in Fournier

Street: 'We never thought of moving or buying something different,' says Gilbert.

'We love it. We'd die in West London,' says George.

'In some ways it is a very extreme district,' says Gilbert. 'It is on the edge all the time.'

George: 'Yiddish was commonly spoken when we first came here.'

Gilbert: 'Now it is a mixture always, moving from cockney to Yiddish to Indian. But it is all quite extreme, the mixture of cultures, and that is very exciting.'

George: 'The man at the string shop used to add up the bill himself. He spoke while adding it up in Yiddish and had to translate it for himself into pounds, shillings and pence. Then he had to translate it into the decimal. Extraordinary!'

Yet again, their knack of being in the right place at the right moment. Spitalfields may have been bizarre when G&G first moved there, but it is even more so today. There is a photograph of them in their suits, with their faces and hands coloured red, while scores of white-robed Muslims leave a mosque behind them. It could have been taken anywhere in the Middle East; rarely in Britain – until now. They have always been accepted by the many different races surrounding them, who are only too familiar with the cruelty of discrimination. 'What is exciting is that in some way they all know us. George always says hello to our Bengali neighbours. We are totally protected. Last night we didn't even have to tell the taxi-driver the address. He just said, "Fournier Street?" '

George: 'Many Bangladeshis are lifelong friends. We already know many middle-aged, or say forty-year-old Asians who speak to us, who we can remember from when they were very glamorous teenagers. And there was a charming incident at the new Indian restaurant we go to. After we left, the handsome young Indian waiter asked a patron who we were. On our next visit he greeted us warmly: "Apparently you are the artists." They admitted it. "Famous artists?" "Probably." "In the newspapers?" "Sometimes."

"Headlines even?" "Occasionally." The waiter was becoming excited. "Rich and famous?" "Not badly off." He looked at us with increasing admiration: "So *how's your love life?*" ' Both, relishing flirtation, hooted with laughter, delighted.

'We always think that around here is very global, that if a space-ship landed and they said we've got five minutes to report on a typical planet-Earth-place, where shall we go? We'd say Spitalfields, Commercial Street, corner of Liverpool Street and Bishopsgate – all within walking distance of our house. The expression in the eyes of the people around here is very up-to-date. In other parts of London it's more typical of the forties or fifties.'

Personally, I find the idea of this district as representative of Britain far-fetched – except that it is multi-racial – but there is no denying G&G's certainty that they live at the hub of the universe, nothing less.

One of the most formidable aspects of G&G is their taste. Considering the coming together of their backgrounds this is hardly surprising; except that it has resulted in a startling contrast between sparsity and largesse. On the one hand they have stripped life to the best essentials, their large fridge containing nothing but good champagne and the special paper they need for their work. They have an electric kettle but no kitchen – 'If we cooked we would have to shop' – yet Fournier Street has two bathrooms, which saves them from mixing up their toothbrushes. Few have seen their bedroom – or bedrooms – with the probable exception of their Jamaican cleaner Stainton Forrest, who is loyal unto death and who would never divulge such secrets. I have always been reluctant to ask him.

Totally derelict when they bought it, the wood-panelling typical of Fournier Street houses has been restored perfectly, along with the highly polished staircase – 'the biggest, most monstrous job of our lives,' says Gilbert. 'There were generations of paint a quarter-inch thick,' adds George. They decided not to furnish the house in the style of the eighteenth century, because that would make it look like a museum. They instead collected nineteenth-century objects, neo-Gothic armchairs of the 1860s, benches, an oak hexagonal table and silk tapestries. A carpet from the Celtic revival movement at the turn of the century fits perfectly, but the overall effect comes close to the very museum they wished to avoid, with themselves as part of the tableau as they serve tea. This is partly due to their passion as collectors of pottery, which would be overwhelming except that their pieces of early Branham pottery made in Barnstaple are the finest of their kind. Tea-chests are filled with further purchases, as if they were unable to resist them. Some of the vases are immense, reminiscent of Ali Baba and his forty thieves.

But this is not the indulgence of buying for the sake of it. G&G's collection reveals their knowledge, and the discretion of buying only the best. Their pride is the pottery by Glasgow-born Christopher Dresser, one of the first industrial designers and an adviser to Tiffany's. What astounded me was the pieces' simplicity, long in advance of the time. They make Tiffany seem old-fashioned. 'These vases were made for four years only, from 1880 to about 1885. Then he closed down,' George explained. Presumably this is why the name of Christopher Dresser is not as widely revered as it should be.

Gilbert opened a cupboard to reveal more shelves lined with pottery: 'These pieces, nearly a hundred years old, are very advanced. If you used them today in a TV series about nineteenth-century London, people would complain that they're the wrong period. You see, they have free glazes – to have running glaze was very unusual.' Much of the pottery is displayed in a glass-fronted cabinet by Augustus Pugin; the triangular brass clock on the hexagonal table was designed by Alfred Waterhouse; Charles Lock Eastlake, who built the oak bookcase, published the first popular book on household taste: 'Before then, there had been no such books for ordinary people.'

Mind you, it would need the most extraordinary people to appreciate Christopher Dresser, unless the brilliance of his work was explained as G&G did for me. Even the simple bench in the backyard, designed by Dresser, has an instant charm. It is his modernity, or rather the co-existence of past and present in his work, that makes it so outstanding: 'That's what Christopher Dresser said was modern for him,' says George. 'Modern was steamship travel, so he could encompass the world easily for the first time. It didn't take months to travel to Japan or San Francisco. The depth of history was just becoming available. They were digging up the pyramids. They were digging up Mayan temples. For the first time you could have a total grasp of history and of the world. Dresser thought that together past and present was very modern.'

Gilbert: 'We believe very much that we are trying to accept the modern and the old at the same time. We don't want to say that only what is modern is right.'

George: 'All history together with today is what is modern, not just the now modern.'

Gilbert: 'The complication of it, we believe, is good.'

The accumulation of the Branham pottery, Dresser designs and nineteenth-century furniture took many years to acquire. Now there is a long workroom at the back of the house, as imposing as a factory, in clinical contrast to the front rooms. George told Sarah Kent of Time Out, as far back as 1982, 'We are now the oldest inhabitants in the street. When we came here all those Bengali factories were Jewish tailors and hatmakers. We are completely at home. We wouldn't like to live in Chelsea. It's more interesting here, more actual – one has one's finger on the pulse and we don't have to compete with every queen on the street!'

But when they first moved in, they were broke. Several factors combined to save them. Determined not to burden themselves with the chore of cooking, they went instead to the Market Café, a few houses away on the other side of Fournier Street. It would be hard to overrate its importance in their lives. With unjustified fastidiousness, I was prepared to brace myself against the greasy caff where they eat side by side, flanked by bottles of HP Sauce and tomato ketchup. In fact it is not greasy at all, and serves excellent English food to the local workers, who always have high standards.

With food no longer a problem, G&G sought a similar simplicity in their clothing. Their remarkably self-contained world provided the services of a traditional East End tailor, also in Fournier Street. They had always dressed in suits. 'Because we came from the country,' George explained, 'you put a suit on for any important occasion – weddings, funerals or holidays.' George sometimes wore a black suit to St Martin's, usually a second-hand one, which was all he could afford. Later, from about 1972, they went to Burtons, the mass-tailoring chain, often despised but of first-rate quality. From there they evolved their own style at the local tailor: the single-breasted, three-button worsted suits which became their trademark.

George says the three buttons were 'normal': 'We always think that if you took a suit from every decade this century and made an average, you'd probably end up like this – not particularly fifties, nor eighties. As for the three buttons, that's to be tidy. Tailors always tell you to leave the top and bottom ones undone; they even tailor it like that now. We change the cut to do up all three buttons, though when I was a teenager I was always told to leave the top and bottom ones undone, or just the bottom one undone.'

Gilbert agreed: 'It's the country style. But everybody copies our suits today! What's exciting is that we have all these photographs of artists from 1971 at parties, all drunk. And we always look the same. The others look like hippies with beards and flared trousers. Everybody has suits now – the young artists, even the pop stars.'

This is disingenuous, as G&G often tend to be. They did not wear dark suits, which would indeed have been 'normal', but pale, lightly-patterned wool suits with trouser cuffs. They stood out a mile – which, presumably, is exactly what they intended.

With the inner and the outer men catered for, they needed someone practical to help them put everything together and move ahead. This proved more difficult. When I first met them, in 1989, they had an agreeable and efficient male secretary, Tyrone Dawson, who had been working for them since 1985. He was followed by an excitable lady, Mirjana Winterbottom, but G&G do not take to such proximity, and prefer to work alone. They had reduced life to basics, with vast filing cabinets meticulously recording their every activity, but they needed a permanent friend. They found him in Stainton Forrest, whom they discovered in 1981 when he was cleaning the Whitechapel Art Gallery. 'He's been with us ever since – our greatest friend and the person we trust more than anyone else. Stainton sees things very clearly and is able to home in on the simple, human truth.'

'We need total supporters,' Gilbert admits.

You could even say they demand it. Of all the people I have spoken to, Stainton gave me the most heartfelt insight into Gilbert & George. He probably knows them better than anyone. Though Madame Cornuel remarked in the seventeenth century that 'No man is a hero to his valet,' I prefer Lord Byron's contradictory couplet:

> In short he was a perfect cavaliero,
> And to his valet seemed a hero.

While Stainton is no twentieth-century valet, though he is their cleaner, he has no illusions about G&G. He met them at a low point in his life, and they changed it. Coming to England from Jamaica as a young man in the late 1950s, he worked in a foundry, on a building site, in a raw metal mill and at Ford Motors. By 1981 his marriage had broken up and he was working as a handyman in the Whitechapel, where Gilbert & George were exhibiting: 'They watch me – see how I operate – and ask me to join them. I hesitate, for I do not understand . . .' He gives a quick smile, but does not elucidate.

Gilbert reassured him: 'We are good people, you won't regret it,' and gave him a card. Outstanding in his job, and with considerable dignity, Stainton also works as a cleaner for the Anthony d'Offay Gallery and the Bank of England – but G&G come first. Stainton relaxed over coffee in the East End, becoming almost voluble: 'They are the two nicest people I ever met in the whole world. The only two humans I ever met. It's hard to explain the feeling – the way they made me feel wanted. When I met them I was really down. Apart from the help of God, they are the only two who help revive me. To me, more than a friend, more than a brother; no words to say how good they are.'

With characteristic consideration, G&G have sometimes included Stainton in their travels, inviting him to accompany them to their exhibitions in Madrid, Bordeaux, Moscow, China and New York. I asked – with such exaggerated discretion that he failed to understand me – if he ever felt embarrassed at being thrown into the high-powered banquets, placed by G&G next to the wife of a gallery-owner or wealthy collector. I had been told how one hostess in France had announced to her guests, including Stainton: 'Now, who shall sit where? Eeny, meeny, miney, mo, catch a . . . Oh, for God's sake [covered with confusion], sit wherever you like!'

I did not repeat this story, but Stainton twigged: 'Prejudice. I never confront that at all. Ever. I wish half the world was like them. Then it would be perfect. If you can bury all the troubles of the world in a hole as they could, everyone could be treated as equals.'

In his turn, Stainton took the usual G&G entourage for a splendid lunch with his sister and family, who now live in Brooklyn. He will never forget his travels with G&G, especially the trip to the Guggenheim exhibition in 1985 with his son, Paul, who appears in G&G's pictures with his brother, Jason.

'I'm telling you – the greatest time in my life. I ask myself this question: "Is this really me, being here with my son, Paul?" And he says, "Dad, if you did come back and tell me all this, I'd have to ask myself, is that really true? But seeing is believing."'

Gilbert & George were in danger of being sanctified, until Stainton allowed them one of their lesser-known defects: 'They don't want things to be too perfect.'

Have you seen them lose their temper?

'Do I ever see it!' he exclaimed. 'I do! And you wouldn't like to see it. When George loses it, he really loses it. When he's calmed down, you wouldn't believe that was him.'

What causes it? Often it's something trivial?

'They are straightforward, but they don't like anyone to come to them with crookedness. If you try to give them less, they don't like it. Their policy is good, but they're really upset if someone tries to put them down.' In other words, they can forgive anything except betrayal. Otherwise they encourage people to do whatever they like, without criticism. When I complained to them once that Francis Bacon could be cruel, and that another friend refused to work, Gilbert exclaimed delightedly: 'But that is all right! That is how they are.' But even for G&G, loyalty has to be restricted; you cannot be loyal to a crowd.

As he knows Gilbert & George more intimately than anyone else, I asked Stainton if he was hurt by some of the labels people stick on them.

'As far as I'm concerned, every man has a life to live. Over the years, I haven't seen anything like that.' He did not specify what 'that' might be, though I could guess. 'People should get to know them before they talk.'

As for the occasional, glibly applied label of 'Fascism': 'They don't know what they're talking about. Some journalists have even suggested that they should move from Spitalfields . . .' His emotion brought him close to tears: 'I don't know. I love it so much. Oh my God,' he declared with a passion surprising in such a reserved man, 'when you mention Fournier Street, I wake up. That's the house!'

Stainton will accept no criticism of G&G, not even of their pictures: 'I wish those who disagree with their work could see them as they really are – two perfect men. People in the past try to fuck them up; if the papers had their way they would close Gilbert & George down, but there's no stopping them now. I feel so happy for them.'

They are extremely generous. Do they use their money wisely?

'They made a book which should sell for £20, but they helped to sell it for only £12. At the For AIDS show people said, "Fools, idiots; no one should give away so much money."

'They changed my life completely,' says Stainton. 'Meeting them makes life worth living. Being with them, walking with them, I feel like I've achieved something in life – a great feeling. I know I'll never meet people like them again.'

It sounds too good to be true, as if Stainton has cast Gilbert & George in the role of Christian martyrs, but when I saw him in a New York restaurant on the evening of the private views for The Fundamental Pictures in 1997, sitting beside his elegant, sharply intelligent wife, with G&G at the end of the table, there was no denying his pride in what he was witnessing.

'If anything happened to either of them,' he told me in London, 'I would take my eyes out and give them to them.'

CHAPTER SIX

THE SINGING
SCULPTURE

In 1968, Stainton Forrest and the full splendours of Fournier Street lay in the future. Now the grants had run out, they were broke and on their own. They knew they wanted to work and be together. They were attempting a new project every week, visiting people who might help, explaining their approach to art – exemplified by their initials, which they wore on their foreheads with small pictures of themselves. Their former teacher Anthony Caro listened attentively, then, after some thought, said: 'I hope very much that you won't succeed,' and after a pause, 'but I rather think you might.' Understandably, they never went near him again. Some of the hostility they encountered took them by surprise. When a friend wrote to Frank Martin, who had created the sculpture department at St Martin's, asking if he could recommend G&G for a project, he replied: 'Dear Madam, Under no circumstances have anything to do with these people.' They still have the letter. 'None of our teachers wanted to know us. Most encouraging!'

Gilbert & George evolved the theory that you could be an artist without the need of a gallery – an original, almost blasphemous

LEFT George's mother, Hermione Ernestine.

ABOVE Gilbert's mother, Cecilia.

BELOW Gilbert (centre) carving Madonnas in his father's workshop.

Gilbert (second from left) with his brother, sister and friends in San Martino, the village in the Dolomites where he grew up.

George (second from left) and friends on their way to the annual carnival in Totnes.

LEFT Gilbert on his friend Heinrich's shoulders with other students at the Kunstakademie in Munich.

BELOW George (second from right) with other students at Dartington Hall School, photographed by Don McCullin for *The Observer*.

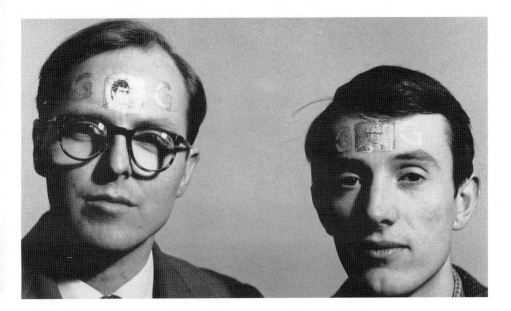

With *Design for Foreheads*, worn during 1969 and 1970 on various social and artistic occasions.

OPPOSITE
ABOVE George demonstrating his spinning painting at the art school of Oxford Technical College.

BELOW A moment of relaxation on the roof of St Martin's School of Art, London, spring 1968.

With Anthony d'Offay, *c.* 1972.

With Illeana Sonnabend at the Musée nationale d'art moderne, Centre Georges Pompidou, Paris, 1981.

OPPOSITE Off to send Charcoal Sculptures to a Paris group exhibition, outside the artists' home and studio in Fournier Street. 1970.

ABOVE In the Market Café, Fournier Street, with Clyde and Phyllis, December 1991.

LEFT In Moscow with Daniel Farson, 1990.

conception at the time. 'We wanted to make living sculpture,' George explains; 'like pop-star artists, just standing there with metallised faces.'

Unsuccessfully seeking permission to erect a tent in Trafalgar Square in which to present their Living Sculpture, they went to the Palace of Westminster, where the then Minister of Works, the late Bob Mellish, took them into his office: 'He chatted away amiably enough, but to our amazement we saw that he was masturbating under his desk. Perhaps he fancied us.'

'He fancied *me*!' Gilbert corrected George indignantly. Years later they met Mellish coming out of the lavatory at Liverpool Street Station. 'He said he would help us, but nothing came of it. All he wanted was a shag; he was rather jealous of young Londoners.'

They rang the Savoy Hotel and said they'd like to present a nativity scene for Christmas, providing a donkey, some sheep and themselves as Mary and Joseph. The Savoy was bemused, but declined. They then presented the same idea to the Tate Gallery. Richard Morphet took copious notes, but again the outcome was a refusal.

G&G had started experimenting with different forms while they were at St Martin's: hardboard and plastic, transparent boxes with things inside, if only dust. One of their most successful pieces was a box with Plexiglas, glass and chromium bars like a prison cell, perfectly executed; inside was one of George's stubbed-out cigarettes. Gilbert recalls placing plaster on the floor of one room, 'to make it like snow. Then we put the objects in and closed off the door with Plexiglas so you could only look through. And when you did you could see all these objects in a snowscape, with the whole landscape of London through the window.' 'The window on the far side framed it like a picture on a wall,' says George, 'like our pictures now. Because you couldn't move very far, it was a still image.' This and many other projects were part of their 'Art for All' experiment.

In 1968 they held a very small show in the staff canteen of a meat-packing factory in Bethnal Green Road, inviting the workers and handing out leaflets at Liverpool Street Station to passers-by in the hope that they would come to it too. No one was interested, except for two progressive young gallery-owners who had the nous to see beyond the norm. I remember Robert Fraser as handsome and dissolute, with enough money to do what he wanted. He generously allowed G&G to make two projects at his Duke Street Gallery, one a back-projection slide show on the gallery's window during the Christmas holidays.

'We made him write "Happy Christmas" on the blank slides [for a moment I misheard this as 'our backsides', which would have been no less surprising]. We bought all the little plaster Christmas-cake decorations we could find and blew them up like immense sculptures. They were incredibly beautiful. Fraser was always nice to us.'

George regards the infamous 'magazine sculpture' of *George the Cunt & Gilbert the Shit* (1969) as the beginning of a lot of modern art. 'We wanted to show it for a day in a glass case and invite people, but the gallery owner, Kasmin, said no, and Anthony d'Offay thought we were pulling his leg – "No, but let's stay friends." Robert Fraser said yes. Of course we had no money, but there was a big antique market in nearby Christopher Place and we borrowed a glass case from a very kind lady antique dealer. Fraser secretly – even to us – invited the collector and film-maker Alan Power to film it from across the street, with people coming in – it was a period of arty farty films – and quite important people came to see it, like the editor of *Studio International*. We wanted him to publish it, and he did so a year later, though censoring the words, and in black and white rather than in colour.' They could hardly have been surprised, for the words were deliberately provocative, but today the two portraits have the disarming wistfulness of two very young men, and movingly reveal how close G&G were.

At no point did they lose their vital touch of arrogance. In 1969, believing that they were on the verge of recognition, they were excited to learn that a major international exhibition, When Attitudes Become Form, was coming to England. Originating in Switzerland, it was touring the world, with a curator in each city to supply additional local artists. Art historian Charles Harrison was London's selector, and G&G were delighted – 'That's fine. We must be in.' Then they were humiliated to hear they had not been chosen: 'We were very, very shocked. We thought, there are only three or four artists in London that he'll add to the show, and we were certainly amongst the leading ones.' Furious at their exclusion, they retaliated by going to the private view, where they stood motionless in the middle of the gallery as Living Sculptures with multi-coloured, metallised heads and hands: 'That just smacked the whole show in, really.'

During the evening, a man they had never met but whose name they knew well, Konrad Fischer, came up to them: 'So, you do a show in Düsseldorf, huh?' They were immediately launched onto a new level of contacts and possibilities. Fischer arranged an immediate show at the Düsseldorf Kunsthalle, where they enjoyed such a success that thousands of people flocked to watch them on the first day. This led to further exhibitions of The Singing Sculpture in Holland, Belgium, Italy, New York, Australia and London. The transition from standing motionless to The Singing Sculpture established G&G as artists to be reckoned with. Their antics were not to be laughed at, like the rigidly posed shop-window mannequins whose sudden movements were greeted by the screams of onlookers. G&G may have been equally bizarre, but The Singing Sculpture was an art to be taken seriously. As the music-hall performers Flanagan & Allen's 'Underneath the Arches' played on the gramophone, G&G, one holding a stick, the other a glove, rotated with mechanical movements, with swivels of their feet, singing along. At the end of the song they restarted the record or cassette at the beginning, exchanged the stick and glove, and began again.

Asked if their metallised faces were inspired by the bronze of conventional sculpture, George explained: 'It's so that you can look at us as persons freely; people can just come up and look, which they can't do otherwise. They'd be embarrassed. They would be too shy to do that. We felt like an object.'

Gilbert added: 'You have to become different, otherwise it doesn't mean anything. It was very important that we came from a tradition of making sculpture.'

George described it as 'Art for All', one of their aims: 'Children would be fascinated by The Singing Sculpture, older people would love it, reminding them of different thoughts and feelings. And it worked!'

Early black-and-white photographs reveal the gradual progress of the piece. First, a card invited people to the Slade School of Art's Weldon Theatre at 3 p.m. on Wednesday, 4 June 1969: 'Gilbert and George, The Sculptors, present UNDERNEATH THE ARCHES — the most intelligent, fascinating, serious and beautiful art piece you have ever seen.' Our New Sculpture had been presented at St Martin's School of Art earlier in the year, on two separate days, followed by another presentation in January at the Camberwell School of Art, which suggests that G&G had more access to the public than they have subsequently suggested. They played the same side of the record twice – although giving the impression that it was being turned over – with a short speech before and after. The Singing Sculpture was shown in the summer at the Lyceum Ballroom in The Strand, and at the National Jazz and Blues Festival at Plumpton in Sussex, though G&G decided that these were not appropriate settings. Perhaps the most poignant presentation was on the first anniversary of the piece they had started to develop at their studio in Wilkes Street in 1968, literally under the arches, in a derelict site off Cable Street: 'The most fascinating, realistic, beautiful, dusty and serious art piece you have ever seen,' with two rough hand-coloured por-trait sketches of themselves. The invitation read: 'We would very much like you to be present at 3 p.m. on 26 October when we present the above piece in the most naturalistic form, revealing to you a clear picture of avant-garde art. Heading East from the Tower of London, along Royal Mint Street, brings you to Cable Street where we have chosen Railway Arch No. 8 for the historical occasion of our anniversary of "Underneath the Arches". Art for All, 12 Fournier Street.'

The bombast of some of G&G's language – 'the most intelligent, fascinating, serious and beautiful art piece you have ever seen' – was typical, but was at odds with the reality of the result. A photograph reveals them in silhouette under the Cable Street railway arch, with a handful of bewildered spectators keeping a safe distance away. 'When we arrived we found two tramps already there,' they told the writer Francis Wyndham. 'They didn't pay any attention to us at all, nor to the few people who came to watch. We thought that was wizard.'

Their triumph at the Düsseldorf Kunsthalle came the following year. It was followed up in the London gallery of Nigel Greenwood, who became a new champion. The closest I came to seeing The Singing Sculpture was years later at the Groucho Club late one night, when a florid new pianist was trilling at the piano. George in the best of spirits, went over to talk to him, and returned delightedly: 'He's going to play "Underneath the Arches"!'

'No!' I exclaimed. 'You wouldn't do it for us, would you?'

'Of course!' said G&G, beaming. And then the pianist came over to say he had forgotten how to play it. So George Melly's first-hand account of The Singing Sculpture is invaluable: 'I can't remember exactly when I first saw Gilbert & George, but my children, although small, were big enough to take along on my second visit, so I'd guess it to be towards the end of the sixties. I remember where it was: a small upstairs gallery in Glebe Place, Chelsea, and Nigel Greenwood was the entrepreneur. Greenwood, later the Diaghilev of minimalism, told me to go and see them.

'In the otherwise empty room was a platform table, a wind-up gramophone, and Gilbert & George. Dressed in drab brown suits, they wore gloves and had gilded their faces. They moved like automata, jerkily, as though programmed. They may have had rolled umbrellas. On the gramophone was Flanagan and Allen singing "Underneath the Arches". I'm pretty sure it was a gramophone and not a tape, because I seem to remember either Gilbert or George winding it up. Actually, Gilbert & George themselves sang the purely orchestral verse, but mimed to Flanagan and Allen singing the chorus. For this they stood on the table, moving jerkily to the music. It was an absurd and touching spectacle.

'What was most impressive was that they started this three-minute routine at 9 or 10 a.m., and continued until 6 p.m., with no variations whatsoever. I became mildly obsessed with them, but however quietly I crept up the stairs they were always at it. I think it lasted for several weeks – certainly a week. They never showed any reaction to the presence of the public, but if you were there at the end (I never was) I believe they offered you a sherry. I brought the children over from NW6 in a taxi. At my suggestion the taxi-driver came up to see them: "They've got to be fucking barmy."'

Melly followed their progress with interest. He heard that in the summer of 1969 they appeared at a concert in Hyde Park after the death of the Rolling Stone Brian Jones, and he received 'beautifully printed little cards in various colours with statements like "To be with art is all we ask" [1970], and a later series, The Pink Elephants [1973], in which they got methodically drunk on different drinks. There was also an invitation to attend or witness a dinner party at which they were hosts to David Hockney, but it was somewhere in the suburbs, and alas I declined.' But the dinner party went ahead, complete with Hockney, candelabra, cook and butler (The Meal, in Bromley, Kent, 1969).

Telling G&G how Melly sneaked back to see if they were still doing The Singing Sculpture even though the room was sometimes empty, and found them still at it, they laughed. 'We were deter-mined to do this throughout the eight-hour day,' said George, 'because we knew someone would try to catch us out!'

Such is the gallantry of dedication.

The Singing Sculpture sounds monotonous, but the presentations varied – posing still and silent in Amsterdam, followed years later, in 1975, by *The Red Sculpture*, based on an hour's recording of messages in which G&G acted out the words wearing a red matt coating on their heads and hands – 'Very powerful,' says George, 'quite different.' But the real turning point came in New York in September 1971, when they stopped the traffic. This was due to the perception of the remarkable Illeana Sonnabend, who in the sixties began showing American artists such as Warhol, Rauschenberg and Johns in her gallery in Paris, and was ready to move to New York and start a new gallery, this time also featuring European artists, in the then-derelict district of SoHo – south of Houston Street. Recognising the need for something extraordinary, she went to see a Brussels presentation of *The Singing Sculpture*, and knew at once that this was what she wanted.

Her shrewdness paid off handsomely – even if not commercially, for collectors could hardly take G&G home and hang them on the wall, though many tried. The publicity exceeded her hopes, as West Broadway became so crowded that the fire department was called in to control it. Today there are scores of galleries in SoHo, but the Sonnabend, with Leo Castelli's below, remains the most famous. Not only did Gilbert & George inaugurate the gallery, they helped to give the lifeless area a new vitality, which helps to explain their popularity in New York ever since.

Their reception was unlike anything they had experienced in England or Europe. They were welcomed by the eminent art historian Robert Rosenblum as representing the last vestiges of a crumbling British Empire. He described them as 'two belated Victorian entertainers', finding a wealth of new meaning in Flanagan and Allen's 1932 lyrics of 'Underneath the Arches':

The Ritz I never sigh for,
The Carlton they can keep,
There's only one place that I know,
And that is where I sleep.

Underneath the Arches I dream my dreams away.
Underneath the Arches on cobblestones I lay.
Every night you'll find me tired out and worn,
Happy when the daylight comes creeping heralding the dawn,
Sleeping when it's raining and waking when it's fine,
Trains travelling by above.
Pavement is my pillow, no matter where I stray,
Underneath the Arches I dream my dreams away.

Rosenblum hailed this 'spectacular debut that seemed to arrive from a distant planet'. The song, he felt, was symbolic of the 'heartbreaking themes of this old-fashioned, bitter-sweet entertainment – homelessness in far away, long ago London'. Perhaps I am mistaken in thinking he takes this too far – certainly he failed to appreciate the savage wit of music hall – but in support of his point he makes comparisons with William Frith's nineteenth-century series Retribution, with inmates of Millbank Gaol exercising in the yard in The Road to Ruin (1880). He even enlists Augustus Egg's Past and Present (1858) in the Tate Gallery, which shows the downfall of an unfaithful wife, 'to lonely squalor literally underneath the arches, where she finds her final refuge'. If you build a thesis like this, it becomes unanswerable: you can prove anything. Yet I am sure that Rosenblum was passionately sincere in finding this echo of the Thames embankment as 'shockingly timely, a jolt from another era and another city'.

The art critic Carter Ratcliff reminded me that in 1971 America was emerging from assassination and drifting towards Watergate. It was an unhappy time, yet the New York art world was positively giddy: 'In SoHo's fresh and bustling success, New Yorkers saw evidence that American artists and dealers were preserving their long ascendance. That the Sonnabend Gallery chose to mark its SoHo opening with a Living Sculpture by Gilbert & George seemed to prove a point the New York art world never doubted: the city was a powerful magnet. Rejecting most foreign art as irrelevant, it attracted the few exceptions worthy of American attention. Hour after hour as the exceedingly foreign Gilbert & George worked their way through the repetitions of *The Singing Sculpture*, New Yorkers were entranced. They were also baffled. Though Gilbert & George looked important, no one could say why. At the centre of art world power, this failing didn't seen reprehensible. Power is blithe and tends not to linger for explanations.'

Ratcliff is right: *The Singing Sculpture* is ephemeral, which is what makes its lasting impact so remarkable. Undeniably, this was a personal triumph for Gilbert & George, an achievement of originality and stamina, and the faces of those watching them revealed interest, respect, the occasional bemused smile, but little emotion. After all, they were robotic.

The success of *The Singing Sculpture* totally eclipsed G&G's other work which was shown alongside it. Yet this other work actually fascinates me more, revealing another side to G&G, a sensitivity which few people suspected, in large blow-ups of rural settings with delicate black-and-white tracery (*The General Jungle*), using a technique that was initially forced on them due to the usual lack of funds. The effect was pastoral, more Samuel Palmer than G&G, and as close as they came to drawing. If there seems a lack of proficiency, this could well have been deliberate, for the appeal of these pictures depends on their naïvety. Dating from 1970, G&G based their drawings on photographic images, and the delicate tracery was enlarged to huge proportions, floor to ceiling, even in the huge Hayward Gallery.

With themselves as the inevitable focal point, the titles of these pieces have a solemnity which verges on the whimsical but does not seem at all misplaced: *Walking is the Eternity of Our Living Moment, and it can never tell us of an End* (from *The General Jungle*, 1971); *Forever We will Search and Give our Thought to the Picture We have in our Mind/We are walking Round Now as Sad as can be* (1970); contrasting with the happier *There Were Two Young Men Who Did Laugh* (1971).

From anyone else this would be self-indulgent, but G&G mean

it when their title asks: *Is Not Art the Only Hope for the Making Way for the Modern World to Enjoy the Sophistication of Decadent Living Expression* (1971). Yet the effect is one of innocence.

Even more startling is the transition to colour (largely greens), such as *The Paintings* (1970), six triptychs with G&G in the centre flanked by trees and foliage on either side, Gilbert with his hands in his pockets, George arms akimbo, wearing dark suits. To enhance the rustic effect, there is a wooden gate in one panel, and a stream in another. These landscapes were made in Suffolk, unlike most of the charcoal works which were made in Regent's Park, Hyde Park and Kew Gardens.

George claimed that they turned to pastoral subjects at first because they did not know how to 'use' the city: 'In the charcoal works there are some buildings, but we didn't really know how to use them. I think that's because we didn't read newspapers or watch television. We never thought about politics or TV or anything, and we believed that whatever these strange feelings around us were – this confusion of life, and fears – we could express by the jungle of nature.'

At first they advanced tentatively. They did not know how to make a big picture with photographic paper, because no one had done it on this scale before. The monochrome appearance was grey, then black-and-white, then red, then yellow, then four-colour, then full-colour.

As Francis Bacon displayed his early Cubist rugs and tubular furniture, so G&G exhibited a table, two benches and a chair, all decorated with drawings of reeds and grasses, with a large picture on the wall in the background showing themselves in the jungle setting, called *The Tuileries* (1974), shown at the time of their retrospective of charcoal works at the Musée d'art contemporain de Bordeaux in 1986.

Overshadowed at the Sonnabend by *The Singing Sculpture*, to which it provided the background, this twenty-three panel rural artwork was bought by Illeana herself. Earlier G&G had shown a large three-part charcoal work at the Konrad Fischer Gallery in Düsseldorf. Konrad Fischer had asked how much it would cost, and, not thinking it was possible to sell such an object, G&G thought of an extravagant sum and said, '£1000 – which was absurd.'

Gilbert: 'Appalling.'

George: 'But he sold it within the next few days.'

Gilbert: 'We were amazed.'

George: 'That was enough money to last for two years at that time. An extraordinary sum of money.'

Gilbert: 'We were drunk every night. We were taking out everybody. That's why we started doing the drinking pieces. The dark shadow came, because it became a nightmare. Doomed. All black. So we did that.'

CHAPTER SEVEN

INTO THE
DARK SHADOW

A sking Barry Flanagan if he agreed that Gilbert
& George are innocents, he remembered them
as 'studied' – and they are certainly that.
Are they disingenuous? Undoubtedly, protesting too much in
order to cause an effect because they know it teases. Often it is
hard for me to tell the truth.

Yet I believe they have always had an innocence of their own.
The wistfulness of The Singing Sculpture and the seeming simplicity of
the rural scenes made with charcoal, though were now overtaken
as they entered their 'Dark Shadow'. With their newly-earned affluence, they admit, indeed they have boasted, that they had 'an
amazingly drunken period from 1971 to 1980'. Gilbert told Wolf
Jahn: 'We went through this big destructive period of the drunken
scenery, exploring ourselves, exploring our dark side, going out,
getting drunk, all those destructive elements, mucking about, being
totally unhappy. We felt it all had to do with us, we were always
looking inside ourselves. And that's why we never even looked for
another person to be in our work. We felt we didn't need it. Like
Dead Boards [1976], it all had to do with us.'

Until 1977, G&G were the only figures in their pictures, but then they started including others. George explains: 'Strangely, the first time we used other persons we took them with a long lens from the window. It was some Asians and some tramps. It never occurred to us that we could actually have someone model for us. So, very shyly, we just took some people like that, with a spy lens. And it took a long time before we actually asked someone on the street if we could take a photo of him. And for an even longer time it was our friend Andrew [Heard] who modelled in an artistic way for us, indoors. And then we started to have strangers come in to model. We had to reinvent for ourselves the idea of an artist's model.'

This is why the young models from that time are shown in rigid poses, standing, sitting or kneeling, but never moving: 'It was based on asking a person if we could take a photo of him standing in the doorway,' Gilbert told critic Martin Gayford. 'We wouldn't ask him to act out something, we wouldn't even have wanted that. We just wanted a person.' The static result, forced on them through their own shyness, became a G&G characteristic.

Far from being tempted to repeat the success of their £1000 picture, they now turned in the opposite direction. Having shown the surface charm, it seems that they wanted to show the underbelly. Their attitude to their models was ambivalent: on the one hand they were sentimentalised, surrounded by blossom to suggest their freshness, striking poses that were positively fey; on the other, in pictures like The Queue (1978), they were shown as lost souls. Gilbert admits to an element of exploitation – though that has been the fate of artists' models from the beginning of time: 'We asked them for instance to lie down on the floor, turn their backs, turn to us, give a dreadful shout, hide their faces, spread their legs, show aggression, look up at the sky, show their bums.'

One hopes the boys were well-paid, though they look pleased enough to indulge in such rampant narcissism.

With their £1000 cheque, Gilbert & George started to socialise as they had not been able to before. George recalls their drinking with other artists through the night, with the sardonic comment that the others would go to their studios the next day and do a 'perfect white canvas with a line down the middle. What the hell was that? Surely you should be doing something you know about, something people can connect with?'

In contrast to the minimal art so fashionable at the time, it was difficult not to relate to the work of G&G, like them or not. Here was the harsh and melancholy reality as they took a closer look at the city surrounding them. Gilbert thinks they were decadent and destructive in their pieces from 1973 onwards, with the drinking pieces, and the Red Morning pieces of 1977 with such sub-titles as Killing, Hate, Flog, Drowning, Dirt, Death, Blood, Beating.

In Cunt Scum (1977, gifted to the Tate Gallery in 1998 by collector Janet de Botton) they used 'dirty' words, as in Queer of the same year, long before the term became acceptable to gays. In Piss (1977), another picture showed winos in the streets. It is hard not to conclude that these titles were intended to be provocative, though George insisted: 'They think it's all right to have an oil painting of fisher boys from Naples, but not to have the boy from the end of the street. We didn't use images of their educated sons ... we wanted something without class – the young person as a symbol of the living human being.'

Gilbert: 'We want to create a reality that doesn't exist in art, like the reality of young persons. Many people try to say that the young people in our pictures are all East End boot boys. Many journalists try to say they're thugs, hooligans, like the ones in the film A Clockwork Orange by Stanley Kubrick. But we don't believe that. We are showing for the first time that a person like that is a total and fantastic being.' He added that they were going against the grain because they were trying to make 'beautiful pictures'. 'I think beauty was regarded as quite beyond the pale at the time. The word beauty had something to do with lower-class greeting cards. It had no connection with fine art.'

This is typical G&G arrogance, blithely disregarding, for example, the richness and beauty to be rediscovered in the National Gallery. But just as they find beauty in *Stream* (1980), which shows a naked boy 'with piss', the same can be said of Rembrandt's painting in the National of a woman lifting her dress in the middle of another stream. One of the most surprising features of G&G's work is this strand of beauty, from these early black-and-white pictures (most disarming when they reveal themselves, smiling) to The Naked Shit Pictures and The Fundamental Pictures.

I was struck by this in their early street scenes, which provided an antidote to Canaletto's romanticised views of London, in which the stinking Thames is made to appear pristine. G&G's London is devoted to the poor, the homeless, the tramps and alcoholics. The streets are filthy with the clutter of market refuse. There is a sense of hopelessness, yet in the simpler pictures like *Here* (1987), with G&G dressed in blue on either side of a street, there is a haunting beauty.

Coming out of themselves, they now started accepting invitations to dinner parties, which proved a disaster as everyone else left, slowly – 'annoyed by our drunkenness, our laughter and vileness, as we realised how we hated being trapped. That's why we love restaurants and why we adopted the rule not to go to people's houses.' (Recently, however, they went to the home of the critic David Sylvester for dinner; but that was only because Sylvester thought it might be helpful for them to meet another guest, Lord Gowrie, then head of the Arts Council, though Sylvester's kind intentions did backfire.) George claims that they have always been more private than people think, but Gilbert admits, 'When we first had money, we discovered life.' They went to the early gay bars and pubs: The DOK, The Pink Elephant, The Vauxhall Tavern, notorious for drag, and The Cricketers in Battersea, where they may have seen Hinge and Bracket.

They complain now that they are not allowed to misbehave, but that did not deter them then. In the mid-1970s, both were arrested for being drunk and disorderly, though on separate occasions. Gilbert was the first, and found it a terrifying experience with the humiliation of the Black Maria and his first appearance in court: 'I thought I was going to be raped!'

'That's Gilbert's definition,' said George, with a lift of his eyebrows. 'Obviously he went about it in the wrong way and upset the poor police. Very silly.'

'But you,' Gilbert spluttered indignantly, 'were arrested yourself a week later.'

'That's perfectly correct,' George agreed.

How would you cope with prison? I asked Gilbert, thinking of the feared 'rape'.

'I'd *love* it!' he smiled.

Have you been mugged?

'Both of us,' said George. 'We don't care about it – we call it self-service dole.'

What is your greatest regret?

'Not having discovered bad behaviour earlier in life.'

But they tried. Liam Carson, who was instrumental in the success of the Groucho Club when he was the manager, told me of an evening in the mid to late seventies when he worked in the Covent Garden bar Blitz, where Steve Strange, Boy George, Pinkitessa, Adam Ant and others sported their latest outrageous outfits. Gilbert & George were regulars, claiming that the house claret, Churchill's Choice, was superior to Simpson's – were they becoming food and drink snobs? 'It was an odd place,' said Carson, 'not at all busy, and the other "regulars" were young men from the East End who ran ice-cream patches along Oxford Street. One night they held a birthday party with twenty or thirty of them with their girlfriends. Gilbert & George were dining too, and I don't know quite what sparked it off, because they seemed to be getting along rather well with them, but I presume that G&G made a pass or an improper suggestion to one of the young men, and a bar-room brawl broke out that would have done justice to a Wild West saloon. The homophobic rage of the East End boys knew no bounds, and Gilbert & George – especially Gilbert – took a severe beating. We eventually managed to control it and I took them to the kitchen to clean up. Gilbert was badly cut – I think the result of a bottle over the head [true] – but he was more worried about spoiling his suit. The evening subsided eventually and G&G paid their bill, leaving an extraordinarily large tip! I have spoken to them since about the evening, and although they were the worse for wear they do recollect it. When they came to the club it was never dull.'

George Melly learnt that when one of them was coshed unconscious by some skinheads in the East End, the other sat by the bed equally (if voluntarily) immobile, until he recovered. But, as Stainton Forrest confirms, there are never any complaints on the mornings after.

After ten years G&G decided that they never wanted to be part of the art crowd: 'We ended up with too many people crucifying us – like one big hangover. If we started going to openings it would immediately start a confrontation – they would have liked to jump on top of us.' When I pointed out that in March 1997 they had been kind enough to come to the launch of *Never a Normal Man*, my autobiography, coinciding with my photographic exhibition at the Roy Miles Gallery, George replied: 'That's a very big exception.' Gilbert agreed: 'Very big. We thought we might surprise you.' They did. The score of gossip-pages snaps as they posed with Edward Heath added invaluable publicity – as they were shrewd enough to know.

Fed up with their own adverse publicity, they started the eighties with new resolve – 'We tried to keep away from the battle, and when they started to discredit us in every newspaper, we retreated.'

It is hard to imagine G&G relaxing, unless sitting opposite each other in Fournier Street, like figures from Madame Tussaud's. I was disappointed, after they recommended *The Old Curiosity Shop* by Charles Dickens, which I then devoured happily for the first time, when as we discussed the character of the evil yet irresistible Quilp I realised they had seen an early film on television (which I suspect they watch more than they admit, with the documentaries as their favourites), rather than read the book.

They do not go to the theatre and have no interest in plays, concerts, ballets or opera. They went to the cinema three or four times a day until the late seventies, seeing everything they could – even Chinese films and comedies like *The Ups and Downs of a Window Cleaner*: 'There wasn't a cinema we didn't go to, but there was a greater variety then.'

Surely three or four times a day was excessive?

'It was. We stopped suddenly in 1979.'

Fournier Street has shelves filled with books. George's preoccupation is collecting every 'sexual' book he can find, reading out the spicy bits to Gilbert, who refuses to read them through. George seems obsessed by the literature of sex – 'all aspects, including medical texts. We have a large library. We think it's one of the most important subjects this century, with the attitudes changing.'

Gilbert: 'The forbidden becoming normal. The books are only male to male. It's the burning issue for the Church, the government, the army . . .'

'And the arts,' interrupted George. 'And the enemy is losing. Even the editor of the *Daily Telegraph* [ironically their favourite newspaper, because it's 'normal'] knows he's losing. He can write whatever editorials he wants [and has done, to their obvious displeasure], but he can't stop thousands of people coming to our shows from all over the world.'

Interviewed by Hans-Ulrich Obrist in 1997 for their book of writings, *The Words of Gilbert & George*, George reiterated: 'The biggest issue of our lifetime has been, and will continue to be, what is a man and what is a woman? We have always believed that, and it became more and more true. We never thought we would live to see an *Evening Standard* headline saying: "It's official: Marriage is Defunct".'

Gilbert: 'We used to say that the heterosexuals can sort themselves out only when they accept, when they are able to understand, the homosexual.'

George: 'At the moment, the so-called straight community is more intent on copying the gay community.'

They stress delightedly their impact on advertising, with the emphasis on men rather than women. George: 'Enormous changes. That is post-G&G. We always fought against the divisions of sexuality. We were always encouraged by the art profession to believe in the idea of gay and straight, and we don't believe in that. We just believe that every person is a sexual person. There literally is no such thing as a heterosexual or homosexual. How many times have you told somebody something that was said to you at a party that was very interesting, without having to say the sex of that person?' He concludes pontifically: 'We are happily capable of being so much more complicated than anyone says, and therefore one has to leave these divisions aside to allow us to be as elaborate as we can be.'

Their preoccupation with these divisions indicates how much they have suffered from being categorised, and how much they resent it. The trouble with labels is that they stick. G&G were right in believing that after 1979 the press had turned against them, using such epithets as 'homosexual artists' and 'fascists', but they brought much of this on themselves. It was hardly a case of being unfairly maligned: they asked for it. Equally, they were unprepared for the extent to which they were condemned: 'We are on the edge in every single way,' says Gilbert today, now that they are established. 'I think that's very important. We always got hurt. People think that we couldn't care less. But we were very hurt by a lot of the stuff. That's good. The hostility became sometimes so incredible. I think for the last twenty years we've always been in trouble. Our art is very confrontational.'

Did they expect polite applause when they released the Dirty Words pictures in 1977 with such titles as *Prostitute, Poof, Bollocks,*

Cock, Lick, Cunt, Fuck, Bummed, Wanker, Queer, Bent Shit Cunt, Shag Stiff, Cunt Scum? It surprises me that they did not create a worse scandal. Here I should declare myself, with some shame, as having been prejudiced against G&G until I began to appreciate their work, feeling that they strove too hard to be shocking. Complaining in a Sunday newspaper in January 1987 about the exclusion of Augustus John from the exhibition British Art in the Twentieth Century at the Royal Academy of Art, I wrote: 'I would rather see a recognisable doodle by John than the squiggly lines of Bridget Riley, the dripping paint thrown by Bruce McLean at his canvas, the photographic collage by Gilbert & George, aptly entitled *Wanker*.'

I still feel it was mistaken not to include Augustus John, and still have my doubts about Riley, but this was ten years after the Dirty Words pictures, and I was wrong. If there is one thing I have learnt from my years as an art critic, it is that when you fail to understand something, it is time to look again.

Fortunately, I looked again, and found myself feeling increasing sympathy for the pictures of the lost youths who drifted through the decaying streets of East London like the hurt graffiti on the walls behind them. The pictures were interpreted by others as an indictment of Britain at the time, though I found them all the more powerful for that.

Just how hostile were the critics? The art historian Frank Whitford, who discussed G&G on my TV art quiz *Gallery*, pinpointed a truth which escapes most of the critics: 'They're so anxious to stress how much hostility their work arouses. They gloss over the fact that more than half the most widely-read critics and almost all the big museum people aren't hostile at all. On the contrary. And the irony is that those who are most hostile are precisely the kind of "ordinary" people who Gilbert & George claim are all for them and for whom they claim their work is primarily intended.'

This is a common form of artist's vanity. In 1994 Ron Kitaj denounced a conspiracy of critics, accusing them of being responsible for his wife's death due to their 'anti-Semitic' reviews of his exhibition at the Tate – apparently unable to accept that they simply disliked the work. As I know from personal experience, Francis Bacon took a perverse pleasure in telling me that he was not appreciated in London and was only admired in Paris, which was wildly untrue, as he must have known. It suited him to believe that only the discerning French really understood him.

Yet, in the case of G&G, there have been virulent critics: like Brian Sewell of the London *Evening Standard*, who has indulged in a personal vendetta against them, exuding a bile which makes one wonder if there is some motivation which has nothing to do with art at all – though that may well be his point. Headlines such as 'Beware of Strange Men who do Funny Things' implied that East End parents should not encourage their sons to pose for G&G as models. Wisely, as always, G&G did not sue.

Undoubtedly Sewell's outrage is genuine, not simulated. He is justified in believing that 'pornography is a private reserve, a matter for personal decisions, and I do not want the catalogue of Gilbert & George to poke my nose into the cleft behind anyone's parted buttocks, and least of all into the sphincter so relaxed that its proper place is in a textbook of medical mysteries'. Sewell's intimate knowledge of such subjects is remarkable, but he is unjustified in his conclusion: 'I understand that Gilbert & George find their subjects in the streets of Spitalfields – local colour, so to speak; imagine the youngster taken home and undressed, Gilbert & George giving their directions from under the black cloth (their photography is dismally old-fashioned and stagey); what must he think of these two artists getting away with the very contact against which he must at one stage have been warned (beware of strange men who do funny things) simply because they proclaim it art and not pornography?' He even accused G&G of taking 'the charlatan's way out'. It is sad to read such hysterical stuff from one of our most informed and entertaining critics. Once, reviewing a book by Sewell on Turkey, I commented on his curious fascination with the pubic hair he found in a shower in Salonika. He never forgave me, though I was complimentary about the collection of his criticism, *The Reviews that Caused the Rumpus*, which I wrote about for *Art Review*. Always consistent, his reaction to The Naked Shit Pictures was predictable – 'Such Tired Old Naughty Boys' – but it dates back to the 1970s. Writing in 1987 about G&G's Hayward Gallery exhibition of recent pictures, he suggested, 'Think of a dirty word for a sexual act, a body function, or a genital part, and you may well find it incorporated in the photo-constructions of Gilbert & George. In 1977 they had a binge of bollocks, bums and buggers (their words not mine) and then went off the boil into what they conceived as modern moralities, with only occasional lapses into the lavatorial vernacular of the Army.'

Sewell once appeared on *Gallery*, an experience he did not seem to enjoy, as he confirmed in print afterwards, resenting – with good reason – the interminable delays and rehearsals. But another guest surprised me by taking Sewell's part wholeheartedly – the late Peter Fuller, whose own vendetta against G&G is less easy to dismiss. Fuller was an interesting, formidable young man, the art critic for the *Sunday Telegraph* and the founder and editor of the magazine *Modern Painters*. I took to him immediately, charmed by his cautious, schoolboy looks, so at variance with the forcefulness of his criticism. We killed time happily before the first rehearsal – unlike Brian Sewell – and spoke generally until I referred to his own dislike of Gilbert & George, and he admitted that he felt a genuine hatred towards them. This had been signalled in Roger Scruton's article 'Beastly Bad Taste' in one of the first issues of *Modern Painters*, in spring 1988, which set the tone:

> Their work, it could hardly be called art, is easy to understand for the simple reason that it contains nothing to understand. Their titles are lifted from the gutter – *Two Cocks, Tongue Fuck Cocks, Friendship Pissing, Shit Faith* and the like – while the images fail to be disgusting only because Gilbert & George are so devoid of artistic talent as to be

capable of producing no emotion whatsoever. They have
little understanding of surface or light; their colours are
those of the playground and supermarket, and their lines
are executed either photographically or in the hard-edged
manner of the comic strip.

This attack on their technique is puzzling: what is so wrong with
the colours of the playground? And American Pop artists like Roy
Lichtenstein proved how powerful comic-strip imagery could be.
As for their photographic executions, this is how G&G work. Apart
from those early rural pictures, awash with greenery, they cannot
be categorised as draughtsmen or painters. But what offended Scruton more than the 'gutter' images was their failure to attract on a
higher level: 'Where there is an absence of beauty, impossibility
of beauty, the overthrow of beauty's empire, there Gilbert & George
stand drivelling their ritual paean of the beautiful, uttering the word
in the same tone of voice as they utter "shit", "fuck", "cock" and
"buggery".'

To this one can only say that 'beauty' lies in the eye of the
beholder; but the validity of Scruton's final conclusion on G&G
cannot be denied, if you are thinking of art in the traditional values
of the past: 'A work can now perform its economic function without
being loved or admired; nobody needs to be awakened by it or
moved by its deeper meaning. The money pours through it unre-
sisted, like sewage through a drain.'

Peter Fuller followed this up with his *Modern Painters* review of the
1989 For AIDS exhibition under the heading 'The Evil of Banality',
to which Gilbert responded: 'But life *is* banal!' Fuller described the
show as the 'tackiest' he had seen in London for two decades.

Other opponents included the charming Giles Auty, then the art
critic for the *Spectator*, who asked in April 1989: 'Can one sensibly
question any calamities that befall a society which makes Gilbert &
George into cultural heroes?' But Auty went too far in impugning
G&G's motive in donating the proceeds of the For AIDS exhibition

to charities helping AIDS research: 'A number of notices suggest that reviewers, acting in a similar spirit of benevolence, have waived their rights to critical comment.'

It is plain that G&G *did* have some justification in believing there was widespread hostility against them in the media – though there is less today. In July 1987 Waldemar Januszczak, then the critic for the *Guardian*, conceded, 'It cannot have been easy being Gilbert & George over the past fifteen years. The shouts of "filthy queers" must have hurt.' Yet, ironically, two of the severest criticisms came from those who were basically well-intended. George Melly said on *Gallery*: 'They proclaim to be little Englanders – strange considering one is Italian – and speak like caricatures of old and particularly reactionary colonels. I've no objection to them being gay or fancying skinheads [This is an assumption rather than a proven fact], but they elevate these same wog- and gay-bashing yobs into heroes. Nor am I impressed or shocked by the graffiti, shit, spunk, etc. in their work, but I am repelled by such symbols as a severed black head. Their own obsessions are their business, but I don't see why I should applaud them for holding them. I find the stained-glass window effect increasingly empty. I see why they're popular. You can tell a Gilbert & George work at a hundred paces or more, and the rich who collect want their acquisitions to be recognised immediately, and Gilbert & George certainly fit *that* bill. But I see no development, no "good" or "bad" examples of their work, simply the appreciation of a rigid system. How serious are they? How much do they mean what they transmit? I neither know nor care. Their recent and generous contribution to AIDS research I applaud. Otherwise, I simply regret their gradual ossification from merry pranks to tendentious and predictable fossils.'

Frank Whitford, a regular on *Gallery*, told me how he enjoyed interviewing G&G for BBC Radio, realising afterwards that they had revealed nothing about themselves. 'They reminded me of actors in a two-handed play, with everything so well-rehearsed that it didn't matter what questions were asked. Only after the interview was over and they were showing me their collection of pots and furniture did they become relatively normal conversation partners: engaged, enthusiastic, genuine. I did, however, get the impression that they are absolutely genuine in their art, genuine above all in their desire to use it to control the feelings of those who look at it. They want to annoy and disgust as well as to amuse and entertain, and it's almost impossible to make art that does this any more. I don't think they're intellectually very sound, but they are enormously clever.'

Whitford recognised their ability to 'amuse', which most critics ignore, probably because it does not suit them to admit it. It is too easy to accept G&G on their own bleak terms – they have described themselves (I think fatuously) as 'lonely, miserable and terrified people' – until you are confronted by *Coming* (1983), in which they look heavenwards at brightly-coloured underpants which rain down from the night sky. This must be one of the funniest pictures of the twentieth century.

When I chose two G&G works to be discussed by the panel on *Gallery*, I expected controversy, but not the extent of the antagonism towards G&G. With their skill at self-promotion they are often hoist by their own petard. I noticed that when we showed a Bacon or a Sickert, the panellists would talk about the painting; shown a G&G, they concentrated on G&G themselves. The artist Maggi Hambling detested the element of 'fascism' which she finds in G&G's work, which they themselves dismiss out of hand. But it is a very sore point indeed: 'They call us drunks, fascists, paedophiles – all kinds of stupid names,' said George contemptuously. 'People say, "Surely you don't mind criticism?" . . . Have you ever been walking at night and you hear a most horrible row going on between a husband and wife? And you get that *dreadful* feeling in your stomach? It's an awful feeling.'

The tag of fascism started with works like *Britisher* and *Patriots* in 1980, and has lingered. George told Lynn Barber, with a degree of anger, that it was meaningless: 'Fascists are what teenagers call their

parents in sitcoms when Daddy refuses to let them borrow the car.'
When she asked Gilbert if his family had supported Mussolini, he
told her, with equal anger, that his family hated Mussolini because
he tried to abolish the Ladino language and culture, and George
said that members of his family fought in both world wars. 'We
hate the blackshirts of the left because they want to dictate what we
can all do, what we can't all do. You used to see them on Brick
Lane on Sundays with their publications *Socialist Worker* and *Militant*,
some crummy disgusting titles – they are dictating all the time. But
our art is just to do with flowers and humanity, that's what we
like: complex life.'

Yet George's old champion Ivor Weeks was dismayed when he
dined with them in the seventies: 'They said some things that if it
had been anyone else, would have made me get up and walk away.
But I never understood whether that fascist stuff was just part of
the game.' Questioned about this, G&G said they remember only
a delightful evening.

Lynn Barber (strangely) was amused to discover that though they
rejected the fascist label, it did not actually *upset* them: the label
they really detested was exposed by her casual assumption that their
work was 'obviously homoerotic'.

Gilbert yelped: 'Not at all, it's not so clear.'

George agonised: 'How can you say that? What do you *mean*?'

She meant, she said, the 'muscular, bare-chested young men who
feature in their pictures; the prevalence of phallic symbols; the total
absence of women and children'. She admitted that the young men
– wimpish rather than muscular, to my eyes at least – were not
blatantly eroticised, as in the photographs of Robert Mapplethorpe,
for example, 'but they are sex objects nonetheless'.

'But they are just boys we find in the street,' wailed G&G in
dismay. 'They are not gay. You can't sex a person in the street,
anyway.'

Gilbert: 'In the eighteenth century, every man was bisexual.'

George: 'It wasn't even called that; it was just being a gentleman.

He would have a wife and a friend. It's only fashion that makes people think that they personally like this kind of sex or that kind of sex. It's conditioning.'

That is a sweeping assumption, but Barber said that this was the first time she had ever seen them, especially Gilbert, so agitated: 'They are far more bothered by the suggestion that their *art* is homosexual than that they themselves are. Why does it worry them so much?'

George: 'We don't like these clichés being applied to us when they're so unfair to life, when they're unfair to people.'

Gilbert declared: 'We never did gay art, we *never* did, *ever*.'

But if they never did gay art, they hardly did heterosexual art either. For the most part the pretty youths flanked by foliage verged on the twee – and there was not a woman in sight. Lynn Barber was unconvinced, especially when they took her to see the 'model' shots in their studio of what they called, oddly, 'normal humanoids' – 'More than two thousand of them, and as boring as reading the phone book.'

'But these are pornographic,' she objected.

'Where's pornographic?' George demanded. 'Is nakedness pornographic? Are you pornographic when you get into the bath?'

Obviously not, thought Barber, but what she found 'really creepy' was not so much the photographs as G&G's desire to show them to her, with George asking, 'What do you think of this one, then?'

During her visit, they showed her (amongst their other treasures) a two-ended phallus, saying, 'This is the Gilbert & George model.' 'Schoolboy stuff,' she concluded, 'but disturbing too, and vaguely hostile.' She still has the hunch, however, that they are not a 'gay' couple.

Does the 'gay' label matter? Not a jot to me, but plainly it does to others, and to G&G themselves, though they have told me they don't like gay militancy, and that though gay liberation was important when it started, now it has run its course and has become too academic, too stilted.

Gilbert: 'They create a ghetto. Even dressing up – big moustaches, leather caps!' He giggled.

George: 'We've always thought that. We think we have a good subversive way for approaching the issue which doesn't alienate anyone. We even dislike the word "gay", which was originally stolen from female prostitutes in eighteenth-century London, though "queer" is perfectly all right. That is a very big movement in America, and we've been a big part of that, but never part of any marching. Our picture Queer [1977] was shown in five US cities. Some gay people were upset. Now you have "Queer as fuck" T-shirts, and Queer Nation is an organised group.'

I asked again, if they were identified as homosexual artists – 'We don't believe in that, we believe in the Nil. We never campaign for homosexual art. Asked, "Are you homosexuals?" we don't accept that; it's too limited a term, a quasi-medical term from Denmark in the last century.' Conversely, it can be argued that they have exploited any prejudice against gays to the great advantage of themselves.

Inexplicably, great offence was taken to their generosity in sponsoring books which were written about them in the early days, and were rich with colour illustrations beyond the means of most publishers. In 1991 I was one of the beneficiaries with my book With Gilbert & George in Moscow, which they designed themselves. Yet their policy of ploughing back the profits sent Peter Fuller into a rage, in particular about The Art of Gilbert & George, published by Thames & Hudson in 1989 at the modest price for such a heavily illustrated book of £12.95.

Fuller started with a celebrated attack on 'banality':

It was, of course, Hannah Arendt who first used the phrase 'the banality of evil' after observing the Nazi war criminals in the dock at Nuremberg; but Gilbert & George's lives and work testify rather to the evil of banality. This was brought home to me when I read a new book about the egregious pair by a little-known German writer, Wolf Jahn ... it carried no health warning, it is, in fact, a piece of 'vanity' publishing by the artists themselves. (It is only because Gilbert & George have poured money into the book that such a large and lavish volume of well over 500 pages, many in full colour, can be offered to the public at this price.)

To which many people might say 'Well done!' G&G make no attempt to conceal such sponsorship, and point out that the handsome catalogues of major exhibitions in leading galleries like the Royal Academy are nearly always sponsored by commercial firms.

Why should such an intelligent man as Fuller be so uncharitable towards artists who are making their way? Partly because of the uncritical admiration expressed by so many of G&G's acolytes, which can work against them. Fuller seized on this as justification: 'Wolf Jahn is not an independent critic, but rather a hand-picked publicist: and his account of the gospel according to St Gilbert and St George makes pretty sick reading. Without any sense of irony, Jahn argues that the "existential aesthetic of Gilbert & George ... is analogous ... to the primordial divine sacrifice of Jesus".'

I have never heard G&G talk like that themselves, and should have debunked them on the spot if I had. They cannot be held responsible for the tributes with which they are showered, though Fuller suggested that they can: 'If Jahn's book was in any way serious, it would pose a graver affront to Christian believers than ever Salman Rushdie directed towards those of the Islamic faith.' Then Fuller asked what could have induced the reputable Thames & Hudson to publish 'such an obscene and blasphemous piece of self-promotion', and gave the answer – 'Money, one can only suppose, has spoken.'

Ah, money! Peter Fuller is the last man I should have suspected of sour grapes, but money makes the world go round, even more than love. Brian Sewell finished one diatribe: 'They have their paws in a crock of gold, and they will do anything to hold on to it.' In fact G&G's sponsorships are a shrewd investment, and they cannot be bought. Offered a huge sum in 1990 to advertise a car on television in a situation that was not belittling, but was neither typical nor humorous, they asked me what they should do.

'Turn it down,' I said immediately.

They smiled: 'We already have. We wanted to hear what you'd say.'

Accusing him of courting publicity, a stranger asked George in a Torquay pub why he had appeared on the BBC chat show *Wogan* (Jonathan Ross had taken over). 'It's beneath your dignity.'

'That's exactly why we appeared!'

Of all their books, the most extraordinary is *Dark Shadow*, of 1974–76, with 'George & Gilbert' (yes!) underneath a crest that looks suspiciously royal. They refer to themselves as 'the sculptors', and the cover also states: 'Art for All, 12 Fournier Street, London E.1.', though Nigel Greenwood is acknowledged inside as the publisher of the limited edition of two thousand copies. It's a very rum affair. 'We have turned them [their daily thoughts]', they write, 'into ink and arranged them as words and pictures to form this living sculpture book.' They are extremely proud of it.

Page one consists of a salute to Gordon's gin, illustrated with the boar's head trademark (all spellings are as they appear in the book):

> The boars head, hallmark of our illustrious down fall and brand new imaginations. Smart and sombre with edges of our clearness. The trade mark rather than the marks of trade, his ears, his nose, nothing between the teeth and eyes left with a steady expression. Easy to turn but hard to turn to the right to make tight. Black for black, white for white but black for bottle-green. Wavy edges, flat top and easy to screw either way, if you know more or less what we mean.

Page two features a photo of Gilbert looking smart in a dark suit, a glass on one arm of his chair, a bottle of gin on the table and a small bottle of tonic.

The next page reads:

> Mother and the Indian together making a perfect tonic. Enough to quell the sea-sickness. Screw-top and non-returnable which is not how one would describe most things.

As if encouraged by these flights of fancy, they go further:

> As black as night and here comes the bottle to head off your chopper. What a strange shape the moon is tonight, quite the little oval. And talking of the oval there is this most marvellous pub down by the . . . but we mustn't keep to the subject. What wonderful shoulders, what a lovely back and such an original tattoo. The milky way of the title, measured and sad. We always spell it out, G for gutsish, O for ovaries and so on through the three names.

Page five becomes maudlin:

> Oh God, nothing, giggle giggle, but nothing, should persuade the normal man to look upon this scene with any normal senses . . . Nobody asked the dear little lemon if he minded, did they. We would not think for a second. Glasses spread out or what and intercourse into the reflections. The influential drink. Awaiting the master-stroke or on the other hand just stroking the stem of a glass in hand.

These last comments are illustrated by an image on the opposite page of fallen and half-filled glasses. 'Influential Drink', with such schoolboyish wit as: 'There was this old fellow who had such good eye-sight that he never needed glasses. He always drank it straight from the bottle.'

The mood becomes more sombre in Chapter Two, also called 'Dark Shadow':

> Glued forever with despondency to this vista of variations of glooms. Nothing is too dark, dreary, desolate or miserable for us. Our black black years stretch out with pleasantness of morbid memory . . . From across the room the mummy tries to speak. Dustily he just manages to say to us the word 'shame'. All then is quiet, vast and grey and lost and lonely . . .

Appropriately, to enhance the hallucinatory effect, the pictures are wildly out of focus. Some of the images are memorable:

> Here comes the first one (shabby thoughts) sticky with pleasurable richness. And hard behind the next a foul smelling perfume of decaying brilliance like a diamond thinly coated with excrement.

Mary McCarthy found shades of Jonathan Swift in William Burroughs' The Naked Lunch: 'There are many points of comparison, not only the obsession with excrement and the horror of female genitals, but disgust with politics, and the whole body politic.' There is the same scatterbrained logic – even in the lack of it – in Dark Shadow, with additional echoes of Edgar Allan Poe, and a poignancy of its own. A blurred yet unmistakable sketch of G&G is complemented with:

> The wicked chaps look bad tonight. They need a trim, they need a shave, their suits are creased and flopping down and all is quite a little the worse for wear. George's lenses are so smoked they would be ideal for seeing the eclipse of the sun through. Gilbert's tie is askew enough for him soon to tell a joke. In another few minutes the round will be up, and the next round must begin again.

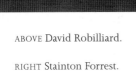

ABOVE David Robilliard.

RIGHT Stainton Forrest.

In Tianenmen Square, Beijing, September 1993, with catalogues for The China Exhibition.

Outside the National Art Gallery, Beijing, with friends and other foreign visitors to The China Exhibition.

Beijing.

ABOVE On the Great Wall.

ABOVE RIGHT In a Beijing restaurant with Raymond O'Daly, Yu Yi-Gang and James Birch.

RIGHT Opening of The China Exhibition at The Art Museum, Shanghai, October 1993.

In New York with Carter Ratcliff and Phyllis Derfner (far left), Daniel Farson (right) and fans at the time of The Fundamental Pictures exhibition, 1997.

OPPOSITE Shitty Naked Human World, Kunstmuseum, Wolfsburg, Germany, 1994.

In Stockholm for the exhibition at Magasin 3, with Daniel Farson (third from left) and Alexander Roussos (centre), 1997.

Brick Lane, London, 1997.

With Daniel Farson in Appledore, Devon, 1997.

The eyes try desperately to give to us some message before passing into shadow. These lips try sculpturally to speak some words but dry and cracked they hardly move. Our moment lost the page is nearly black yet was his that voice we hear call softly – this tis his – he whispers to us the word, 'shame', 'shame', 'shame', 'shame'.

What is it all about? What does it mean? (I am old-fashioned enough to like things to mean something.) I am not sure. I doubt if they could have achieved the drunken effect when drunk themselves: such undisciplined prose needs the height of discipline, and if there is madness in this book it is rather fine, a confessional. Significantly, two of their major black-and-white pictures of 1980 and 1982 show two demented images of G&G with a dragon-like shape tilting forward above them (*Living with Madness*), while *Deatho Knocko* depicts huge beetles hovering above two armoured figures with swords and shields jousting below. Plainly this was a period during which G&G knew moments of the utmost melancholy. This changed dramatically in the mid-eighties, with a burst of colour – the time of the dark shadows was over. They began their 'Ascent'.

CHAPTER EIGHT

WITH GILBERT & GEORGE
IN MOSCOW

In 1988, James Birch of the Birch & Conran Gallery in Soho had organised an exhibition of Francis Bacon's paintings at the New Tretyakov Gallery in Moscow, the first exhibition in the Soviet Union by a major Western artist since the war. Bacon was enthusiastic about the idea, and I was eager to climb on such a historic bandwagon, persuading the *Daily Mail* to pay my fare, while the British Council made a modest but welcome contribution towards my expenses.

Then something went wrong. I am still not entirely sure what it was, but suspect that poison had been dropped in Bacon's ear by a few people who opposed the project – probably because they had been left out.

I saw Bacon one evening in the Groucho Club, and he looked so testy when I mentioned Moscow that I realised he was changing his mind about the whole project. He had lunched with a couple of representatives of the British Council and found them so boring that he refused to allow them to pay the bill, doing so himself though he was the guest, as a typically inverted form of self-punishment. Now he told me that he doubted if he would go to

Moscow because he felt he was being taken advantage of, and James Birch, who had organised the exhibition, had not warned him about the protocol involved. Realising this was a delicate situation and that I needed to be circumspect, I reassured him that Birch had behaved impeccably, and that he was equally fed up with the British Council, who were taking the credit for something he had initiated. Knowing that Francis would veer off in the other direction if anyone attempted to lead him, I stressed: 'You must do exactly as you want. That is all that matters. If you don't want to go, don't.'

'Well, I don't.'

Disingenuously, I pointed out that the young Russian artists would be disappointed.

'That's rubbish. They know my work already. They send me letters. They don't need to see me.'

I gave a nervous laugh: 'You might enjoy it.'

'I doubt that greatly.'

'You could do whatever you wanted; they could even hold the press conference without you . . .'

He leapt up furiously, as if I had upset my drink all over him. 'What press conference?'

Oh God, I thought, no one has told him that this would be part of the first day's programme, though it was listed in the British Council's detailed itinerary.

I suggested that just possibly the visiting artist might be expected to say a few words, but assured him that it would be quite unnecessary in his case: 'You must do as you like.'

'Anyhow,' he concluded, 'there's my asthma.' He complained that this had recently become worse, but then went into reverse, adding that his doctor was travelling to Moscow too, so there was nothing to worry about if he did have an attack.

'But Francis,' I protested, 'if you're suffering from asthma, the flight could be disastrous.'

Having raised the subject, he dismissed it: 'I don't know; it's just a few hours.'

Probably his mind was already made up, for I had never known him to change it. He sent a message of his personal regret, with asthma as his alibi, and I returned my cheque to the *Daily Mail* – for my planned story was no longer valid without him.

All this in-fighting should have been avoided. Francis had originally been so keen to go that he had been studying Russian from cassettes for the previous six months. After the exhibition, James Birch told me that he had breakfast with Francis before he set out to Moscow with John Edwards, his close friend whose portrait adorned both the exhibition poster and the Russian catalogue. 'We had bacon and eggs in his studio, and you could tell that Francis was excited. Afterwards, John told me, "I bet if he'd had a visa he would have hopped on the plane with us."' Instead the British contingent included Lord Gowrie, the former Arts Minister, and Henry Meyric-Hughes, then director of the British Council's Fine Arts Department, who spoke at the obligatory press conference. But the artist himself was absent. This is why Gilbert & George's attendance was so important for their own exhibition in 1990 at the New Tretyakov Gallery.

As I carried my luggage from my bedroom, the night porter appeared. 'Gilbert & George are here,' he said.

In person?

'Very much so!'

I had expected them to wait in a hired limousine while the chauffeur was sent to fetch me, but at that stage I did not know them well. They stood outside smiling, and helped me carry my luggage to the taxi.

I had met them only once, a year or two before at their home in Fournier Street, where I went to interview them for my book *Gallery*. As I was early I stopped for a drink at the Jack the Ripper on the corner, a beastly pub which became briefly notorious in 1988 when the Canadian landlord served 'Ripper-tipple cocktails' to celebrate the centenary of the murders. The brewers had been forced to change the name back to The Three Bells, but it was no less rough, and when I asked the landlord the way to G&G's home, he scowled: 'Oh, you mean the gay couple?' I felt that he would have preferred the bloodstained Jack as a neighbour and wondered if this was the general opinion locally.

When I found the house, G&G's pleasant assistant Tyrone Dawson asked if I drank coffee, as if this were a rare ritual, then showed me upstairs into a panelled room where G&G awaited me like figures in a Victorian photograph, with George seated and Gilbert standing. I felt I was on trial, which was probably the case.

'The critics are 100 per cent against us!' said George with some satisfaction.

They were evidently sounding me out, and when I asked the naïve but inevitable question why their work was restricted to men, they were prepared.

'If there were a poster for "Nudes", people would assume they were female nudes,' said Gilbert.

'The male nude is still shocking,' said George – I noted that they spoke in relays – 'Nudes have always been women because men have the money; look at advertising. If a woman artist painted women, her work would not be described as lesbian.'

They laughed as they referred to the theme most interviewers returned to – the naked men, though in fact most of those who appear in their work have their trousers on.

'If women had the chequebooks, art would be filled with naked men!' George said. Yet at the same time, they referred to women disparagingly as 'tarts'.

I relished their craziness and contrary logic, though I was feeling my way too.

But by now they trusted me, and as we bowled along the Hammersmith flyover on a perfect April morning we seemed like old friends embarking on a spree – as it certainly was for me. Even Heathrow held none of the usual horrors: not because of any VIP treatment, but due to G&G's quiet discretion as they checked in with everyone else. Even I relaxed, without the usual impatience induced by airports, and stocked up on the duty-free gifts so precious in Russia – chocolates, plastic half-bottles of Johnny Walker, cartons of Marlboro cigarettes. These Western goods are the most valuable currency – far above roubles – and I added them to my arsenal of soap, socks and books. A saleswoman of startling elegance waved a new brand of eau de cologne on special offer, pitching her talk so skilfully that I bought some partly to please her, and she threw in several samples for good measure. A few nights later I was to use one of them to freshen up, unaware that it was undiluted perfume until James Birch reeled away from me, clutching his nose.

I was disappointed though not surprised that she had not heard of G&G, but a smartly dressed young man asked for their autograph, which George gave with such a flourish that Gilbert turned to me with a shrug of irritation: 'Oh, George, he does make such a thing of it!' before signing his own name, Gilbert, before & George, revealing that he was less keen on the razzmatazz. Thanking them politely, the young man walked away with no attempt at conversation, not even to ask where they were going.

Travelling Club Class – this time my fare was being paid by the Sunday Telegraph – we were fuelled with gin and tonics, and it seemed only a matter of moments before we arrived in Moscow, in such an advanced state of euphoria that I left one of my duty-free bags on the plane. Before I could stop him, George hurried back to retrieve it. He did this instinctively, with none of the irritation which would have been displayed by, for example, Francis Bacon, who detested inefficiency and fuss.

While G&G were swept away in a Rover 2000 (apparently one of only two in Russia) I followed with James Birch and Judy Adam from the d'Offay Gallery, who had come to meet us in a mini-bus which overflowed with exuberant Russians: Sasha, short for Alexander, the driver, and Sasha Rozin, Moscow's leading art critic, a joyful, volatile personality who insisted on stopping at the first lay-by where he produced a bottle of Georgian cognac of such ferocity that it melted the paper cups even when three were stacked one inside the other. Sasha had blazed the way proclaiming his enthusiasm for G&G in the magazine *Creativity*: 'I write that I like them for their total humanity. Not just the Russians, not Jewish, everybody!' This was echoed in the first of many toasts, with Sasha constantly on his feet, glass in hand, toasting the fellowship of nations, peace for mankind, wives, children and childhood friends. It was all very Russian, yet there was the unmentionable edge that the country was on the verge of a change as devastating as the 1917 revolution.

As I watched the passing Russian countryside and the glades of shimmering silver birch, I had a sense of vicarious *déjà vu*; not only from the great Russian novelists and playwrights I had read when I studied the language for a year at the age of sixteen, but from what my parents had told me. My father knew Petrograd in the Tsarist days of 1914, when he tried to sell American munitions to the corrupt officials responsible for the Russian army. Intending to stay for three weeks, he remained for three years, constantly frustrated by graft. Even so, he was to write: 'Petrograd during the first years of the war provided the perfect life of dissipation. I'm not so sure it did not provide the perfect life all around.' He witnessed the Kerensy Revolution; the great American journalist John Reed became his closest friend; and he covered the USSR between the wars as foreign correspondent for the *Chicago Daily News*.

My mother, Eve Stoker, a VAD nurse, was working in the new Anglo-Russian Hospital in Petrograd. In 1916 she was photographed at the feet of the Empress on the day of the hospital's grand opening, eighteen years old, wide-eyed and wistful. One night the Crown Prince Dimitri, who owned the palace which had been converted into the hospital, burst in with prince Felix Yusopov smeared with blood, packed a few things, and fled to internal exile in the Caucasus. They had just murdered Rasputin.

My mother loved Russia as much as my father, and they often revisited the country after they were married, until their inevitable disillusionment with Communism.

Now, in April 1990, Moscow was at rock-bottom. The people were close to starvation, yet the whole city was trembling with the anticipation of change.

After checking into the Hotel Ukraine, a Stalinist-baroque, wedding-cake edifice with twenty-eight storeys and no bar, I left my luggage in my surprisingly comfortable room and joined the others in the drab ground-floor lobby we would grow to know well. Then we were driven to the headquarters of the Union of Artists, a fine old mansion once owned by a friend of Turgenev, who had stayed there, and I was photographed in the back garden with G&G and Judy Adam beside more silver birch. The atmosphere inside had the informality of the Chelsea Arts Club, and there was a volley of toasts to G&G, which they accepted gratefully, George murmuring, 'Very kind, very sweet, extraordinary!'

James Birch recorded G&G's progress in his notes: 'They like Dan for he is a good drinker [no longer]. Everyone is very excited. Dan gets emotional and starts crying because there is a wedding in the next room. Misha [Mikheyev, Head of Art Promotion at the Union of Artists] is upset with Richard Salmon [one of the British collectors who had flown in] because he said he worked for the KGB. Afterwards somebody insists we go to the Armand Hammer Centre, which is not very nice; everyone is a bit drunk and starts dancing. Dan, who already had been dancing at the wedding, is now dancing with Judy Adam. One of the guests showed me a photo of her parents, who are dressed completely in ethnic clothes. She dares not go out on the streets at night because she is from the Republic of Azerbaijan. George is v. drunk and keeps dropping his gins and tonics. Then everyone comes back to my room.'

I remember that wedding well, with the young couple so stiff and wistful, and an amusing aunt who insisted we should dance. Then dancing with Judy Adam with such abandon that my shoes finally gave up and had to be thrown away, which meant that for the rest of the trip I had to wear my blue mountain boots, which I had intended for my later visit to the Caucasus. Each morning I polished them vigorously, in the hope of making them look presentable – though they might have come from Lobb's as far as the ill-shod Russians were concerned.

Dancing in Russia requires little finesse, but my stamina at 3 a.m. surprised me until I remembered it was only midnight by Greenwich Mean Time. I finally called it a day – or night – at five o'clock, and was guided down the labyrinthine corridors of the hotel by Misha Kurzanoff of the Union of Artists. Reaching my bedroom, I gestured with embarrassment at the various objects scattered on the table – cigarettes, whisky and soap. 'Please take whatever you like,' I said – though I hoped he would not take the lot.

Misha studied these assembled riches, but then his eyes fixed upon my open sponge-bag and a carton of those nasty little sticks with which one cleans out one's ears, known as cotton-buds.

'Could I have these for my children?'

'Of course.' I felt ashamed that I could give him such pleasure with something so pathetic, and was pleased that I had a small bag of chocolates to give his children as well. But the embarrassment was all mine; James later told me that when Misha returned to the party he brandished the cotton-buds as if they were Fabergé eggs. Even so, the constant reminders that the everyday items which we took for granted could only be obtained by Muscovites, with immense effort and graft, continued to worry me. To photograph G&G joining a patient queue for some squashed and soggy strawberries seemed an impertinence. To offer a grown man a bar of soap, an obscenity. When I asked Sergei Klokhov of the Union of Artists if their privations had made the Muscovites devious, he laughed: 'They have to be, for they have nothing.'

Recently I reminded George of the wonderful time we had had in Moscow, in spite of everything.

'But it was the most dreadful shit-hole of a place!'

'Surely that's why – because we were thrown together.'

With so few places to go to, and no bar in the Hotel Ukraine, we used James's bedroom for dormitory feasts at midnight, fuelled with the food and drink we had prudently brought from England.

Over the next few days I had the revelatory experience of seeing a major art exhibition come to life. It was like a military operation, and I realised I had had no idea of the logistics involved, nor of the team of experts who had to be flown in to see that it all worked. The pictures were transported across Europe with an art handler from the d'Offay Gallery, Paul Barratt, who had left London on 10 April.

In addition to the forty pictures, many of them enormous, there were fifty-eight five-litre cans of white emulsion for the walls of the New Tretyakov Gallery, rollers, brushes, ladders, drills, a crate of Bell's whisky and enough food to last the workers for a fortnight. The two drivers who transported all this, Tomas and Michael, came from West Berlin, and spoke no English, while Paul spoke no German. Their longest delay came right at the beginning, at Dover, where they had to wait four and a half hours for customs clearance. From there they caught the ferry to Zeebrugge in Belgium, and the Germans drove in shifts, taking turns to sleep in the back of the lorry. They reached Berlin at 4.30 the next morning, and Paul slept for most of the day while they waited for the catalogues to be delivered by the German printers – five thousand copies, weighing seven tons.

The next day they set off again. Paul was so ravenous that they stopped at an East German supermarket, where Tomas bought some cheap sausages whose wrapper bore the single word of warning POLAND. Sure enough, they were inedible. In Warsaw they stopped at a motel which had no food, plugs or light bulbs, though the woman at reception offered them some stale cake which she had hidden under her desk. Perhaps the language problems were to blame, or perhaps they were just ill-prepared. The next day was

Easter Sunday, and every town was celebrating. 'By now I was so hungry I would have gone to communion service just to have the wafer,' said Paul, 'but we pressed on, reaching the Soviet border at three o'clock in the afternoon.' They were greeted by an officer whose grin revealed a mouthful of gold teeth. This was their escort, arranged by the Union of Artists to ensure a safe journey on to Moscow, but the only near-accident came from the driving of the escort himself, who shunted cars out of the way, suddenly roaring forward then halting abruptly. The explanation became obvious when he stopped and leant into the lorry's cab to talk to Michael: 'He was as drunk as a skunk.' They reached Minsk at 9 p.m., thankful to join a party in the Intourist hotel. Offered black market money, two girls, a steak, a leather jacket and a fine Soviet army watch, Paul settled for the steak. They finally got to Moscow at 2.30 the following morning, and Paul checked into the Ukraine Hotel, reporting the safe arrival of the pictures to the advance party from London.

In addition to the problems of actually transporting the works to Moscow, there was the high cost of insuring them, which even then was growing more alarming with every major exhibition. Without subsidy, or reciprocal gallery loans in the case of artists like Velásquez or Van Gogh, the amount of money at risk prevented many shows from going ahead. But in the case of Gilbert & George in Moscow the expense of the exhibition was shared with the d'Offay Gallery, a remarkable – perhaps unique – arrangement, considering that not a single picture was for sale.

Gilbert & George's work has always had one unusual asset. The pictures, designed on a grid system with black edges (frequently compared to the lead in stained-glass windows), are composed of as many as 250 panels. When these are dismantled they fit neatly into large wooden crates, making their transportation across Europe possible.

Once in Moscow the pictures were reassembled by a team of eight Russian workmen supervised by Raymond O'Daly, a smiling young Irish-Canadian who has hung every G&G show since Rome in 1984. Moscow was his tenth, and the most difficult.

'I needed ten days,' he told me, 'and they gave me three, due to an unexpected exhibition of Lenin commemorative stamps, the most boring show I've ever seen. Then I had problems with the walls, which were made of such a hard material I thought it was asbestos. Each panel had to be screwed in to the scream of drills. David Goodwin [of the Tate Gallery] was there to observe, and he didn't have to help but joined us in the late-night work – an absolute saint.'

I found it admirable that the Tate had flown in David Goodwin simply to ensure the safety of their quadripartite picture *Death, Hope, Life, Fear* (1984). After making sure that it was properly installed, he flew back to London. That's professionalism – and care.

With no hint of the difficulties overcome, when the exhibition opened the Russian crowds wandered through the Tretyakov Gallery astounded: how could pictures of this size have been transported? Where was the Aeroflot cargo plane or juggernaut big enough? Many remained mystified to the end.

Nothing had been left to chance, starting with the maquette which G&G had made the previous year after a flying visit to Moscow to take the measurements of the gallery's rooms. They showed it to me in the back yard at Fournier Street, with tiny reproductions indicating where each picture should be hung. G&G supervised everything, including the design of the catalogue, which was translated into Russian and printed in Germany, where the quality of reproduction was superior.

Then, like the provisions of an advancing army, came thirty-two thousand postcards; stickers for taxis, which delighted the drivers; badges for lapels; and hundreds of posters for the show, depicting a picture entitled *Shag* (1988), translated tactfully as 'a small furry animal', accompanied by the buckets, brushes and paste needed to plaster them across the capital.

Most sought-after were the G&G T-shirts, whose exceptional

quality made them irresistible to young Russians, particularly students. Those who were lucky enough to procure one wore it for days both as the height of luxury and a status symbol.

On the day before the opening Judy Adam rushed to the airport to greet the VIPs who were flying in to attend it. Thirty-four people in all, most of them collectors, who had been pleased to loan their pictures for the exhibition: not one refused. I had a few incomprehensible words with Massimo Martino, the Italian owner of many G&Gs. Several others had equally exotic names, and I have little idea who they were or where they came from: Isy Brachot, Ascan Crone, Désiré Feuerle and Wim Beeren – names which might have sprung from a novel about the *Titanic*. Jean-Louis Froment, former director of the Musée d'art contemporain de Bordeaux, and Illeana Sonnabend had been unable to make their flight to Moscow due to an air strike in Paris. Mirjana Winterbottom, as lively as her name, was flown in by the d'Offay Gallery with the sole objective of arranging a good restaurant where everyone could celebrate the following night, a tougher assignment in Moscow at that time than could be imagined.

Rudi Fuchs, then of the Gemeentemuseum in the Hague, was welcomed by G&G as one of their closest friends and very early supporters. So was Wolf Jahn, their friend and author of *The Art of Gilbert & George*.

As so often, the least conspicuous were the most important. Anthony d'Offay sidled in almost unnoticed. This was my first encounter with the formidable man whose gallery bears his name. At first smirk it could be assumed, as Nancy Astor said of ghosts, that appearances were against him, yet he is one of those men who are irresistible to women, although other men cannot understand why. Perhaps it is the famous aphrodisiac of success. He moves around the world surreptitiously, and was described in a profile in the *New Statesman* in the week of his arrival in Moscow as 'a man whose business takes him to New York one week out of four, and who travels to Europe four or five times in the same period'. This slightly envious comment amused him, and he remarked that he may well see his friends and clients from Cleveland, Ohio, more frequently than those from South Kensington. That's business. Yet some resist his charms: Gordon Burn wrote a few months later in the *Sunday Times Magazine* that d'Offay's manner suggests 'both flaccidness and blind ambition, both the chapel of rest and the private vault'.

People often condemn ambition as 'blind', when in fact it needs to be far-sighted, and Anthony d'Offay is certainly that. Not once during his time in Moscow did he attempt to impose his authority, and he had evidently taken the trouble to do his homework beforehand. When he pays a compliment, he aims it like a dart. I had been warned of this, and was amused when he praised my unremarkable shirt as enthusiastically as if it had been designed by Bakst, or at least came from Turnbull & Asser. I have no recollection of the shirt itself, because it hardly merited remembering, but he was fulsome.

'Am I right in saying that the d'Offay Gallery is one of the top three or four galleries in London?' I asked.

He stared at me, incredulous that anyone could be so naïve.

'I should hope so. We are the *only* large gallery dealing in contemporary art.'

'Is it true that your annual turnover is £17 million?'

He pounced: 'Where did you get that figure?'

'Less?' I suggested.

'More. Twenty million would be closer.'

Phew! I thought, beginning to appreciate that in no respect should Anthony d'Offay be underestimated. His relationship with Gilbert & George is puzzling, more of an armed truce than a glorious alliance, yet in many ways they are inseparable, and they are clearly good for each other. His reputation in the international art market had been invaluable to them, while their unique contribution to modern art has enhanced his gallery. Because he deals only in the best or most controversial – Joseph Beuys and Andy Warhol, amongst others – one wonders what is actually sold at some of his exhibitions. But the mere fact of his being an artist's dealer can lift the price to astronomical proportions when a sale is made, even if it is not in the gallery itself. He recognised G&G's potential after seeing their *Red Sculpture* (1975): 'This totally changed the way I looked at something,' he explained. 'I liked the tension between them; I liked their endearing quality of innocence on the one hand and knowingness on the other.'

Pointing out that critics had sometimes been provoked unnecessarily by G&G's apparently puerile titles, I wondered if he had ever tried to dissuade them.

'Oh, no. It's very important that they deal with subjects that haven't already been burnt into the realm of art today.'

The fascist labels?

He stared at me unblinkingly: 'They're nice working-class boys who care for the people.' (I wondered if he really believed that.) 'If Gilbert & George were completely accepted, then they'd have cause to worry. Is any radical art completely accepted in its time? Beuys was not accepted in Germany, Warhol not in America. There is an interesting comparison between Warhol, Beuys and Gilbert & George, who in their various ways have turned their lives into works of art. Those are the three artists who attract very young people.'

Yet it is an odd relationship, each circling the other like suspicious dogs. I would guess d'Offay and his artists are loyal to each other, if only because of their mutual dependence. Anthony d'Offay's commercial flair did not prevent him from donating his profits, along with G&G's, of the 1989 show to AIDS charities, a gesture not properly appreciated by the press at the time. Certainly the d'Offay organisation were instrumental in bringing us to Moscow, sharing in the cost. Did he regard the show in Russia as that important?

'Oh, yes! A vast resource of humanity, untapped for contemporary art. A great longing need for art.'

I discovered later that though none of the pictures was for sale, the fame of the Moscow exhibition boosted G&G's prices in New York. 'We are incredibly lucky to be here,' d'Offay told me then, perhaps already aware of the potential attached to such prestige.

There is a personal element too in the relationship: at the opening of The New Art at the Hayward Gallery in 1972, George told d'Offay, 'Why don't you give Anne Seymour [curator of the exhibition] a kiss?' As Anne Seymour was exceptionally attractive, that was no hardship, and she soon became the second Mrs d'Offay. Her knowledge of contemporary art, acquired when she was Assistant Keeper of Modern Art at the Tate – complements that of her husband. She came to Moscow too.

Jill Ritblat, a well-known collector, was interested in seeing G&G in the alien setting of Russia: 'Would they turn out to be the prejudiced, racist, sexist, truculent drunks of repute?' she wondered. 'The inscrutable hosts in Fournier Street or the affable guests they had been in my own house?' There was never any cause to worry – there seldom is, except that G&G arrived so late for one dinner that it was rumoured they were exhausted. In fact the hanging had been difficult and the Russian lighting inadequate. However, their entrance was perfectly timed – and as ever they were polite to the unfamiliar, affectionate to their intimates. George poured vodka and gossiped expansively. They were human – a part of them in every one of Jill Ritblat's preconceptions.

My personal favourite among the guests was Dolly J. Fiterman. As soon as I heard that name, I introduced her in the mordant tones of Walter Matthau: 'May I present Mrs Dolly Fiterman of the Dolly J. Fiterman Gallery in Minneapolis.' She rose to the occasion gallantly. Dolly's energy made the rest of us look like limp lettuce. I was not surprised to read in her press cuttings that as a child she used to turn cartwheels all the way to the store in the small Minnesota town where she was born. 'She was a sheer ball of energy,' her sister recalled. 'She could move heaven and earth for whatever she wanted.' Dolly was a drum majorette at high school; less predictably, Minnesota's first 'Wild Rice Queen'. With the eagerness of a child returning from holiday, she showed me snaps of her home. It had a health spa off the master bedroom, with Turkish bath, Finnish sauna and jacuzzi, and a fifty-four-foot lap pool suspended from the second storey beneath a glass ceiling, where she swims under the stars. She must sound a horror, described like this, but she had two assets which always impress me: innocence and wealth. Her late husband Edward Fiterman had been a financier, and though Dolly is not Jewish she inaugurated the Marc Chagall Memorial Forest in Israel on his death in 1984, after twenty-seven years of marriage, and pledged a million dollars to the Temple Israel for a wing called the Dolly and Edward Fiterman Building.

'Do you think, Mrs Fiterman,' I asked after we had announced our engagement, 'that you will be able to keep me in a style to which I am unaccustomed?' This time her laugh was mirthless, for money is never a humorous subject to those who have it.

Dolly had shrewdly acquired work by Picasso, Frank Stella, Andy Warhol, Milton Avery, Jim Dine, Robert Rauschenberg and Jasper Johns: 'My goal was to have a high-quality gallery on a par with the East Coast.'

Why had she come to Moscow?

'I have two masterpieces by Gilbert & George, and just had to be here. I'm so happy to be part of it.'

This was a common reaction. Yet when I met her in the Ukraine lobby she was lost, and on no one's list, having made her own way from the airport. I tried to make up for this lapse.

Mirjana Winterbottom had triumphed in finding the ideal restaurant, probably the only one in Moscow. The Kolkhida served good Georgian food in an intimate atmosphere, with a charming old violinist who performed such wearisome party tricks as playing the violin on top of his head. As we sat down I noticed that Dolly was missing, and Mirjana raced back to the hotel to collect her. When Dolly arrived she sat down beside me without a word of complaint at being forgotten, and when she admitted that she had

never met G&G, I introduced them. They rose with their usual
attention and George's murmurs of 'Extraordinary . . . so kind . . .
how sweet!' She came back after several minutes, her journey made
worthwhile by the encounter.

It was a great night at Kolkhida, with the exuberance everyone
had hoped to find in Russia, but had not before now. But after all,
the restaurant was Georgian. The small room was crowded. At a
corner table were three Armenian couples. The men, who looked
like grizzled bears, fluctuated between tears and fisticuffs. The violin
wailed and the vodka flowed, though the waiters tried to persuade
us to drink the Caucasian wine which was far more expensive. The
evening ended with the Russians bobbing up and down from their
chairs as they indulged in volleys of toasts which gave them the
excuse for throwing back the vodkas in a single gulp. Rudi Fuchs
of the Gemeentemuseum danced on a tiny table, and the climax
was reached when Gilbert followed with a pirouette worthy of
Chaplin. He is usually a careful drinker, and I had heard him
exclaim, 'Christ, this is crazy!' when someone poured him a lethal
cognac. His dance was greeted by shouts and cheers, and though
the celebration was over the night was too special to be allowed
to run down.

I went ahead with Dolly to the bar in the Belgrade Two Hotel.
For some curious reason, a Russian had presented *me* with a bouquet
of flowers, and I handed them with a bow to Dolly, who was
wearing a sensational dress by Zandra Rhodes. She entered the hotel
with head held high and her dancer's gait. In her mid-sixties she
looked sensational, and was promptly arrested by the glum young
Russian soldier at the door, who mistook her for a very high-class
hooker. After I had talked her in, she turned to me gratefully:
'Daniel, this is one of the *nicest* evenings I've had in all my life!'

Throughout all this, James Birch was the catalyst. His position
was invidious: he was the inspiration for both the Bacon and G&G
Moscow exhibitions, largely due to his friendship with the artists,
though Francis failed to reward him with a picture, as he had

promised. He was not employed by the d'Offay Gallery (everyone else seemed to be), and lacked its influence. Above all, he was bypassed by the British Council. James had paved the way on the earlier flying visit with G&G to take the measurements of the Tretyakov Gallery, but the British Council were sceptical and suspicious. With a minuscule annual budget of about £20,000 for Russia, their inability to help would have been forgivable if they had been in the least diplomatic about it. Instead, one of the Council's representatives asked the Russian organisers of the exhibition why they were promoting the work of 'two homosexual fascists'. If he was trying to frighten the Russians, he underestimated their own brand of deviousness. All too familiar with the wiles of malevolent bureaucracy, the Russians assumed this was a case of double-bluff, and ignored it. Also, they trusted James, who was shocked that the British Council, whose aim was ostensibly to promote British culture abroad, could have acted so stupidly: 'I knew such deviousness existed in Russia; instead I found it coming from England.' James had forged a close relationship with Gilbert & George, cemented by their shared schoolboy sense of humour. After collapsing in his hotel bedroom at dawn, he would be woken by a cheerful call from George telling him to hurry up and join them in the breakfast room, where he would be confronted with a revolting sausage which George recommended as 'delicious donkey dick'. They even evolved a secret language: a sudden cry of 'Oy!' would always convulse them, despite the strained smiles of onlookers.

The brief advance visit had consolidated James's particular friendship with Mikhail Mikheyev, Head of Art Promotion in the Union of Artists, and he spread the word that Gilbert & George were acceptable.

'Presumably you had to change some of the titles for Russia?' I suggested to George. When he feigned surprise, I mentioned *Queer*, *Smash the Reds* (particularly unfortunate) and *Fucked Up*, and he conceded that *Coming* was first retitled *Orgasm*, and later *Arriving*. This prompted one serious Russian student to interpret the falling underpants in this 1983 picture as an invasion from the West. 'Extraordinary!' said George.

For the most part, though, the Russians were not disturbed by the pictures' titles, but amused. When George asked Mrs Mikheyev if she preferred Blooded or Shitted, she chose Blooded – 'Aha! All women say that!'

James explained to me why he regarded G&G as the natural follow-up to the Moscow Bacon exhibition: 'It was my theory that the Russians were used to social realism and would find Gilbert & George similar, and that this would make the exhibition popular; neither difficult nor abstract, but art for all and possible to understand. I could not have been more wrong! They were sick of social realism, having had it rammed down their throats for years. Fortunately they loved Gilbert & George anyhow.'

From our privileged position within the G&G entourage, it was easy to forget how traumatic the whole event was for the Russians. For decades they had been subdued, suppressed, denied the smallest of luxuries, and we reminded them that life was fun, or could be. Bridget Kendall, the BBC's Moscow correspondent, had noticed a new phenomenon among Russians in recent times: 'a resentment of foreigners and what they are missing, and anger that they have been deprived of so much'. She added that the living conditions in the country were now worse than they had been when she was there as a student.

I began to dread invitations to Russians' homes. Usually they would turn out to consist of one neat but crowded room in an apartment block, overlooking a dirty courtyard with trees which had long ago cried 'Surrender!' Tremendous efforts would have been made by the hostess to prepare something special – perhaps a biscuit – which we would greet with cries of appreciation which she took literally.

Over dinner on our first evening I told Sergei Klokhov's father, seated beside me, that the red caviar and smoked sturgeon was a wonderful treat. 'It certainly is,' he agreed sardonically, 'for us!'

I knew that I could not have endured life in Russia and would have made every effort to escape. No wonder the average Muscovite resented the hotel restaurants crowded with foreigners and rich Russians with hard currency. While I was waiting in the Ukraine's dining-room with James one lunchtime, a ferocious, tough young man lurched towards our table and demanded of James, 'You are Russian?'

'No,' said James calmly. For a moment I thought the man was going to strike him in the face, but he moved on. Obviously he had been drinking, and this had aggravated a deep resentment of people feeding their faces while he was excluded. I would have felt the same. Seldom had I encountered such class-consciousness, in forms unknown to us. Consequently, in a sense the G&G exhibition was historic, a breakthrough.

Mikhail Mikheyev feared the project was too daring when it was first suggested, but after meeting Gilbert & George in London, all his reservations disappeared. Transferring personal sympathies from a painter onto his creation is a dangerous path for a critic to follow, though it seems to me that the individual social standpoint of the artist is always reflected in that which he creates. G&G do not aspire to rise above their audience, to condescend or to withdraw. On the contrary, in every work they stress that they are no different from us – only I believe they are more daring, more talented, have greater foresight and are more generous than us.

The climax of the trip was a special luncheon held in G&G's honour in the fine Union of Artists mansion. As everywhere in Russia, protocol was still paramount, but the president, Thair Salakov, made a startling admission in his brief speech: 'A few years ago, during the period of stagnation, we would not have been allowed to stage a show like this at all, and certainly not before the First of May. That's what makes it so marvellous.'

'Extraordinary!' said George while we wondered about the significance of the First of May, the day of the annual parade in Red Square. None of us had the answer, but the mention of 'the period of stagnation' lingered, for it seemed there was a feeling that it might at last be coming to an end.

The start of the exhibition's opening day was inauspicious. We had enjoyed the usual midnight feast in James's dorm, but decided it would be advisable to go to bed earlier than the customary dawn slump. This was to prove a fatal mistake, for we were still suspended between clarity and confusion. After having delivered James a sleeping pill, I padded along the interminable hotel corridors until I reached my room, where I heard the phone ringing. Thinking it was probably the *Sunday Telegraph* phoning from England, I struggled with the lock and reached the phone, only to hear a hooker asking for Marlboro cigarettes. 'No!' I shouted.

After reading for a few minutes I turned out the light and slept soundly. I needed to. Even James, who was so much younger than me, usually recorded 'Feel terrible' as the start to his daily notes, but this morning I felt restored, until I was suddenly stricken by the chill of panic. My camera case had vanished, complete with all my money and my passport. I wondered for an improbable moment if someone had entered the room during the night, then I searched every corner, hoping it might have fallen behind the chair, under the bed, behind the curtain. Finally I remembered the ringing phone, and how in my haste to unlock the door I had put the camera case on the floor. Could it have lain outside in the corridor all night? I did not suspect that a member of the hotel staff might have taken it, but I did have doubts about the curious mix of foreign guests.

I opened the door, to find the corridor empty. Perhaps the case had been handed in to the forbidding lady who sat at a desk near the lifts, where she kept our keys. I ran down the corridor in my bare feet, which caused her such consternation that she called out in alarm to her friends, as if she had never seen a man with bare feet before.

'Forget my feet,' I said testily. 'Have you seen my camera case?' As she spoke no English, I had to mime my predicament – unsuccessfully. She waved me to a grander supervisor who was polishing her nails a few doors away.

Irritated by the interruption, she told me 'Niet,' with all the satisfaction the Russians display when they are able to say no.

I returned to my room, sat on the bed and took stock. The situation could hardly have been worse: I had lost two cameras, including my beloved Rolleiflex, my documents and my money. Suddenly there was a knock on the door, and there stood the ugliest woman I had seen in Moscow – and that was saying something – though her face was partly concealed by huge bifocals. She moved the camera case towards me, and it leapt into my arms like a long-lost dog. As I embraced this suddenly beautiful cleaning lady, she indicated in dumb-show that she had found the case outside, and had looked after it. I hurried to the drawer where I kept my cigarettes and gave her two packets of Marlboro, thanking her profusely. Two packets for restoring my livelihood? I padded down that corridor yet again in pursuit, and found her in a cubby-hole. I pressed two £5 notes into her pudgy hand, and she burst into tears.

As I was relating all this to Gilbert & George in the makeshift dining-room over breakfast, we were joined by James, who as usual looked like Dracula at dawn.

'Are you sure that was a sleeping-pill you gave me, and not an upper?' He explained that the pill had had no effect, and that as he lay wide awake on his bed he heard this strange noise coming from the corner of the room: Crunch, crunch crunch. 'My bedside light didn't work, so I turned on the bathroom light, and there was this giant rat devouring the last of my choccy biccies.'

'Oh, come on,' said George. 'You had the DTs.'

James ignored this: 'I put on my socks and shoes and lay there clutching the iron crucifix given to me by a Russian lady earlier in the day.'

'You mean you were going to raise the crucifix, as if it were a vampire rat?' I asked.

'Don't be ridiculous. I was going to club it to death.'

'And you couldn't get to sleep?' I added fatuously.

'Not a wink.'

Gilbert had been listening to the tales of our night's adventures with increasing impatience: 'Serves you both right – you should never, ever, go to bed *half*-pissed.'

The sleepless night left James exhausted. I could see the impression this made on the Russians, who found his apparent melancholy infinitely romantic, unaware that his bedroom eyes looked as if they needed polishing only because they yearned to be tightly closed, fast asleep in his hotel room without the vampire rat.

Last-minute problems persisted into opening day, but they were few. G&G had maintained their patience throughout, though they were a little irritated when I asked them to pose for photographs outside McDonald's, Moscow's new status symbol, and playing chess in Gorky Park: 'We would never pose outside McDonald's in London, and we don't play chess, so it wouldn't be true.'

Gilbert was concerned that the lighting in the gallery was too bland, especially as the walls were beige instead of glistening white as intended, because there would not have been time for the white paint to dry after the removal of Lenin's commemorative stamps. But the rooms were brightened up by spotlights, and Gilbert was satisfied, though the extra electricity they required caused a power cut, plunging two districts of Moscow temporarily into darkness.

The pictures were finally in place, and Gilbert & George congratulated Raymond O'Daly and his Russian team, recognising the efforts they had made as they worked throughout the night. Such work is rarely appreciated by the public, who expect everything somehow to be perfect the moment an exhibition opens. Though he was pleased he had beaten the deadline with a couple of hours to spare, Raymond looked exhausted. While workmen cleaned up the debris, Anthony d'Offay and Rudi Fuchs attached the labels to the walls beside the appropriate pictures.

It was all worth it. The final result was sensational: cascades of vivid colour erupted from one room to another, the whole effect carefully documented by photographer Keith Davey, who frequently records G&G's exhibitions. I felt that in this particular case the Russian public would not take the hanging for granted, because they would not be able to understand how it had been achieved – mounting an exhibition on this scale was clearly far removed from nailing a pretty still-life to the wall.

Art should shock, if only to delight, and this was truly the shock of the new. The four-part Tate picture covered an entire wall, the length of a small aircraft hangar: a phalanx of marching men; *Three Ways*, three youths under foliage; three sets of G&G in front of a cross; *Tears*, four green leaves; *Hope*, seventeen youths with a minuscule G&G on the horizon (I wondered if the boys had been allowed to keep the T-shirts they wore).

Seeing the work displayed like this was a turning point for me, but what would the Russians make of something so alien to everything they knew? Would they be shocked by the pictures' sheer exuberance? I asked Marina, our interpreter. Like all interpreters, she chose her words cautiously, as if she were looking over her shoulder, anxious not to commit herself: 'Not shock. Only interested in the freedom of expression and technique. Something quite new to our country. Later there may be other impressions: maybe compare them to mass culture . . . maybe . . . Why only men in the pictures?' She shrugged, perhaps fearing she had gone too far. 'But technically *fantastic!*'

As so often, Gilbert's astringent wit supplied the best answer when I asked him how he wanted the Russians to react: 'I want them to say: "What the fuck is that?"'

It was good to see Gilbert & George so happy, and I was glad I had come to terms with their art, and was able to share in the excitement. It would have been odious to have had to pretend. I had always felt that the critics expected G&G to deliver a message which they in fact had no interest in delivering – a common critical vice. George's verdict was probably wide of the mark. 'British art critics are racist,' said George, 'because they are only interested in art which comes from wine-growing countries.'

'Everything circles around sex,' added Gilbert, which struck me as irrelevant now, as I looked at the pictures.

'The general public accept it quite easily,' said George. 'That's why we like flowers and plants. Everything's fucking.'

Gilbert: 'Every young person who goes to an art gallery is looking for his freedom. I believe our art form is the most modern, and will be the form of the future.'

When I said that their arch-enemy, Peter Fuller, complained that their work lacked feeling, it was one of the few times that I ever saw Gilbert annoyed: 'Our pictures are filled with feeling, that's why people either love it or hate it.'

While we patrolled the rooms, James went to supervise the kitchen staff. With his knowledge of Russian bureaucracy – 'Go to the bottom rather than to the top officials, who would only delay' – he had negotiated for food over the past two days, paying 1,500 roubles to the staff, with the inevitable two hundred cigarettes and four cans of lager for the cook. With cigarettes rationed to a hundred a month, such bribery was universal.

We needed to return to the Hotel Ukraine to change, but it had started to snow, and the taxis either swept by or were hailed before they reached us – exactly like London. Finally we stopped a private car by waving the ubiquitous packet of Marlboros, and were driven back by a happy Russian. Our strict instructions to be back at the gallery by three for Keith Davey's group photograph were endangered by the continued lack of transport and the disappearance of Dolly Fiterman, who had asked me earlier if she should wear her 'plain black ensemble' or another Zandra Rhodes outfit – 'It's not flashy,' she assured me, 'though it's decorated with snails [at least that's what it sounded like] and . . . striking.'

'That's the one,' I told her. 'It is a celebration.' And her decorated dress did indeed manage to be striking, yet surprisingly restrained. James wore a tie, Stainton Forrest a white jacket, and G&G, of course, their customary three-button suits. They travel abroad with three spare suits each. We were an unusual-looking group for Moscow.

The press conference followed at four, and I began to realise that Francis Bacon had had a point when he said he dreaded such events. If you have ever seen the newsreels of the Nuremberg Trials you will understand why I found the proceedings so funny: James sat in a dark costume and grey face, with G&G expressionless in the dock beside him, all looking as guilty as hell. Sergei Klokhov, the bearded driving force behind the exhibition, wore a peasant's smock that made him startlingly reminiscent of Rasputin, whom he resembled already. He alone had been given a painting by Bacon after the earlier exhibition. He had taken it directly to Sotheby's, and had bought a flat in Belgravia with the proceeds. Some people had been shocked that he failed to present it to the Pushkin Museum; others, like myself, admired such nerve.

At the end of the table sat a Russian lady interpreter, prolific in frills and furbelows, though less so in the English language, as soon became obvious. Altogether, about a hundred Soviet reporters were present.

'Are you going to make any speeches?' I had asked G&G beforehand.

'Our speeches are on the walls,' replied George, to which there was no answer.

James spoke on their behalf. He told me afterwards that he was so exhausted and shaken from tiredness that he felt none of the usual fear as he read out his speech. I noticed how meticulously he observed protocol, carefully thanking all the Russians involved. In his turn, Mikhail Mikheyev was very complimentary to James. Sergei Klokhov glowered alone. It was easy to believe that he owned a snake farm in the Urals. Asked earlier if there were homosexuals in Moscow, he had replied tersely: 'Yes; all in Lubianka.'

Gilbert & George started to answer the reporters' questions, which proved surprisingly tactful, concentrating on their technique rather than the pictures' subject matter. I wrote some of their answers down.

Gilbert: 'We believe the camera is the modern brush. We believe in the picture looking at the viewer, not the viewer looking at the picture.'

Jointly: 'We are making pictures like people always made pictures, but we are using modern forms relevant to our time.'

'Are you well-known?' asked a journalist.

'Yes, of course.' George smiled at such naivety, though this failed to raise a titter from the other reporters, to whom G&G were totally unknown.

'Is your work decadent?' The inevitable question, at last.

'What is decadence? You tell me,' Gilbert responded.

'We believe that art that only speaks about art is decadent,' George elaborated. 'Art which talks to specialists, art which is elite is decadent. Our art is appreciated by different people and nationalities, therefore it is a kind of moral art.'

Gilbert broke the tension with his wit, so carefree yet aimed so carefully: 'We are not against being decadent ourselves.'

Another reporter asked why so many of the pictures were based on themselves — a fair question.

'We are showing the world our inner souls,' Gilbert replied.

When someone mentioned Blake, George interrupted: 'Blake was a kind of genius, but we're not interested in being influenced in that way.'

'You're not very social?' a reporter suggested, and the real G&G whom I had grown to know burst out: 'Just wait for two or three hours!'

Finally the ordeal came to an end, and we went upstairs to the official grand opening, which was described by Mikhail Mikheyev as one of the most lively and intriguing he had ever seen. Admiring the catalogues, badges and posters, he declared, 'Such dedicated and thorough work could not have failed to bring results.'

Protocol reared its sanctimonious head again with a plethora of speeches, though the British Ambassador, Sir Roderic Braithwaite, had had the nous to decline to speak. He listened to the other speeches intently nonetheless, even to Sergei Klokhov in his Rasputin outfit who emerged from the shadows, seized the centre-stage and the microphone too, and launched into a lengthy and – to me at least – incomprehensible speech. Sir Roderic retained his diplomatic smile throughout. I photographed him later, and he was polite but evasive when I asked if he had any comment to make on the exhibition: 'No, not yet.' He admitted a few minutes later in a whisper, 'Not quite my cup of tea.' Lady Braithwaite had no hesitation in telling me, 'Frankly, I'm foxed!'

The one person Sir Roderic upset, unintentionally, was George, when, indulging in small talk, he asked him how long they had been in Moscow and what had they been doing. 'What on earth does he think we've been doing?' George exclaimed afterwards. '*Sightseeing?*' In fact they did no sightseeing whatsoever, and showed no curiosity when I returned from the great Pushkin Museum: 'We haven't come here to look, but to be looked at,' said Gilbert dismissively.

Before Sir Roderic made his exit, I introduced him to Dolly: 'Your Excellency, may I have the honour to present Mrs Dolly J. Fiterman from Minneapolis.' No fool, his eyes swept across her outfit, and he shot me a cool look for having placed him in such a position. He shook her hand, though he was plainly bemused, so I thought it wise to add, 'Dolly is a friend of our Prime Minister.' This was confirmed by Dolly, who described her recent visit to Downing Street and how kind Mrs Thatcher and Dennis had been to her. The Ambassador listened with new respect, and as he left he gave me an uneasy grin. Thousands of Russians poured into the opening. Even their numbers were not as remarkable as the excitement: G&G were pinioned into a corner as the crowd jostled for their autographs in the splendid catalogues, whose black-market value was increasing by the minute. The exhilaration could be seen on their faces, especially those of the young and such famous collectors as Tania Kolodzei, who owned a thousand works of Russian art, and Francesca Thyssen – of whom Klokhov was in hot pursuit. The sense of occasion was evident: one student told me he regarded this as 'a turning point in the history of art. Every time I see their work I feel alive.' Later, the attendance swelled to three thousand a day, helped by glowing reviews in *Pravda* and *Izvestia*, which wrote: 'Their art warns of the possible catastrophe and its inevitability if people do not listen to the voice of reason, do not become more generous, purer and more charitable.'

If the average Russian failed to understand the work, one could well ask, what was there to understand? Certainly no arty label like 'man's inhumanity to man', which dogged Bacon, or any message about the Holocaust.

Mikhail Mikheyev concluded: 'It would of course be unfair to say that the Gilbert & George exhibition had total success. It seems that the position of an average Moscow consumer differs little from that of a London one – in both cases intellectual apathy is replaced by a pose. Perhaps the Moscow consumer can be marked out by his greater severity in passing judgement, as for more than a century unenlightment and narrow-mindedness were considered good taste.'

G&G could certainly be absolved of good taste. Russian art was in the doldrums: pretty flower-pieces and river scenes replacing the Stalinist realism of peasant workers and laughing girls bringing in the harvest (always a wishful fantasy). Unlike contemporary Russian literature, the country's art veered away from the truth, which was too painful. It will be years before it comes closer, and then the depictions could be terrifying. As it was, I felt that as always with G&G, even if the viewers did not understand entirely, at least their eyes had been opened.

We descended to the party below, where the violinist from the Kolkhida welcomed the guests, and G&G were announced as 'Gilbet' and 'Jojo', and at one alarming moment as 'Gilberta' and 'Georgia'. As if by radar instinct, the swelling masses sensed the second that the doors would swing open, and then poured through them like the storming of the Winter Palace, though their objective was food and drink rather than revolution. The security guards backed away helplessly as gatecrashers thrust past them in their desperation for food. The violinist was knocked down, but rose up, playing his instrument on his head. The plates were cleared as if by starving prisoners, with some of the Russians drinking three glasses of champagne simultaneously, difficult though that might sound. In a few minutes the 162 bottles of French champagne were empty. But nobody seemed to object to the gatecrashers, who enjoyed the party more than anyone. It was a great, if brief, success.

There was another official party, given by the British Council, perhaps in an attempt to salvage their reputation. Having been scornful of the exhibition from the outset, they sensed belatedly that it was proving historic, and that they should have been involved. But they could not have got things more wrong: the members of the Union of Artists were not invited, and were conspicuous by their absence, though Klokhov turned up with a bevy of girlfriends. The restaurant where the party was held served some of the nastiest food I had seen in Moscow – which was quite a distinction – and the staff served it with a surliness which suggested that the British Council were lousy tippers and their least favourite customers.

A speech was made by a pale, perspiring, overweight official who apologised profusely for having arrived too late to greet us. Of all the fumbling speeches I have ever heard, this one was so inept that I rather enjoyed it. The man informed us that he had been travelling with some minister – as if we cared – which was why he had not actually seen the exhibition, though he was told it was very good. Hold on: he had not actually seen the exhibition? A grim silence descended and he perspired the more, congratulating everyone on the work involved, apologising for the lack of help from the British Council, but they were understaffed . . . and so on. He was grovelling.

A pall had fallen on the room. 'He should have lied,' Gilbert said. 'People have flown in from all over the world, and the man from the British Council could not even bother to see it. And why do they suddenly want to know us? It's only because we shocked the knickers off the natives.'

The man from the Council realised that his effort had been humiliating, and sat down in silence. Sergei Klokhov rose imperiously and complained that inadequate acknowledgement had been given to the d'Offay Gallery. In fact the Council man had expressed his admiration for d'Offay, who was sitting beside him, but that was forgotten.

Then George rose slowly and tapped his glass, with such a severe expression on his face that I cringed in anticipation of the outburst to come.

'We have some very important news,' he announced. 'It is Rudi Fuchs's birthday!' At this the room dissolved in uproar as we sang 'Happy Birthday dear Rudi!' for all we were worth, followed by Dolly giving a solo rendition of the little-known second verse. The man from the British Council crept out.

Afterwards, I flew to the Caucasus in a battered Aeroflot plane. Someone had been sick on the seat beside me, so at least I had some room. James and Judy Adam continued to Kiev, and the G&G entourage flew back to England. The collector Jill Ritblat was among them, and she wrote to me that my feature on the exhibition had been given a full-page spread in the Sunday Telegraph, with the photograph I had taken of G&G posing in front of the heroic sculpture of the Soviet Worker and Peasant Girl by Vera Mouchina, which caused a sensation when it was reassembled in 1925 for the Paris Exhibition. Jill said that a copy of the article – presumably left behind by an incoming passenger – had been 'passed around the plane several times' and read with considerable pleasure.

Then someone had turned to the next page of the paper and gasped. Peter Fuller had been killed when his car had overturned while he was being driven back to his home in Bath from London. His neck had been broken, his young son was hurt, as was his wife, who was expecting their second child, and who had miscarried. It was unrelieved tragedy, with the terrible irony that Fuller's father-in-law, knowing how tired Peter was, had insisted on arranging for a chauffeur to drive them.

The accident had happened the previous day; a few hours later Peter's appearance on my television art programme *Gallery* was transmitted, with Channel 4 unaware that he was already dead.

The final irony was the most brutal: Peter Fuller had been due to fly to Chicago to give a lecture, the title of which was 'Goodbye Andy Warhol, Farewell Gilbert & George'.

George's comment: 'Because someone is dead, it doesn't mean you hate them less.'

CHAPTER NINE

WITH GILBERT & GEORGE
IN SHANGHAI

E arly in September 1993, Gilbert and George became the first living British artists to be granted an exhibition in Beijing. After Moscow, James Birch had asked them, 'Where would you like to exhibit next?' Without hesitation they replied in unison, 'CHINA!'

George explained: 'I don't think we meant it really. It just seemed even more outrageous than Moscow.'

'It seemed like an impossibility,' added Gilbert.

So they gave James a pile of catalogues and told him to show them to the Chinese government, thinking that would be the end of it. James came back and told them the Chinese Embassy were prepared to have a show in three months. In the event, of course, it took longer. The following year James flew to Beijing to search for a suitable space, and signed a letter of intent. All the pictures which the artists proposed for the exhibition – none of which included them in the nude, like their recent shows – were approved at once.

'The artists' selection of pictures aroused no comment, good or bad,' said James, 'so we assumed they were accepted. I think the

Chinese couldn't ignore the respectability Gilbert & George have won in Europe and America. The Chinese want to be broad-minded.'

This anxiety to be regarded as 'modern' was confirmed by Madame Qi from the Exhibition Agency, who accepted the show. The next one she had in mind was a Dalí exhibition, but she was keen to 'discover' living artists: 'We want to introduce the best artists and the best art in the world to Chinese people. They want to know more about art in the Western world. I think this work will influence Chinese contemporary art and it is very important that the artists shall accompany their work to Beijing where people can talk to them and learn to understand what they see.' She conceded that to the Chinese G&G might sometimes 'seem strange in their dress and behaviour, but that they are very kind gentlemen'.

Surprisingly, G&G's reputation preceded them. They were astonished on the day after their arrival in Beijing to be stopped by an enthusiastic young artist who almost fell off his bicycle when he spotted them in the street. 'Are you the artists from England?' They assured him they were, and he burst into delighted laughter.

I had decided to join them in Shanghai, which sounded more romantic to me than the capital city, and I suspect that my hunch was correct. This time it was even more of a jamboree than Moscow, with 120 dealers and collectors from all over the world, including twenty-five from Britain, anxious to see the once-forbidden city. The journalists included Martin Gayford of the *Daily Telegraph*, and there were two camera teams. One of them, directed by Jill Ritblat's son, David Zilkha, made a revealing short film called *Normal Conservative Rebels*, which was shown at the Edinburgh Festival in August 1996. The other documentary, made by David Langham, has yet to be shown.

The impact of China was overwhelming for the Western arrivals, not only because it was strange, but because it was so vast, modern and cosmopolitan. There were nine banquets altogether, the first after the exhibition's opening at the Jade Ballroom of the Kempinski

Hotel, described by Gayford as 'a spot of such up-to-the-minute smartness that it might have been transported bodily through the air from Dallas'.

At every official occasion, G&G made a curious little speech, in unison and in turn, each of them reading from a piece of paper and speaking almost robotically:

> WE ARE GILBERT AND GEORGE. WE AS
> UNHAPPY ARTISTS ARE VERY HAPPY TO BE
> ABLE TO HOLD THIS EXHIBITION OF OUR
> PICTURES IN CHINA. OUR ART FIGHTS FOR
> LOVE AND TOLERANCE AND THE UNIVERSAL
> ELABORATION OF THE INDIVIDUAL. EACH
> OF OUR PICTURES IS A VISUAL LOVE LETTER
> FROM OURSELVES TO THE VIEWER. THIS VISIT
> HAS BEEN A HUMAN REVELATION TO US. WE
> HAVE NEVER BEFORE SEEN SO MANY GOOD-
> LOOKING PEOPLE – [building up to a climax]
> AND BEIJING IS NOW OUR FAVOURITE CITY.

They even recited this on the Great Wall of China, filmed by David Zilkha.

As usual the logistics of the show were mind-boggling, the insurance costs so high that G&G needed the sponsorship of the Willis Coroon Group, as well as their own subsidy (shared by d'Offay), which included hotel accommodation for many of their guests.

Transporting the fifty-five pictures by sea would have taken three months, so they were flown over in crates, unpacked and reassembled by Raymond O'Daly. The first crisis came when Chinese bureaucracy forbade the drilling of holes in the walls of the National Art Gallery. It was only resolved when Gilbert & George devised a new hanging system. There was a near shipping disaster with the catalogues, stranded mysteriously in Singapore, and James was already shaken when he was summoned to meet Qin Gang, the Foreign Affairs Minister, who said he had urgent news for him. 'My heart sank. I found him looking intently at *Headed* [1992], a large picture of George's head with a tiny Gilbert lying on top of it. The translator interpreted the "urgent" news: "The minister will be a little late to make his speech at the banquet."'

Throughout their time in China G&G were their impeccable selves, delighting everyone with their courtesy, wearing new light-weight tropical suits, which proved a wise precaution, as the temperatures reached ninety degrees, with high humidity. Martin Gayford noticed: 'The rest of us sweltered in shirtsleeves, but some-how – perhaps due to the superhuman self-control that goes with being a Living Sculpture – never a bead of sweat appeared on the besuited Gilbert or George.'

Far more sophisticated than the Muscovites, the Chinese took G&G's work at face value: 'It's OK – very colourful'; 'It's very elegant, but modern'; 'It gives me a big impression'; 'England is a very courteous country but suddenly you produce rock and roll.' One student admired the way G&G were questioning tradition, which received their approval. Gilbert: 'We are trying to break down taboos.' George: 'The artist is nothing if not unconventional. We wanted to experiment with Art for All.' They then immediately returned to their odd alleged unhappiness: 'We want to be as miserable as the most miserable person on earth.' They were good enough actors to look miserable as they said it.

There was no sense of apology from the people of Beijing, as there had been in Moscow. One had only to see all the new buildings to know that the West had already arrived. Many of the comments from the Chinese were self-assured and critical: 'There is more alienation in the West than the East'; 'I feel Western society is very nervous.'

The opening had the added frisson that only a week earlier an exhibition of young Chinese painters was closed after officials ordered that the more controversial works be removed. One artist protested, cutting off his long hair; he was arrested.

Lynn MacRitchie described the opening in the *Financial Times*: 'The gallery was packed to bursting with an extraordinary mixture of art world types, both Western and Chinese, dressed in everything from vests and cotton trousers to impeccable business suits . . . a mini-riot broke out around the catalogue desk. And all fuelled on bottles of pop, drunk through a straw – no alcohol, probably fortunately, was served.' G&G found the occasion 'very emotional, historic', but one older Chinese man exclaimed: 'What's so wonderful? There's no beauty there. Everyone is standing upside down.' 'G&G are very bad English artists, and we don't like them in England,' said another dissident, but he came from Aberdeen.

The British Ambassador gave an interview, stressing perhaps the most remarkable aspect of all. 'This exhibition would not have been possible three years ago. It would have been considered too disturbing, too alien.'

Only three years? Such was the speed of change. Our guide books might have been describing another place. Gayford wrote that none of the G&G retinue was prepared for a city with such an abundance of luxury hotels, a nightclub called Maxim's with a first-rate jazz group at Parisian prices, and a gigantic Kentucky Fried Chicken takeaway.

G&G were excited by their welcome, especially as a show of Western art from South Korea had been cancelled a year or so earlier: 'The artists here were amazed that the authorities allowed it to go ahead. This opening is the best-attended since the Chinese avant-garde show in 1989, but, sadly, that was also soon closed and the pictures removed.'

Grandiloquently, George declared that Chinese art would never be the same again. But he had the grace to add that they would not be the same again either.

At first I had been reluctant to go to China, feeling it would amount to support for a regime which killed its students; caged bears in wooden cages too small to turn round in, in order to extract the animals' bile; and imprisoned thousands of its citizens for daring to think for themselves.

This was English arrogance at its most insular, always pointing the accusing finger while believing ourselves to be genuinely superior to other races. At least if I go, I told my friends, I can make a small protest, and they warned me, 'Keep your trap shut, or you'll end up in a Chinky clink, and they won't let you out.' I resolved that my trap would indeed stay shut, but this was not the right mood in which to embark on a promising new experience.

My mood was not improved when I spent the long flight to China squeezed between two large Dutchmen who insisted on watching Whoopi Goldberg on the in-flight TV, first in English, then in German. In the early hours one of the Dutchmen went to the lavatory, and I leant across to lift the shutter, revealing an astounding dawn vista above the clouds, so dazzling, so breathtakingly beautiful that my spirits immediately lifted. I drew the sight to the attention of my phlegmatic companions, but they preferred Whoopi. The flight took sixteen hours altogether, with an interminable transfer at Hong Kong, yet the moment we landed in Shanghai I was reinvigorated.

Sadie Coles, then of the d'Offay Gallery, had been travelling on the same plane, and we were met by a van which whisked us through innumerable back streets, scattering cockerels and children pecking or peeing in the refuse. Ah! This was the Shanghai of which I had been dreaming – reeking, literally, of the East. Then we turned a corner: a curved boulevard stretched away – neon lights, modern buildings. The contrast with the muddy alleys we had left just seconds ago was shocking.

The Park Hotel, with a panoramic view from my room of the boulevard teeming with people, was modern and comfortable, but G&G were waiting for us in the Jazz Bar of the Peace Hotel near the Bund, where we would have liked to stay, but it was too far from the exhibition. The hotel's jazz band was famous as the first to emerge in China after the Cultural Revolution, with some of the same now aged musicians, in white shirts and black ties. They were terrible, which added to the fun as British expatriates cavorted on the dance floor with the ungainly clip-clops and swirls which they perform when they let their hair down, watched by the Chinese with boggled eyes. George greeted me warmly, pointing out the decorations, which reminded him of a Gothic hotel in Oxford, while to me they suggested a Hammer film set for Dracula. Gilbert added that some of the details were reminiscent of the back streets of Istanbul or the avenues of Paris, but that the whole was unique. 'If you were led blindfold and then allowed to look, you would think you were anywhere except Shanghai. Extraordinary!'

George agreed: 'Naples without the pickpockets.'

The Peace Hotel was built by Victor Sassoon in 1930, which helped to explain its bizarre appearance. By now the musicians were in full swoop with the Tennessee Waltz, which encouraged the fat and perspiring British expats to new enthusiasm.

'Yu is our friend nephew,' George whispered. I was flattered by this curious ungrammatical statement until I realised he was referring to the young Chinese sitting between G&G: Mr Yu Yi-Gang. Radiant with enjoyment, Yu was so delighted by his new 'uncles' that he was already echoing their cries of 'Extraordinary!' and 'Very kind!', a teasing which was new and delightful to them. Apparently Yu had met Raymond O'Daly when he was buying some cinema tickets and needed help. Since then he had attached himself to G&G. Someone warned them that Yu was a government spy, but they were unconcerned: 'If Yu is a deliberate plant,' said George, 'it might be for our benefit. Certainly, he's helpful in arranging restaurants for his uncles. Anyhow, our Chinese nephew is very sweet.'

Gilbert leant towards me confidentially: 'George likes him because he reminds him of me when I was young.' I could just see this: the similarity was enhanced because Yu seemed to be wearing one of G&G's suits, and a beautiful pale blue tie. He never stopped smiling.

Over the next few days I gathered that Shanghai is as different from Beijing as Liverpool is from London. The capital's English-language *China Daily* slipped under my bedroom door introduced a sceptical note as an antidote to the general euphoria: 'These two artists are said to capture a typically British genre of painting. This show is said to help Beijing's bid for the 2000 Olympics.' If that was a motive, it failed, and I was told that the Chinese cried on the streets of Beijing — or were told to cry — when the news was announced that the bid had failed. In Shanghai they could not have cared less.

The following morning at 6 a.m. (had I slept?) I saw the face of the Chinese as they performed their martial arts exercises in slow motion and dumb-show, some twirling wooden swords, a few men confronting bushes in silent contemplation as if they were considering a pee. They were mostly middle-aged and dressed drably in grey costumes, and the music was solemn in contrast to that in Beijing where they performed to modern music like Breakfast TV aerobics in Britain, as filmed by David Zilkha.

G&G were used to the morning ceremony by now, but I found it disturbing, as if a single command from a loudspeaker could turn these unsmiling men and women into automata who would obey without question.

In the afternoon I took a long walk down the busy shopping centre of Nanjing Lu, which stretches from the Park Hotel to the Bund, and saw the other face of Shanghai as I walked, blissfully alone among thousands of people. What was so stimulating was the city's evident sophistication compared to Moscow's naivety. While the Muscovites seemed resigned to failure and were grim, dirty and hopeless, Shanghai exemplified the future, and apparently it worked. There was just a hint of the past as I looked over the great river at the Bund, with the Westminster Clock on the former British Customs House which was stopped by Mao in 1949 when he founded the People's Republic. Before the war the Bund was synonymous with decadence, with rich Westerners who corrupted everyone in sight, and rich Chinese who kept the engines of their cars warm with their sable coats while others froze to death for lack of clothing, and the coffins of the poor were shoved into the Huangpu River to drift to the Yangtze and the sea. Prostitutes, or Chinese 'chickens', were rampant, and transvestites performed their cabaret on the quay. This was the Shanghai of Clive Brook and Marlene Dietrich, who, asked if she had an affair after they split up, replied: 'They don't call me Shanghai Lil for nothing!'

The Bund will never have quite the same romance again, but there was still a special atmosphere as I looked out over the river. I was approached by a charming man of eighty-eight, smartly dressed with a white shirt showing at the top of his black-buttoned costume, complete with cap and wooden walking stick. He had lived in Washington and spoke good English, and had no hesitation in telling me that the Cultural Revolution was 'the worst of times', an announcement which caused a frisson among the young people who had gathered round to listen. After he walked away, a girl took me aside and whispered passionately, 'This is a heartbreaking city.' I realised how superficial my first impressions of the city's modernity had been.

But it was unavoidable the next morning when we drove in G&G's minibus to see the new bridge. At every turn I saw the living transformation: the streets beneath us would be rubble by the evening, and new foundations would be built tomorrow. Duck-boards and flagstones provided a shaky causeway across the muddy water and debris to a new house opposite. By now I doubt if much of the old city is left. The Yoyuan Bridge with the wooden Zigzag Bridge was built in 1559, and is one of the few such landmarks to be preserved. It is still a favourite with the Chinese, who acted there like any tourists anywhere.

To gain a panorama of the awakening city we continued across the river over the Nanpu Bridge and took the lift to the top of a new skyscraper: part of the massive foreign investment which made Britain's finger-wagging over Hong Kong seem ridiculous when all the Chinese had to do was pull a lever and turn Shanghai into the new financial centre of the Far East.

That evening we escaped from the entourage and took a lift to the top bar of the modern Jin Jang Tower. On the floor below was a revolving restaurant – the height of chic. Looking across the city's new skyline, George said it was like Los Angeles. 'Extraordinary!'

Gilbert agreed: 'But it *is* extraordinary. A fantastic big *orgasm!*'

'Beijing a great Chinese city,' said George. 'Shanghai a great world city.'

As we left the spacious foyer I noticed a small Chinese boy who had wandered in on his own, looking up at the high ceiling which was animated by moving shapes and patterns more open-mouthed than anyone I have ever seen. Again I could not help noticing the contrast with Moscow's hotels, where the unfortunate locals were not allowed inside the restaurants without a special pass. The difference between the degradation there and the optimism here made me think with a wistful affection that they were all so *human.*

The exhibition opened at the impressive Shanghai Art Museum, off Nanjing Road, at 10 a.m. on 21 October. A band played 'When the Saints Come Marching in', and the museum was so crowded that I thought I might be pushed over. As I came in, an elderly man hurried out smiling: 'It's so modern!' Inside, a girl told me: 'It's like fresh air.' I repeated this to Gilbert, but he corrected her: 'It *reeks* of fresh air.'

While the Russians had seen G&G's work in their own way, the Chinese were more intuitive. They could see how the pictures were assembled, and did not care if they did not understand them. Instead, they showed an affinity with the work, laughing, exclaiming, touching. G&G were delighted when a student told them, 'I feel like that picture!' and when two friends mimicked the picture *Tongues* (1992) behind them, striking a similar, exaggerated pose.

I had not appreciated that G&G's work was already popular in

China from books and magazines over the last ten years. George said: 'We always say our art does not reflect life but is forming our tomorrow – and that's very Chinese.'

Gilbert agreed: 'They just want the new. No sentiment for old wicker-baskets.'

George: 'The young people are amazed by modernity, they see a new visual language and take to it like children – and children are always right.'

On the second morning the huge crowds clapped G&G as they entered, which had never happened to them before: 'Not in New York, not in Paris. Extraordinary!'

Their elation was such that Gilbert told me later, 'In some ways it feels like having a show on the moon, and it works.'

George added: 'And we're the Martians. They'll never see work like this again.'

On the third day of the exhibition I was woken by an urgent summons to hurry to the gallery and see Edward Heath. I had met him before, and had warmed to him: a beached whale politically, but shrewd and amusing personally. The Chinese took him very seriously as a former British Prime Minister (unlike the last Governor of Hong Kong Chris Patten, who had lost his seat in the 1992 British general election and was therefore considered a failure), which Sir Edward relished, and he travelled extensively in style. He still has presence, and everyone seemed pleased to see him at the gallery, where I found him bemused by the pictures.

'A bit big for Roy,' he whispered, referring to the Roy Miles Gallery in London, one of the places where we had met. He was puzzled, but had the wit to ask the right questions. G&G explained that they take thirty to forty thousand images, and evolve a theme as they go along from the black-and-white negatives which they assemble into a big picture, using a blocking-off technique, dying the panels in vivid colours with a cloth. Heath asked how many staff they employed.

'None,' said George. 'Everything is made by hand.'

After Heath asked where he could see their work in England, they mentioned that they were having a show in Sydney. 'Should be Melbourne,' he told them: 'more artistic. In Sydney they're only interested in money. But perhaps you are too?'

'Oh yes,' said Gilbert quickly. 'Spending it.'

Escorting Heath out of the gallery, I asked his advice: as a visitor, should I ignore the oppression that lurks behind the smiling Chinese façade? It was a foolish question, but he answered patiently, pointing out that he knew Beijing when the place was a primitive town, and it is now one of the most modern: 'After three thousand years a new society is emerging so quickly, affecting so many millions of Chinese, that we need to make allowances. I went to a lake last night and saw the happiness of the Chinese relaxing with their families. After all the heartache of previous regimes, this is an astounding liberation.'

He deplored the way that the British failed to appreciate the importance of what was happening: 'I drove through the city and everywhere I saw huge advertisements for French and German imports – not one for Britain!'

Back in England, Heath, who is knowledgeable about art and who owns a prized Sickert, invited Gilbert & George to lunch at his home in Salisbury, so this was the start of a curious friendship.

Perhaps predictably, G&G had no qualms about the Chinese regime: 'No Western country is clean enough to point the finger blamefully,' said George. 'Be gentle, that's better. If we want China to be part of us, we have to be friendly. For us, having the opportunity to show here will help. This is the most open response we've seen.'

Gilbert said vehemently: 'We prefer to fuck today instead of tomorrow. We are trying to break down the narrow-mindedness of British Western art. I don't give a shit what they do in England, it's all provincialism.'

G&G's entourage of loyal hangers-on in China included a striking

Dutch actress of indeterminate age and dyed red hair, who had burst into tears when told she was being cast as a mother in a local TV show, instead of the juvenile lead she was hoping for. There was also a Canadian with a bandaged arm as a result of a fight, who claimed he played the 'baddies' in Chinese B-films. I would have believed this, but he was so broke he had nowhere to sleep, and tried to occupy the other bed in my hotel room until the Chinese staff, who seemed to know him, told him to leave. He was devilishly handsome and charming, but I did not trust him, and warned some students at a party that he was a 'bad man'. 'Batman!' they shrieked, and he preened himself with pleasure, accepting the accolade. On one occasion when I was playing host for once, with the help of Mr Yu, everything went wrong when 'baddie' arrived with a group of noisy Germans and upset Yu by walking out of the restaurant which he had chosen so carefully. Unfortunately Yu had booked our group a special separate room, which could have been anywhere. The food was excellent, but I had hoped for a tea-garden in the open air, complete with tumblers and musicians.

The inevitable evening banquet was given at the Dragon-Phoenix Hall and really was a banquet, though much of it was still alive: shark fins with bamboo shoots; shrimps with precious fried nuts, sizzled to leaping death on a hot plate; river crabs; mandarin fish with noodles; silver thread soup; and four fair play dumplings were some of the dishes.

G&G were, as always, impeccable, wearing their lightweight suits and ties patterned with birds and pandas from a selection of thirty made for them by their Swiss admirer, Fabric. A girl whispered to me: 'I've never seen artists before who look like gentlemen!' One of their secrets.

James Birch – who confided to me privately that he found one of G&G's pictures, in which they appear in their underpants with manhole covers on their heads 'very funny', but is not sure the artists would agree – thanked everyone punctiliously, especially the director of the Cultural Agency, who was sitting beside me. He told me he had conducted the Chinese orchestra at an acrobatic show in London twenty years earlier. He beamed good will as he replied: 'This is the first British exhibition to come here. The most moving sight was the people crowded together to ask Mr Gilbert and Mr George to sign their names. It helps our reform. When our own artists tried to broaden themselves five years ago, "they" could not accept it.' He did not explain who 'they' were, but we could guess he was referring to the officialdom which had stifled life for so long – until now.

The British Consul, and his tongue, described G&G's work as 'disturbing', which caused a rustle of displeasure, though it seemed a fair comment to me.

Then G&G rose to loud applause: 'We as unhappy artists are very happy to hold . . .' and so on, until the peroration: 'This visit has been a human revelation to us. We have never seen so many good-looking people, and SHANGHAI ['Beijing' had been crossed out, along with 'Crakow'] is now *our favourite city*.'

I admit I felt a twinge of irreverence. Were they playing games? Certainly their declaration of 'unhappiness' was belied by their smiling selves. Was the speech condescending, with their 'favourite city' simply the one they happened to be in at that moment? If so, I concluded, there was no harm in it. It was another aspect of their Living Sculpture, as they chanted in unison. But the performance was, as Barry Flanagan pointed out, 'studied'.

What was undeniable was that they carried out their role as British ambassadors perfectly, winning friends all along the way. Their appearance, their courtesy, their personal attention to every- one they met, left a lasting impression which was invariably to the good. In this sense they were modern explorers blazing new ground, opening doors, opening eyes.

After their speech G&G insisted on being photographed with the entire restaurant staff in their white-and-black costumes (as they had been with the girls who worked in the gallery). Again, I wondered for a moment if they were being condescending, until

I saw the pleasure on the faces of the waiters and waitresses, who clearly took it as an unexpected compliment.

One English visitor to Shanghai warned me that our hotel rooms were bugged, which led to a delightful fantasy from G&G after they had closed the door behind them: 'That Consul, he should have *adored* us, Daniel. He's too much! But who's a sissy, refusing to go to the snake market because the snakes were chopped up alive!'

Several of us went on, as we did every night, to an amazing disco the size of an aircraft hangar, with five floors and several thousand young Chinese bouncing up and down. Even at my age I found this irresistible. The atmosphere was one of pure joy. Suddenly a group would form a ring and sweep me along with them, as if I were a teenager. To my surprise the disc jockey came from Enfield, and I felt I should interview him, but he agreed only with evident reluctance, and proved yawningly boring, only being interested in disco music.

Seeing the young so happy, it was easy to be seduced by Shanghai, and to forget the other face of that 'heartbreaking city'. We were present at the birth of an economic revolution.

My one regret about the whole visit was having to wait for hours on end at the hotel before being summoned to a press conference or to be interviewed interminably for David Langham's documentary, which was never shown and which must have added to the cost G&G were confronted with at the end of the venture, during which not a picture was for sale. Much later, George told me: 'We didn't want to sell a picture – it would only have been lost or destroyed.' I regret those wasted hours of waiting, when I should have been tougher and escaped on my own to take the three-hour trip along the Huangpu River.

The party was finally over, and I crawled back home on a flight via Hong Kong and Zurich while G&G flew on to South Korea to meet their favourite waiter from a Korean restaurant in London, a Mr Chung, who had started a Viennese pastry shop in Seoul. Saying goodbye at the airport they looked as crisp as ever – and their friend-nephew Yu shed tears to see them go. Gilbert & George have kept in touch, and Yu continues to write to his 'Dear Uncles' regularly.

CHAPTER TEN

URINAL

I n October 1990, always experimenting, G&G
returned to postcard pieces for their exhibition
Worlds and Windows. They were brilliant tech-
nically, as might be expected, and imaginative: the cover of the
invitation card to the private view showed nearly a hundred heads
of someone (it was hard to say if male or female) with coloured
hair and wearing a vest, interspersed with soaring flights of the
RAF's display team Red Arrows.

The private view, followed by a lavish party at Anthony d'Offay's
home in Regents Park, was enhanced by an admiring crowd of
supporters, and a less admiring television crew, who asked me if
the postcard pieces had any merit whatsoever. Privately, I had been
reminded of a vain attempt of mine to make some collages on a
special theme one Christmas, which ended up as a complete mess,
but I suggested that the postcard pieces were fun and eye-catching,
and that not too much should be read into them.

With his customary loyalty, Carter Ratcliff came close to making
this mistake in his introduction to the Hirschl & Adler Modern
catalogue in New York that year. Correctly, he reminded us that

during the 1980s we grew so used to thinking of G&G as monumental artists (with works up to forty feet long) that 'it is a mild
shock to be reminded that they make objects of every size. Always,
though, the scale of their intentions and meanings remains the
same: immense. Yet smaller works like their postcard sculptures
are intimate in a way that their photo pieces cannot be.'

I am not entirely persuaded by his interpretation of the postcard
piece of the Edwardian actor Henry Ainley, whose 'strong-jawed
yet delicately molded . . . face . . . might have turned up in Pre-
Raphaelite paintings four or five decades earlier. You could call his
gaze piercing. Or you could say that his eyes are liquid . . . it would
draw attention to Ainley's actorish power to transform himself.'
Relating this to G&G, Ratcliff claimed: 'With this postcard piece
Gilbert & George showed themselves to be fascinated by – and
acutely sensitive to – the nuances of public presentation . . . G&G
have that same ability.' He found another resemblance, which must
have been unintentional when they made the work: 'Look past the
differences between Ainley's roles and you see the same face, sixteen
times. Look past that sameness, and you see another kind of difference, for Ainley ages here, under one's eyes. Gilbert & George
have done the same and just as publicly . . . Now their self-images
reveal them to be relentlessly serious middle-aged men, and the
full transformation from youth to maturity was reflected in Henry
Ainley when the process had only just got under way.' Ratcliff
even interpreted Ainley's scribbled 'So sorry cannot get round this
morning hope to see you soon. D.' as a parallel to the chatty
but formal tone with which G&G manage small-talk on public
occasions.

Could it be, I wondered, that G&G had acquired the postcards
of the actor and mounted them simply because they liked them,
rather than because they wished to convey any temporal message?
Significantly, the postcard pieces date back to 1972, and the Ainley
to 1980, which shows how much they mean to G&G, but, ultimately, the Worlds and Windows are merely postcards, not even

images taken by G&G themselves. Yet they provided a vital chance to pause and mark time before the next onslaught.

The Cosmological Pictures were created in 1989, and exhibited over the next three years at Crakow ('This is now our favourite city!') Rome, Zurich, Vienna, Budapest, The Hague, Dublin, Barcelona, Liverpool (the Tate) and Stuttgart, curated by Rudi Fuchs of The Hague's Gemeentemuseum. Fuchs, one of G&G's closest friends and supporters, declared that the twenty-five works 'demonstrate a fierce independence in formulation and expression that is quite unique in contemporary art'. He found a candour and warmth in this new work which made it clear that G&G cannot accept

> the rather miserable idea that modern man is cool and tactical – or, in Cézanne's case, aesthetic: that is unsentimental.
>
> Gilbert & George passionately want to be popular artists – though in a more general, more evocative way than Van Gogh who, in the social context of his times, was directly concerned with the misery of the peasants and the urban working class.
>
> For that reason Gilbert & George have chosen sentiment as their theme and mode of expression. By that bold choice they have distanced themselves from the dominant drift of art in the twentieth century.
>
> They do not play games. [Oh yes they do!] They are passionately serious, since only seriousness can be convincing. They exposed themselves. That left them with nothing but their individual honesty.
>
> The Cosmological Pictures are in a sense more flamboyant than anything they have done before; these are dramatic scenes in wonderfully rich and glowing colour,

and yet one sees that a strong sense of ceremonial sym-
metry underlines the compositions.

This is the advance: the vivid colours and urban backgrounds of
Edger – *Look* – *Smoke Rising* – and a rare view of London's waterfront
in *Crush* (all 1989), with a crouching boy in the centre and the
view above him depicted upside down. But there is a new note of
solemnity, noticed by Fuchs as a blunt frontality, which reminds
me very much of the elaborate formal designs of the portals of
Gothic cathedrals.

> One can also think of early Renaissance altarpieces where
> saints, perfectly in line with the sight-lines of the perspec-
> tive, stand to both sides of the enthroned Madonna; but
> there is a marked difference. Not only is the posture
> of these saints often seductively coy (unlike Gilbert &
> George); they also seem to beckon the beholder into the
> space of the picture. In Gothic tympanums, as well as in
> pictures by Gilbert & George, the image is very flat and
> frontal.

This leads us to *Urinal* (1991), one of their New Democratic Pictures,
exhibited at the Aarhus Kunstmuseum in Denmark in 1992 and
purchased by the Boymans van Beuningen Museum in Rotterdam.
This is one of their most important pictures to date, and it signalled
the way ahead.

I think G&G have an uneasy relationship to Christ, with whom
they have been compared by one of their sillier admirers. On the
one hand they are contemptuous about Tony Blair's attendance at
church on Sundays; yet I suspect that they are fully aware of the
twitch of the thread, which could one day pull them back. After all,
Gilbert's childhood was steeped in religion: 'I was totally Catholic,
absolutely. I went to church every Sunday until I was nineteen or
so. I never committed a mortal sin.'

'Plenty of venial ones,' interrupted George, 'but no mortal ones.'

George is irreverent, describing Jesus as 'the first dandy, poncing about with several young men on a beach till he was crucified for it'.

Conversely, Gilbert spoke for them both when he told an interviewer in 1987: 'We accept and would like to honour Christian power – we're happily in debt to the Christian tradition. We do not say we're sophisticated atheists, let the peasants go to church, which is what all people of intelligence said this century. They had a classist attitude towards religion. We don't even know where we stand exactly, we're trying to work it out – our religious pictures are both pro and anti religion.'

George: 'When we first did our Jesus pictures in 1980 some of our biggest admirers thought we were cuckoo. Now everybody talks about religiosity, morality or politics in art. We are interested in the power of the individual and the freedom of the artist. In the past they were either serving the Church or the toffs – they did their Christian pictures or pictures of the toff's house, his family or animals. There was very little in the way of serving people. We are at last free and we have a sense of service, of purpose – we want to give in exchange for the gift of life. We don't do it to please ourselves – we're just these miserable chaps trying very hard to give. No joke.'

I think their major picture of 1991 was Urinal. It was not intended as an acknowledgement to Marcel Duchamp, who started conceptual art – and some might say the rot – in 1917 when he exhibited a urinal upside down and called it Fountain; art has never recovered. G&G's Urinal was something more personal, arresting, strangely impressive despite the blasphemous subject-matter. In the sombre context of a deserted Gothic cathedral, the vaulted ceiling tinted yellow, they have replaced the rood screen in the centre with a ruder screen: a tripartite urinal in black and white flanked by Gilbert & George stark naked, their bodies also tinted yellow – apart, curiously, from their private parts. It takes a moment to see that behind George, who looks unusually nervous, is a massive blow-up of a naked man, presumably himself. His penis is exposed, but not the upper half of his body. Gilbert stands in front of the backside of another naked man, his head almost fitting into the cleavage of the buttocks. Surprisingly, the picture is simple and unpretentious, without the garish red dyes that, to my mind, overwhelm *Ill World* (1994), which looks even more magnificent in a black-and-white reproduction than it does in colour.

Writing of *Urinal* in the *Independent* on 8 December 1992, James Hall found the 'general scheme of things is pretty clear. They are making the time-honoured parallel between sacred architecture and the architecture of the human body. Not only do Gilbert & George slot into the grid, but their relationship to the blown-up bodies, and to the Gothic architecture, is like that of medieval sculptures to their setting.' This is lifting them onto a new level.

George told the interviewer Hans-Ulrich Obrist of a passage in the Bible: 'Be aware of the men who sit on the wall and eat their own dung and drink their own piss.' 'Those words appear in the Bible twice [2nd Book of Kings 18:27; Isaiah 36:12]. In Barbara Thiery's book *Jesus the Man*, she says that one of the original texts says that Jesus was taken from the cross and laid temporarily in a urinal. This is so interesting because our picture *Urinal* shows a urinal set in a church.

'Shit and faith put together, like in *Shit Faith* [1982] or in the big shit cross in The Naked Shit Pictures should be great unifying themes. All people, wherever they live, have some involvement with shit. All people have some faith or attitude towards faith.'

Gilbert: 'But the combination is dangerous.'

George: 'It is exciting. Do churches have lavatories?'

Obrist: 'There is an interesting church in Vienna, in a psychiatric hospital in Steinhopf, built by Otto Wagner. He made the floor slanted so that water could directly pour off the excrement.'

George: '*Amazing!* Every church must have a lavatory presumably.'

Gilbert: 'Normally they don't.'

Obrist: 'Maybe a private one for the vicar.'

George: 'An elitist lavatory. Surely Christians say this is the house of God, so if it is a house it must have a lavatory.'

This basic point had never occurred to me; where can the congregation go, particularly children, if caught short? This could partly explain why religion is such a turn-off to the young.

It is odd, and G&G noticed it, that in works like *Urinal* and The Naked Shit Pictures, people were less outraged by the nakedness than by the shit – possibly because the sight of two naked, middle-aged men could hardly be thought of as deliberately erotic. They explained that the viewer was looking at his own nakedness as well: 'It's not just us. They realise their own nakedness under their clothes at that moment. In that way the pictures are as much about the viewer as about us, really.' And it is a nice twist to the Emperor's new clothes, for G&G know they are wearing nothing, and so does the viewer.

Nakedness and excrement is the legal definition of obscenity in America, according to Gilbert & George, who wanted to see how far they could go in breaking such taboos.

CHAPTER ELEVEN

ALL ABOUT SHIT

On 15 October 1992, Gilbert & George celebrated their One Hundredth Birthday Dinner – their combined ages. The event was in itself a contradiction, as they had declared that they never celebrated birthdays – 'What would we want to do that for?'

In spite of this, these two 'unhappy', 'tormented', suffering artists threw a party which typified their gift for fun (when they are not being interviewed). It was held at their new favourite restaurant, La Gaulette in Cleveland Street, with champagne in the bar downstairs before dinner in a private room, comparatively stark, which they had taken over for the evening. There was nothing simple or stark about the food and drink, starting with Dom Perignon, followed by the most beautiful Pouligny Montrachet. This happens to be my favourite drink, and it was superb, further enhanced when Nicholas Serota, Director of the Tate Gallery, who was sitting opposite, leant across and urged me to have some more beluga caviar, which he shovelled on to my plate. That alone would have been blissful enough, but every course was accompanied by another wine, typical of G&G's talent for making everyone else happy, if not themselves.

When the party finished, long after midnight, Troy, a young admirer whom I knew from Moscow, took me to the latest 'in' club, a converted cinema close to Victoria station, whose existence I was unaware of. From the circle I looked down on what looked like a thousand heaving bodies, most of them naked and all of them male, which sobered me up alarmingly. Two days later I heard the club had been raided and closed down.

The two exhibitions in China had given G&G the international prestige they wanted. There had of course been no commercial return, but they were not interested in that – they were building for the future, like the Chinese. Significantly, their latest work revealed a new range, with the vigorous colour that was so appealing to the young. I found it remarkable that anything which started with a process as mechanical as photography should end with such exuberance. They insisted that their pictures might look 'mechanical' but were really the opposite, yet they go into reverse as they add that 'there is no magic. We are very anti the hand. Brush-stroke is not interesting to us,' as if they are denying their inspiration. They like a 'vision', but deny that they start with a preconceived concept: 'The most important part is when we actually go into the studio to design the pictures. The most key thing to everything is that we go empty-headed at that point. We have to go completely zonked, completely blank. And then how we are as people will dictate how the pictures will be. Ideas are no good. Our development is not a stylistic one. It is about the development of us as people. Our pictures are a life's development.'

The pictures for China took them two years to create, and the results are what mattered. G&G's rate of productivity – hardly speedy – means that they are incommunicado when they are working, concentrating on the pictures to the exclusion of every outside interruption. They do not answer the phone personally; they eat in the Market Café; they do not socialise: 'We have to keep our lives empty,' says Gilbert. 'We are too crazed, too driven; we concentrate twenty-four hours a day on our work.'

And then they accompany it around the world, an activity people take for granted, but which is one of the reasons for their international success. 'Public exhibitions of living artists are extremely rare,' Gilbert points out, 'and no one seems to realise that.' They regard artists who refuse to attend their private views as very selfish: 'It is the responsibility of the artist to bring their work before the public while they're alive. We want to know what it is like to feel that love.'

In 1994, a year after their visit to China, they started their revolutionary Naked Shit Pictures.

Why their preoccupation with shit? They are quite blithe about it! To start with they were pushing the frontiers back as far as they could go, in active response to their critics: 'What they want us to do is to take out everything that offends people. Take out the flowers because that's kitsch; shit, take that out; young men, take them out; garish colours . . . You'd end up with a still life of a bowl of flowers, and then they wouldn't discuss it at all. You wouldn't even get an exhibition. You'd never be heard of again. We believe that if we want to have a totally free society everything has to be included, and if we do a piece called Shit and they still believe it is shocking, then we have to de-shock them. Because there is nothing wrong with shit.'

Gilbert said these words in 1994, but G&G's obsession with shit began years earlier, in 1969, with their magazine sculpture *George the Cunt & Gilbert the Shit*. *Shitted* and *Shit* followed in the early 1980s, and George admits that they were more aggressive than The Naked Shit Pictures of the 1990s: 'In a way they were,' he told Wolf Jahn, 'because shit-eating is very aggressive. But if *Shit* [1982] had been a camera negative it would have been a lot more aggressive. It's a photogram.'

Gilbert: 'One is called *Shitted* because we're being shat on. I think there's no more extreme situation you can have than being shat on; that's the ultimate disgrace, insult. I think we felt attacked like that. We were using that.'

George: 'To say, "We can take it, do your worst." Then we wanted to make it more disgusting. That's why we coloured the tongues shit-colour, even. Now we normalise it more, in a way. The shit is in the pictures the same way everything else is. For instance, a lot of young people would love to be able to do what we're doing in Flying Shit [1994], to make themselves a skateboard or a surfboard. They actually like that, they'd love to arrive at a party on a shit, they'd be so happy. The reality in the world is that if you manufacture little bar stools, shit-shaped, like in Flying Shit, you can make a very famous bar with that, they'll all go there and sit down and have their gins and tonics. That's the reality.'

Gilbert added: 'And it's interesting that the pictures with shit in them cause people to comment who wouldn't otherwise comment. With shit, they feel they have to look, they have to say something.'

Initially, my response was twofold: that this is reducing life to basics – all of us shit, and some of us look at the results floating in the lavatory. But, equally, isn't this preoccupation rather childish? Exactly. Gilbert told the musician Dave Stewart that 'the first piece of art you ever do – as a baby even – is to form the shit. In fact it's the only sculpture that exists naturally in the world; it's modelled in that way. It's people's first adventure in form, and it's one that everybody in the world understands, whether they are rich or poor, come from a desert or a city, or are three years old or seventy. It's the first clay that you have. Children naturally make sculptures out of shit.'

Stewart pointed out that their parents told them not to; but that might be part of the attraction, both to the child and G&G.

Gilbert: 'We don't believe that there is anything wrong in doing pieces to do with shit, because shit is part of us. Or to do with nakedness – especially of men. It's strange: a naked lady is wonderful, two naked ladies, very interesting, but two men naked are more naked than one. Many collectors only want to buy middle-class art; they love meaningless, empty-of-feeling art. The moment that art says something they are terrified. That's what happened with our Dirty Words show in '77, which had pictures with titles like *Bent Shit Cunt*, *Fucked Up* and *Communism*.'

George: 'Even some of our biggest fans thought that we'd gone nuts.'

Dave Stewart, one of Britain's most celebrated modern musicians, who founded the Eurythmics with Annie Lennox in 1981, collects pictures by contemporary artists like Damien Hirst, who designed the cover for his 1994 solo album *Greetings from the Gutter*. He told G&G that he had had a lot of trouble with their picture *Shag* (1988), which hangs in the deconsecrated church in north London he has converted into a recording studio: 'It gets rented out to all sorts of people, a gospel choir sometimes, and people walk in and say, "You can't have that picture in here."' Which is odd, for the title is discreet for G&G, and the picture is not offensive, unless you wish to interpret it as being so.

George was indignant: 'How ridiculous! People are always shagging in churches – I remember my days in the choir.'

Laughing, Stewart told them how he loved their pictures to such a point that Annie Lennox and he had copied G&G during their time as the Eurythmics, searching out suits like theirs.

'Very flattering,' said George.

'And instead of playing live we would just sit on the stage and let the record play,' continued Stewart.

George: 'Amazing. I'm sure it was very effective.'

Stewart's reaction to The Naked Shit Pictures seemed to disconcert them: 'I was in Cologne recently and I saw your new show and I just fell about in hysterics. I thought it was hilariously funny.'

George: 'So you saw *Flying Shit*, in other words?'

Gilbert: 'It was quite an amazing show. But you have only seen excerpts; the reality of the whole show was much, much more powerful.'

Indeed, they took the Shit pictures very seriously; the only levity could come from them. 'I think we're extremely freaky, weird people to do pictures like *Shitty World* or *Naked Shit*,' Gilbert told Wolf Jahn, as if he were boasting. Probably he was, for he added: 'Nobody ever did pictures like those. Even when we showed The Naked Shit Pictures in Cologne in 1994, people were trying to tell us that it must have been so much fun doing them.'

George: 'We replied, if it's all such fun, how come the whole population of Cologne isn't doing it? It's obviously not that.'

In 1997 the interviewer Hans-Ulrich Obrist said that he doubted if their work would threaten people so much if it were not beautiful.

George: 'I think if all the [Naked Shit Pictures] were done without using our negative form, if they were done with charcoal and some brown paint, and done a little rough, not so polished as ours are, I think they would have no impact. No service to people whatsoever. None. They would provide nothing to help one single person. If they were collaged, with a little bit of polythene, even if they had some real shit and lavatory paper stuck to the pictures, they would mean nothing. They wouldn't have the connection to the inside of the person.'

Gilbert: 'We think that through the form we use, through the negative that becomes so hard and so polished, the pictures become so powerful and aggressive in some strange way. We always say that our flowers are totally aggressive.'

George: 'Recently people said that we even made shit beautiful in some way, that we gave them a way of looking at it.'

Gilbert: 'The first time they can actually look at it. I think that's incredible.'

George: 'To the people who say, "Surely you've manipulated these shits to make them look like penises, I don't believe they are actually shits," we say, "Have you looked at yours? Because if you look at them every day, come next Thursday you probably will have one like that." If you never look at the shit, you cannot say that it shouldn't look like that.'

Gilbert: 'The morality that we are allowed to eat but not allowed to look at our shit is morally wrong.'

This could be seen as G&G hyperbole – we are hardly forbidden to look at our excrement by an Act of Parliament, and most of us have the occasional glance before flushing; but Obrist took the point literally as a 'big theme', quoting Roland Barthes, who said 'Photographic shit doesn't stink.'

George agreed, but insisted that people 'think ours does'. 'We recently had an article where it said: "The artists and their pictures stink." [Surely this was intended as a critical observation, rather than the literal truth?] It's interesting that people are alarmed, as probably we are as well, by the combination of naked and shit. It is interesting that that should be alarming, because the fact of life is that you have to be at least partly naked in order to shit. You cannot shit with all your clothes on. So it's very natural, the combination of these two subjects.'

Gilbert: 'It is based on degrading ourselves. Then critics cannot attack you in the same way!'

Obrist told them he had seen an exhibition of Aztec art with beautiful ancient earrings in the form of shit, at a time when shit was also taboo.

'How marvellous!' said George, delighted. 'What a commercial item that would be today. They would sell like hot cakes. We think it is important to say about taboos that a lot of people think we are very free, crazy fuckers who want to impose our free way of life on them. This is not at all the case. We are filled with taboos. We are terrified of shit. It is an adventure together with the public, together with the viewer.'

Knowing that 'shit' is taboo – the very word is unmentionable when used literally and not as an epithet – G&G proceeded cautiously, testing the water. They introduced seven of the new pictures (out of sixteen altogether) in an exhibition of their work at the Kunstmuseum in Wolfsburg in December 1994, including full-frontal images of themselves stark naked, with nothing concealed.

Ironically, few people took exception to being confronted by a pair of naked, middle-aged gentlemen. The critic David Sylvester surprised them by saying that other modern artists (such as Lucian Freud) tried to do naked pictures, but only succeeded in doing *nudes*, whereas G&G showed them *naked*.

Gilbert was amused by the hypocrisy of some people complaining of an image of them with their trousers half-down: 'It is not the nakedness that is taboo, it is having the trousers half-down.'

In November 1994 they showed The Naked Shit Pictures, which Dave Stewart found hilarious, at the Jablonka Galerie in Cologne. Few people complained, either about the nakedness or the shit, and G&G began preparing to mount a major show in London.

The trouble began when they took part in a mixed exhibition at the Serpentine Gallery in February 1995, and two of their pictures were rejected. G&G wrote to the director, Julia Peyton-Jones, expressing their dismay:

> We write to tell you of our horror and deep distress at the banning of our two pictures. We understand this happened at a meeting chaired by vice chairman Felicity Waley-Cohen.
>
> This banning is totally unfair in the light of previous Serpentine exhibitions like [Robert] Gober, the Hirst group show, Helen Chadwick and Man Ray to name but a few.
>
> The human subjects discussed in these pictures have been common currency for many, many years in art. Richard Hamilton's 'Girls Shitting Prints' [i.e. *Soft Pink Landscape* (1971–73) and *Sunset* (1973)] were shown long ago at the ICA. Hamilton's IRA shit picture is in the collection of the 'very public' Tate Gallery. The Whitechapel Gallery at this very moment is showing images of pissing and pierced vaginas and nipples.
>
> If it's the shit that is the concern we would like to

Retrospective exhibition at the Solomon R. Guggenheim Museum, New York, 1985.

The Sexual Pictures (1982–83), in the exhibition Pictures 1982 to 1985, Kunsthalle, Basle, Switzerland, 1986.

The Naked Shit Pictures, South London Gallery, 1994.

The Fundamental Pictures, Sonnabend Gallery, New York, 1997.

The Fundamental Pictures, Lehmann Maupin Gallery, New York, 1997.

Retrospective exhibition at ARC Musée d'art moderne de la Ville de Paris, 1997.

ABOVE *George the Cunt and Gilbert the Shit* magazine sculpture (1969).

RIGHT Charcoal on paper sculpture, from a five-part charcoal on paper sculpture called *The Nature of our Looking* (1970, 348 x 236cm).

FOREVER WE WILL SEARCH   AND GIVE OUR THOUGHT TO   THE PICTURE WE HAVE IN   OUR MIND.
WE ARE WALKING ROUND   NOW AS SAD AS CAN BE

LEFT *Bloody Life No. 3* (1975, 247 x 206 cm).

BELOW *Henry Ainley* postcard sculpture (1980, 106 x 92cm).

The Singing Sculpture (1991).

LEFT *Cunt Scum* (1977, Collection Tate Gallery, London, 241 x 201cm).

BELOW *Fallen Leaves* (1980, 241 x 201cm).

ABOVE LEFT *Four Knights* (1980, 241 x 201cm).

ABOVE *Living with Madness* (1980, 241 x 201cm).

LEFT *Stream* (1980, 241 x 201cm).

remind you that the curator for this group exhibition [Hans-Ulrich Obrist] was invited on the strength of his highly successful exhibition entitled *cloaxa maxima* which dealt exclusively with human waste. Moreover it should be realised that Kensington Gardens has public conveniences and a special area for dogs to shit.

The two banned pictures are from a group of sixteen we created in 1994. They have been exhibited during the busy Art Fair period in Cologne and in greater numbers at the Kunstmuseum in Wolfsburg. In both places fully-illustrated catalogues were produced together with postcards, posters, badges and news-sheets which were distributed to every single household in Wolfsburg.

Now to return to your *banning*. We know we have done *nothing* wrong and cannot accept these two pictures being banned. These pictures were the most intensely difficult and emotional we ever created. They do not show violence, they do not show or suggest any sexual act, they exploit no one. For us they are deeply humanistic pictures which people in Britain should not be *prevented* from seeing.

G&G's reaction was obviously completely sincere, with no deviousness whatsoever. Significantly they did not refer to possible support for their stand from the media, for they were anxious to avoid any scandal or police interference, which could threaten their major show planned for later in the year. They suggested to Julia Peyton-Jones that the banning was not due to the pictures' subject matter, and wondered if there was some other unspoken motive: 'We don't believe these pictures would be *banned* if we were overseas artists and we can't help but feel that you wouldn't ban them if they were not by Gilbert & George.' In this they might have been being invidious, but they pointed out that it was strange that no other works in the show had been banned, though one artist was exhibiting a vibrator and another a swing with an anal device. They concluded:

> We are determined to *reverse* this dictatorial censorship – even if we have to recruit the support of the art world. [Their only threat.] Please, *please*, for the sake of art and freedom, and modern thought and the British art public, *reverse* this oppressive horrible ban.

Typically, they finished: 'Lots of love, Gilbert & George.'

In fact this was all a case of much ado about nothing substantial, though G&G clearly saw it differently, as deliberate censorship. The Serpentine Gallery has large windows which look out over Kensington Gardens, and any nice little old lady or gentleman walking their dogs might have been startled if they had looked up as they passed, to be confronted by two naked men surrounded by excrement. The explicit Gober exhibition of 1993 had already attracted the attention of the police, who were anxious to protect the public from too severe a shock.

The eventual solution was to substitute two other Naked Shit Pictures, *Ill World* and *Human Shits*, for the two pictures in question. I was present at the private view, and G&G's pictures definitely enhanced the occasion. If they had been hoping for a scandal they would have been disappointed, but they were not.

Now they were able to proceed with the big Naked Shit Pictures exhibition, which opened at the South London Art Gallery in Peckham that September. The project was agreed, catalogued, and hung within three months: sixteen massive pictures in Renaissance blues, reds – and browns. 'People don't yet realise how extraordinary it is to do this show,' said Gilbert.

Having avoided the possible scandal of a police raid at the Serpentine exhibition, G&G were prepared for controversy, but what happened was not what anyone expected. Suddenly they found themselves being deified.

A distant gallery in South London – tube to the Oval and then a

35 bus to 65 Peckham Road – was hardly an auspicious location, but this drill-hall of a place, active once again after a break of a hundred years, proved perfect for the height and size of the pictures, some twenty feet long, hung in double tiers. As I entered on the night of the private view there was all the excitement of a great occasion. Anne Seymour (Mrs Anthony d'Offay) hurried towards me to say she was reminded of the Giotto frescoes in the Scrovegni Chapel in Padua. Looking around me, I could see her point. Stacked from floor to ceiling in this immense room, the effect was of murals rather than of separate pictures. David Sylvester showed me the feature article about the show he had written for the *Guardian*, which concluded: 'I find it difficult to drag myself away from this chapel, feel compelled to remain in the presence of a disturbingly weighty vision of the world.'

This was an astonishing accolade. Every artist needs the right patron: Francis Bacon had the support of Sir Robert and Lisa Sainsbury from the very beginning, while Gilbert & George had such loyal gallery owners as Illeana Sonnabend and Anthony d'Offay. Every artist needs the right gallery, and though Erica Brausen at the Hanover had brought Bacon to the attention of the Sainsburys, it was the Marlborough Gallery which established him internationally, helping to organise the first, historic exhibition at the Tate in 1962. The Konrad Fischer Gallery in Düsseldorf, the Sonnabend in New York and, later, the d'Offay Gallery in London did the same for Gilbert & George. Without establishing a reputation in America, an artist is doomed to be relegated to the second division. Even Sickert and Stanley Spencer were restricted to being known as 'British' artists. Lucian Freud's status was transformed when a new agent set out to conquer the American market and succeeded in doubling his prices.

Every artist also needs a champion. Graham Sutherland, so fine but so British, was unfortunate in having as his champion a waspish, wealthy Australian collector, Douglas Cooper, who owned a large number of paintings by Picasso, who was a close friend. For a time it seemed, to Sutherland at least, that Cooper was the most influential supporter he could have had, especially when Cooper turned against Francis Bacon, largely because of personal dislike, and transferred his allegiance to Sutherland. But Cooper was devious and treacherous, and came to decide that he had mistakenly overrated Sutherland. Like many tremendously ugly men, Cooper was vain, and he felt his doubts about Sutherland were confirmed when the artist made the error of making Cooper's portrait not quite flattering enough.

Partly as a consequence, Francis Bacon replaced Sutherland to be regarded as 'Britain's leading artist'. He had the championship of David Sylvester, whose published interviews, which came after my first television interview in 1958 – the only recording was destroyed when Associated-Rediffusion lost their franchise in 1964 – did much to further Bacon's reputation. Sylvester was a heavyweight, the serious biographer of Magritte and Giacometti, and his judgement was respected.

When I arrived at the Pompidou Centre in Paris in June 1996, Sylvester, who was the curator of the brilliant Bacon retrospective (the colours proving more brilliant than I remembered), took me aside to discuss the hanging and the reflections from the glass, which some people objected to, though I suspected that Bacon would have liked them. Sylvester confided that he hoped his next major exhibition would be devoted to Andy Warhol, Bacon and Gilbert & George.

As this was hardly the occasion, I did not indicate to him how explosive I feared Bacon's reaction to such a proposal might have been. When he had told me once that he was sorry that no new interesting work was coming up, I dared to mention Gilbert & George, hoping to provoke him. He went as flat as a fallen soufflé, responding suspiciously, 'What about Gilbert & George? I don't really know about Gilbert & George. Do you think they are any good? I ask you the question!'

'I'm not sure,' I said, intimidated.

'Well, I'm *certain!*' Surprisingly, he accused them of wanting to make money – which was neither relevant nor true – 'but if they were any good they would be exciting – and they're not. I just do not find Gilbert & George exciting.'

At the same time, he was interested to know how they worked – 'Do they use some sort of cipher?' – and grunted a doubtful 'Oh yuss!' when I insisted that their pictures could not be judged properly in a small space like the room they occupied at the Tate, but needed to be seen at various distances to gain the full impact. Over a lunch given by James Birch, I tried to bring Bacon and G&G together. At first Francis said it was impossible. At my insistence George phoned him a few minutes later, introducing himself politely, but Francis remained adamant. I suspect he was busy with the young Spaniard with whom he was having a last affair, and can hardly blame him, but this was a sadly missed opportunity, for I am certain they would have enjoyed each other's sense of humour. Francis, though, was surprisingly jealous and dismissive of other artists (like G&G themselves), and the meeting could only have succeeded if art was not mentioned – unless to run it down, all contemporaries dismissed, and sex extolled.

At this point, David Sylvester had expressed no interest in Gilbert & George. Bacon was the one British artist he revered, although he maintained amicable relationships with Lucian Freud, Frank Auerbach and Michael Andrews, a band of brothers in the early days of Soho and the Colony Room, absurdly described by Kitaj as the 'School of London'.

Now Bacon was dead and, in a devastating reversal, Sylvester had changed his mind about Freud and Auerbach, deciding that they were not up to much after all. He had become the champion of Gilbert & George, which made his assessment of The Naked Shit Pictures vitally important. G&G had shown him the new works already, and he had studied them in silence for several minutes before telling them softly that they were G&G's 'greatest Old-Master pictures'.

'What?' replied George. 'You've come halfway across London to insult us?'

Sylvester confirmed his admiration in his review for the *Guardian*, in which he admitted that he was old enough to be amazed by comedians who joked on the BBC about masturbation, menstruation and fellatio, but were not daring enough to come out with jokes about excretion, which were part of his prep-school culture: 'Gilbert & George are chronic troubleshooters. They seem to have made it a point of honour to take on subjects from daily life that other artists have found too hot to handle. [He could have mentioned Bacon as an exception.] This time they have faced up to a process which, besides mattering as much as breathing and besides causing intense anxiety when it isn't working smoothly, is also, unlike eating or sleeping, a notorious source of embarrassment.' Writing of G&G's very different backgrounds, he concluded: 'But as artists their separate identities were completely dissolved and fused, in that their *modus operandi* was presented as being inextricably collaborative. As artists, they were almost a Holy Trinity – two persons but one Creator.'

Referring to the controversial matter, he described the work as G&G's 'most daring':

> As is their wont, they take the difficult subject in their stride. The faeces they present us with are perfectly formed compact units. Blown up, they look like rocks and are put to excellent use by G&G for the construction of totem poles, crossed and the like. Employed thus as building material, human excrement becomes as sociable as cowdung. And as sacred as Hindu linghams.
>
> If this transformation could be taken to have sanitised the subject, this does not mean the subject has had the sting taken out of it. The real theme of these works is not shit and shitting but a subject that this evokes. A man is never so little the master of his fate as when he is

defecating. A series avowedly about shit is effectively about man's fate.

As to their total achievement, they seem to me out-standing in every context in which they might be assessed. Among their contemporaries – Nauman, Boltan-ski, Kiefer, Long, Cragg – they are not surpassed. Among exponents of photo-based art, going back to Hartfield, they come second only to Warhol. Among English artists, they are the chief successors, along with Malcolm Morley, to the line of visionary painters that runs from Fuseli and Blake and Palmer to Watts to Spencer to Bacon. They have become perhaps the only artists who have managed to profit from Bacon's large triptychs.

Sylvester reminded his readers that it was Bacon's sight of a dog's turd on a pavement that aroused the sense of the immanence of mortality that is so crucial to his work. He disagreed with Martin Gayford in the *Spectator*, who claimed that Lucian Freud was dealing, like Bacon, with mortality and 'the brutality of fact':

But Bacon hit upon that phrase when trying to define a key quality which he found in Picasso and found wanting in Matisse, a quality that clearly involves a sense of the human condition, which in turn demands a measure of universality. Freud seems to see the world at close range through his own eyes only, painting attractive prospects or repulsive sights according to his personal whim. Gil-bert & George, in contrast, for all their fooling around, look at humanity at large with an instinct for the typical and a mature compassion. That is why they are not fool-ing around when they take it upon themselves to pose together (in *Naked Eye* and *Ill World*) in what look like paraphrases of Masaccio's *Expulsion from Eden* and Michel-angelo's *Rondanini Pièta*.

This remarkable comparison is all the stronger for the admission that G&G do 'fool around', or did so. This work offered a new dimension, and the chapel-like setting enhanced it. Surprisingly, the blown-up turds which Sylvester compared to totem poles gave no offence once you accepted them. Conversely, Ill World has a touching vulnerability: Gilbert & George are naked, clasping each other in a long street with parked cars and graffiti on a dark wall, with two full-length but diminutive figures of themselves, fully dressed, on either side. This has nothing to do with shit, but much to do with love.

Reviewing the exhibition in the Sunday Telegraph, the respected critic John McEwen also found a spiritual content:

> In such exposure there is a degree of risk, of self-sacrifice for a higher cause, which is purposely moral and indeed Christian. What they defiantly declare is that there is nothing shameful in nakedness. As the Bible states, naked we came into the world and naked we shall go out of it. The true shame is to snigger or condemn.
>
> The evangelical point is confirmed by references to the Crucifixion and the Garden of Eden, where the seed of shame was sown. That these cruciforms are composed of images of the artists' shit, literally their own faeces, is their ultimate assault on conformity.

This exceptional tribute came four days after Richard Dorment's review in the sister paper, the Daily Telegraph. Many of Dorment's readers regard him as the doyen of art critics; circumspect, fair, knowledgeable, the complete professional, sufficiently respected by Nicholas Serota to ask him to curate the 1994–95 retrospective of his fellow-American and fellow-Anglophile James McNeill Whistler at the Tate. In many ways one would expect him to be the last critic to come out in G&G's favour, and indeed he has admitted that their work has repelled him. But he has also discovered his appreciation for it, and shortly after joining the Telegraph he devoted half a page to their 1987 exhibition at the Hayward, acclaiming them as part of a 'uniquely English tradition' and comparing them to Sickert, with his affection for the slums of Camden Town.

> Although, like artistic dandies from Whistler to Dalí, they cultivate a highly-controlled and mannered public image, the themes of their assemblages have been preoccupied with the very opposite of control, being about sex, boredom, loneliness, madness and death. Gilbert & George are poets who use everything that happens in their lives as material for their art. They insist that *all* their feelings and thoughts are legitimate subjects for sculpture, no matter how embarrassing for them to reveal or for us to see. [This was written ten years before The Naked Shit Pictures.] They are deeply disliked by many critics because they omit the element of self-editing that most people automatically incorporate into their lives.

Dorment concluded that each G&G picture was a fragment of 'an immeasurably huge mosaic' that they were still putting together, and in this he has been proved correct as well: 'In some respects, the only way to see Gilbert & George is in these large retrospectives which are, in some senses, a single work of art.'

These comments were followed in the next day's *Telegraph* by a piece of editorial malice which must have left Dorment gasping and exposed him to ridicule. 'It's a Joke but at Whose Expense?' was the heading of the paper's 'Sixth Column', by the late Martyn Harris:

> They [G&G] are, in fact, an enormous joke at the expense of the art world. They have become hugely famous in the twin citadels of pretension and credulity – the French and American art markets – and are now winning grudging acclaim from British art critics who have looked at

them aghast for the past decade, hoping they might go
away.

Such a rebuke was cruel to the paper's new art critic. It also confirmed G&G's capacity to provoke; few artists are universally loved
in their lifetime – think of the years when Picasso was considered
a fraud by the likes of Sir Alfred Munnings, who asked: 'What are
pictures for? But to fill a man's soul with admiration and sheer
joy, not to bewilder and daze him.' Notoriously, he and Winston
Churchill said they would have enjoyed kicking Picasso in the backside in the unlikely event of seeing him leave their club.

Dorment was undaunted: 'It's much harder for the British to
understand G&G than the Russians. They hit a nerve in England.
They do not paint what the British want to see, still less what they
want to believe about their country. They tell the truth. That is
why foreigners love them and they are so vilified at home. What
other British artists treat such subjects as the filthiness of London,
alcoholism, AIDS, and the racial hatred on the one hand, and on
the other the grandeur and beauty of a city in decline? They rarely
do a piece that is entirely one-sided. If their subject is London they
will include the glories of its architecture, but also the dogshit in
the streets.'

Dorment also made the point that while somebody like Howard
Hodgkin is never confused with Hodgkin the artist, G&G were
attacked as individuals, as if what they do and who they are were
the same thing. When I suggested that their craving for self-publicity
encouraged such identification, he compared them to T. S. Eliot,
who wrote passionate poetry while assuming the bland appearance
of a bowler-hatted bank clerk: 'They are the English "everyman".'

I mentioned the fervent dislike of G&G felt by so intelligent a
critic as Peter Fuller. 'Ironically,' said Dorment, 'of all critics, Peter
Fuller had the most in common with Gilbert & George. He was all
for returning humanist content into contemporary art. It was very
strange to me that he appeared not to understand that in addition

to the strong visual punch the For AIDS pictures carried, they were all about death, grief, love and fear. It was all terribly moving, and yet Peter couldn't get beyond the titles, which he claimed shocked him.'

Then Dorment made what was, to me, an astonishing claim for G&G: 'They are the successors to, but much greater than, Francis Bacon. Francis Bacon is able to express his own predicament; Gilbert & George can do that, but go much further, beyond the self-obsessed private world of Bacon's paintings, which are in a certain sense self-portraits. One feels one knows a lot about Francis Bacon, but not Gilbert & George. They've achieved a device which allows them to express universal subjects; their art has developed in a most extraordinary way, as Francis Bacon's never has.'

When I queried his belief that G&G will be remembered in a hundred years' time, he confirmed it vehemently: 'Oh yes. More than Francis Bacon. They belong to the Northern tradition that includes Brueghel, Munch, Otto Dix – the opposite of reassurance. There are very few artists whose exhibitions one wouldn't dream of missing – Gilbert & George are the exception.'

Conversely, I would say that Bacon was the 'opposite of reassurance' indeed the embodiment of disquiet, and that he will certainly be remembered in a hundred years' time himself. But Richard Dorment made me aware, as I had not been before, of the way G&G's art reflects contemporary London and the desolation of the East End: 'Their celebration of London has not been recognised: their works on the sculpture of London are some of the most beautiful things they have ever done; their East End seems to go back to Dickens and certainly to Hogarth's *Gin Lane*. They do not pretend that London's parks are leafy glens; you can sense the alienation of nature barely hanging on. They're also in the great tradition of William Blake – the visionary side – two people looking at this urban hell. Like T. S. Eliot there is a passionate poetry behind the façade – they have constructed their own *Waste Land*.'

In fact there are numerous 'leafy glens' in G&G's work, as for instance in *Lone* (1988), where a youth in pink jeans strolls across an armpit surrounded by cherry blossom. And I doubt that – as Dorment asserts – the young men in their pictures are 'deliberately repellent, evoking the First War scandal when so many conscripts were revealed as shockingly undernourished', nor do I agree that G&G were intent on portraying British youth today. I find their young men slight but perfectly formed, twee rather than erotic, with scarcely a muscle between them, chosen because they were local, available models and fitted into G&G's images rather than with the object of conveying any social message.

Only with *Here* (1987) do I agree with Dorment's view that G&G depict London as an 'urban hell'. The picture shows the gigantic figures of G&G in blue, their palms outstretched, with a panorama of Spitalfields behind them. It has the element of despair which Dorment refers to, a haunting quality, yet it's only fair to comment that the refuse of the Brick Lane market after it closes down is virtually identical to that of markets all over the world when the activity is over, and is not restricted to London alone.

As for the number of people who hate G&G's work, Dorment says: 'They're not new. They've been around since the early seventies but recognition comes late in England. Within twenty years' time they'll be much loved, when people actually look instead of listen. *They are the most important British artists alive.*' They may well end up with knighthoods, if such honours still exist.

Look instead of listen. This applies to their most vociferous critics, who did not even see The Naked Shit Pictures, while denouncing them in newspaper editorials. Yet again, Dorment's review was at variance with the editorial in his paper, the *Daily Telegraph*, though I suppose it is healthy that such divergent views should be published.

Dorment started his review by reminding us that works of art are not always easy to look at, citing the sores on Christ in the Isenheim altarpiece (a work greatly admired by Francis Bacon) or Otto Dix's mutilated soldiers:

This week I am going to write about a group of pictures that actually repel me, but which I nevertheless believe are works of art. Indeed, when the history of twentieth-century British art comes to be written, there is no question in my mind that the artists who made them, Gilbert & George, will be seen as the most important artists of their generation. Motivated by nothing less than a desire to reproduce in their art the entirety of human reality, their life's work is to make an inventory of all that is bestial in man, as well as all that is cerebral and spiritual. But whatever they do they don't play by the rules.

That Richard Dorment should have praised G&G so highly to me is one matter, but this was an extraordinarily bold declaration in the *Daily Telegraph*, conservative to the core. But then Dorment begins to qualify his enthusiasm, admitting that he found The Naked Shit Pictures hard to take, because he was fastidious: 'Pictures of naked bodies I don't mind; but I can't look at giant brown turds without revulsion.'

He then hits the target by admitting:

And that, I'm afraid, is the whole point of this exhibition. At the moment when we begin to ask ourselves why the human body and its functions should so appal us, we begin to understand what Gilbert & George are all about. Far from being gratuitously offensive, these pictures are the contemporary equivalent of medieval representations of corpses in the process of decomposition. And when we ask 'To what end?' the answer is that these pictures proclaim a messianic, visionary message: nothing human is disgusting. We are all the same.

We are all the same – that was the triumph of the exhibition at Peckham, though Dorment concluded that he did not find the same subtlety that he had with the For AIDS exhibition in 1989: 'If people can't look at an artist's pictures, he has made them in vain. In this group, it is all too easy to turn away.'

He accused G&G of preferring 'confrontation to acceptance', but this did not detract from his earlier praise, when he called them the most important British artists of their generation. Not even Bacon received greater acclaim than the tributes G&G had from David Sylvester, John McEwen and Richard Dorment, which must have been dismaying to the artists themselves, always so quick to complain that the critics did not love them. If they needed a backlash of abuse, it came at once. Just as it had done with Dorment's first review, the *Daily Telegraph* published a lead article on the editorial page on the day following his second: 'The Gilbert and George Talent for a Load of Tosh', by John Casey, Fellow of Gonville and Caius College, Cambridge. As usual, there is no indication that Casey actually took the trouble to visit the exhibition in Peckham. Comparing the artistic fashion for a 'concept', Casey claimed that Salvador Dalí was partly responsible – 'a horrible but talented painter, who liked to think up titles such as *Virgin Auto-Sodomised by her own Chastity*'. He conceded that Dalí did not attempt to illustrate such titles literally. But Gilbert & George *did* – and surely that is the point. Casey concluded: 'The admirers of Gilbert & George (and this included the *Telegraph*'s own art critic) claim their loathsome images show the artists are possessed of a dark and prophetic vision of the human condition. I cannot help wondering whether they are not, rather, possessed. They are tosh as well, of course.'

Let Philistines rejoice!

This was followed by a delightful article in the *Spectator* of 16 September 1995: 'Is my Loved and Respected Brother-in-Law Determined to Make a Fool of Himself?', by Auberon Waugh (whose sister, the novelist Harriet Waugh, is Dorment's wife), who at least has the merit of high intelligence and humour, though even he professed himself appalled by the new pictures (again, I am not sure that he ever actually saw them). Taking up Dorment's assertion that G&G were telling us that we are all the same, he wrote: 'If there is any such message contained in these pictures of enlarged stools, we should resist it violently. We are not all the same, we are all different both physically and in our characters; many human things are disgusting, including shit, which is one of our lowest denominators. There is nothing remotely messianic or visionary in the message. It is socialist, discredited and wrong.'

Why 'socialist'? Don't Tories crap? And in attacking G&G for reducing human life to the lowest denominator, Waugh failed to appreciate that this was exactly their achievement. They had succeeded triumphantly in *de*-shocking those who came to Peckham. Waugh asked why McEwen and Dorment had praised G&G, McEwen writing of their 'ultimate assault on conformity', and Dorment of 'pictures which alienate the entire British middle class'.

> Has Dorment tried them on a taxi-driver, or on his daily cleaner? Only some six-month old babies like the stuff. For years I struggled to teach my children that nothing is funny which makes a loud noise: *a fortiori* nothing is funny which makes a bad smell, and shit stinks.

He concluded that the joke was no longer against the middle class:

> The question 'Is it art?' must be answered: 'Only if art has become something very silly indeed,' and the truth is that the reputation of contemporary art has fallen much too low among intelligent, educated members of the middle class for anyone to be shocked by anything done in its name.

Dorment replied on the letters page in the following week's *Spectator* that G&G's art was like Waugh's journalism — 'a habit of saying what nobody else dares to say about life in modern Britain. That earns them a huge popular following, at the cost of outraging the intelligentsia on both Left and Right.' Plainly his brother-in-law's facetiousness had hit a nerve:

It amazes me that he can be so prissy about The Naked
Shit Pictures when he recently treated the *Spectator* readers
to what emerged from his own bottom after a delicious
dinner in a Korean restaurant . . . [when] he calls me a
fool, he should first be absolutely certain that he knows
what he's talking about. Remember that his grandfather
denounced the poetry of T.S. Eliot, his father the paintings of Picasso. Yet somehow − inexplicably − the first
continues to be read and the second admired, more than
half a century after their savagings by the Waughs.

Good knockabout stuff, with Dorment perhaps taking his brother-
in-law too seriously, for there is always a wicked glint of wit in
every sentence Auberon Waugh writes. As for G&G, who would
have thought that their new works would spill so much blood?

Inevitably, Brian Sewell in the *Evening Standard* was hostile, and
even complained that the show was not about shit at all, but turds:

Turd has the precise sense of a stool, of excrement in
the form excreted, and though in the 1500 years since
the polite society of Saxony brought it here in their
intellectual baggage, it has fallen from grace, this is still
its essential meaning. Shit, on the other hand, another
word of low Teutonic provenance, has spread far further,
and from its original application to the generalities of
voiding the bowels, is now in much wider public use;
turds do not hit the fan, nor is one ever in the turd; in
vulgarisms for the lavatory and anus, turd does not com-
bine with other words; turd is not used as a term of
criticism in art, literature or intellectual argument, and
when striving for the unattainable, no one shouts the
exhortation 'Turd or bust!'

Apart from showing off, what on earth is Sewell on about? This
seems like academic nitpicking which needs to be sprayed with

turpentine. Some people shit 'bricks', but not all the time; and what does it matter? And, yet again, there is no indication that Sewell ever went to Peckham. 'Shock is still their weapon,' he continued, 'for in their close resemblance to late ordinands in a low church, with trousers about their knees, buttocks pulled apart, fingers pleasuring the anus, and unexcited genitals blowing in the breeze, it is eroticism that G&G abandon, not pornography.'

At least Waldemar Januszczak admitted in the *Sunday Times* that he would not go to see the show: 'They're rubbish, they're the worst side of it all, sensationalist attention-seekers. They've gone down the Madonna road: take all your clothes off, show what you've got and leave yourself nowhere else to go. It's puerile.'

The most vociferous critics are entitled to their views, but what an outcry there would be if book reviewers attacked books without even reading them.

At that time I was the art critic for *Night & Day*, the supplement of the *Mail on Sunday*. I sometimes felt that I should have been described as the '*alleged* art critic', or 'art correspondent', as my lack of training in art made me feel like an impostor. I always tried to relate specifically to readers who had as little knowledge of art as myself and wanted to be guided and informed, rather than to be exposed to my opinions, and I thought I had done a good job of that over the years, although I received no guidance from the paper as to what was expected of me, and never had any idea if my work was going down well with the editor. Apparently not, for after reading my review of The Naked Shit Pictures he phoned me – for the first or second time in two years – to tell me how good it was, but that he was not renewing my contract. Foolishly, I took this badly; but he was perfectly entitled to sack me, and I had to admit later that my successor was excellent, perhaps too good for the readership I had cultivated. So my personal experience of the Peckham show was traumatic. In my review, published under the title 'Shock of the Poo!' (witty, but not mine), I described it as 'the most sensational show in town. Whether you love or hate it is another matter.' My main concern was to get people to go to Peckham and see it.

The day after the exhibition's opening, which was followed by a party at the notorious gay club The Fridge, in Brixton, I found G&G ecstatic. But I felt I needed to ask them – on behalf of readers who might well be wondering – why they felt the need to alienate people with such repulsive subject matter. I was correctly scorned as a prude. As an interviewer, you frequently have to ask the wrong question in order to get the right answer.

'Don't you have a lavatory in your house?' George demanded.

'Yes, but most of us lock the door,' I replied.

I wrote in my review that: 'Our disgust is due to a rigid denial and revulsion at the word "shit", though, as they point out, no one has complained that many of the pictures show them stark naked.'

'These,' Gilbert told me proudly, 'are the most tender, vulnerable, human pictures we have ever done. We are able to accept our humanity. This is liberation on an amazing scale.'

George added: 'No one in the world can find anything wrong in these pictures of shit, and we have proved there is something right. No young person is alienated. Three young couples came last night and asked us to hold their babies for a photograph. Incredibly gentle, very sweet.'

'Extraordinary!' echoed Gilbert.

Surprising support for the exhibition had come from the Vicar of Lubeck, in Germany, who wanted to show some of the pictures in his church, stressing, 'You've got to humiliate yourself to nothing, and then you can become a total person.'

We moved on to a busy Spanish restaurant in Spitalfields to celebrate. G&G knew this was a turning point for them, and as it turned out, the exhibition blazed the way to the next – the exhibition of The Fundamental Pictures in New York in 1997. As for myself, this was my last column for Night & Day. After a spell as 'art critic' for the Sunday Express, I decided that this particular role in life had run its course, and felt immeasurably relieved, though I was so visibly shattered at the time that G&G did their utmost to cheer me up: 'What a ghastly person that editor must be,' said George loyally, if unfairly.

Gilbert was almost hopping with glee as he hailed me a cab afterwards: 'We were on the edge and it worked! Unbelievable!'

CHAPTER TWELVE

WITH GILBERT & GEORGE
IN NEW YORK

'Gilbert & George?' I asked the receptionist. 'What are their surnames?' She gave me an oversweet smile.

'They don't have any.'

'They must.' The smile was fading.

'I know they must, but they don't.' I pointed out that they were staying in the hotel – the SoHo Grand on West Broadway – and were easy to recognise because they dressed in identical worsted three-buttoned suits. At this her smile vanished altogether, and when I added that I was desperate to go to my room and change, having just arrived from England, she asked me icily for my credit card. I explained that I was not the sort of person who carried them, but that Gilbert & George would vouch for me if they could be paged. Now, deep suspicion set in, and though she admitted that I had indeed been booked into a room upstairs, she could not possibly allow me to use it.

It was 2 May 1997, and though Gilbert & George had left England some days earlier, I was determined to stay for the General Election, cast my vote, and watch the results coming in on television. I was also cracking up: prostate trouble (non-malignant); a tumorous melanoma on my back; and probably cirrhosis of the liver. The tumour had just been removed, and I shamelessly asked the publicity office of Virgin Airways to upgrade me, especially as I had been commissioned to write a feature on G&G in New York for *The Times*, although it was never published. In the event the flight was so crowded — just after the election and just before the May bank holiday — that I was squeezed in between two burly Americans; but at least I had been fêted in Virgin's VIP Lounge, not only fuelled with smoked salmon and champagne, but able to watch the new Prime Minister Tony Blair's arrival in Downing Street.

My discomfort at the hotel was increased by the fact that there was no message from G&G about the party being held for them that evening by the critic Robert Rosenblum. Relief finally arrived when David Maupin, the co-director of the Lehmann Maupin Gallery, where one of the G&G exhibitions was being held, tracked me down in the elegant SoHo Grand bar to tell me that the party had been postponed. Instead, he gave me the address of an exclusive cocktail party being given at that moment by Leo Castelli, and the sympathetic barman, noticing my confusion, gave me a dry martini (gin) on the house.

Hailing a yellow cab, I hurried to the party, only to find I had the wrong address. I returned to the SoHo Grand and was given the right address (around the corner from the wrong one), but by the time I arrived the party was over, and no one was left. Disconsolately, I walked into the next avenue, where I found G&G surrounded by friends in a pleasant restaurant. Jet-lagged and taxi-lagged, I was thankful to be allowed to reach my bedroom in the early hours.

The following morning I joined G&G for a leisurely breakfast, and at last everything came together, with George insisting that I try the 'homo-fries'.

It was a treat walking down West Broadway with Gilbert & George. After fifteen shows in America they were known to strangers, if not to the hotel receptionist, and people were stopping them in the street to congratulate them. They were invariably rewarded by G&G's infinite courtesy: 'How kind! Fantastic! Extraordinary!' spoken in unison.

Never have I seen G&G's composure ruffled, though I suspect there are times when they have been thankful for the privacy of a hotel room before an evening's onslaught. Their New York visit had begun with a banquet at the Museum of Modern Art hosted by Melvyn Bragg, who introduced his two-hour *South Bank Show* devoted to G&G, directed by Gerald Fox. They were still in a state of euphoria: 'We've never got a full house like this! Extremely impressive.'

Trying to bring them back to earth, I asked them about the food.

'Buffet,' said George succinctly. 'Posh modern, a stick of asparagus getting friendly with a dead carrot.'

Walking anywhere with G&G is a constant surprise, because George, in particular, is exceptionally observant. I am at my best walking in cities, possibly because as a photographer I always look around and above me, instead of staring straight ahead as most people do. I walked on my own that afternoon, the length of Fifth Avenue, but I preferred the more rackety streets, with their garish signs that would have looked tawdry in a London suburb, but somehow seemed exotic here, flanked by fire-escapes and those immense glass mansions which to all appearances are totally uninhabited. One morning George drew my attention to a charming small house, dwarfed by its gigantic neighbours. It turned out to be a burlesque theatre, its doors already open at midday on a Sunday. The effect was so old fashioned I half-expected Lillian Russell to come outside and wave. Burlesque! I began to love the incongruity of New York, the friendliness, everyone casually dressed, the freshness of the air.

The critic Carter Ratcliff gave me a hilarious account of G&G's first visit to New York for *The Singing Sculpture* in 1971 when he, his wife Phyllis Derfner and their friends thought it would entertain G&G to cruise around the island of Manhattan, just like other first-time tourists. Carter was not sure if they should point out the less-known features of the skyline, in contrast to the Statue of Liberty, but they did.

'That's the 52nd Street pier.'

'Marvellous.'

'Super.'

'Would you like anything to drink?'

'How terribly kind.'

'It's a nice day, isn't it?' probably asked in desperation.

'Oh yes, absolutely splendid.'

Carter said that G&G used conversational forms they had found ready-made in the lyrics of 'Underneath the Arches', yet had adopted no Duchampian condescension – their refusal to be ironic was militant. Describing the weather or the view as 'absolutely splendid', they were as utterly earnest in their tenth as in their first use of the phrase. Gilbert & George did not so much converse as offer rigidity, impersonality, monumental representations of what proper conversation should be. They were talking as Living Sculptures ought to talk.

The Fundamental Pictures would open that night at two nearby galleries. The Lehmann Maupin is on street level, so you walk straight into it. To enter the Sonnabend you take a lift that opens inside the gallery – typical of New York. In contrast to the in-fighting of the London art world, the two galleries worked together on the exhibition, shared the profits, and gained from the other's success, due to the exceptional rapport of the people involved. The Lehmann Maupin at 39 Greene Street is younger (like the owners), spacious and elegant. It was designed by Rem Koolhaas, a fashionable Dutch architect known as 'Mr Extra Large', though in this case he was 'Mr Fairly Small': 'I do big and small with equal interest,' he says. 'It's all about planning, whatever the scale.' David Maupin had originally invited him to visit some artists' studios, but soon they were talking about a gallery space – 'Then it was more like getting design advice from a friend.'

Rachel Lehmann had grown tired of Switzerland, where she had run the Galerie Lehmann in Lausanne. On the advice of Illeana Sonnabend she had flown from New York to London to see The Naked Shit Pictures, and she felt that their religious atmosphere was ideal for the new gallery which she was opening in New York with David Maupin.

An attractive, youthful woman with cascading hair, Lehmann does not look the tough businesswoman that she undoubtedly is, unless you see her in her office, surrounded by phones and secretaries. Her background is startling: she was born in Ethiopia where her father raised cattle after the war – he was German, her mother half-Italian. Mysteriously, she has four passports: German, French, Swiss and Ethiopian. She still goes back to Ethiopia, although her home there no longer exists, bombed in one of the recent wars – 'It was such a nice place.'

'Is there any rivalry with Sonnabend?' I asked her.

'None at all. We never have problems, but increase the possibilities for better results. For us the object of the rat-race is entering a different race altogether, to get the best results.'

We continued to the Sonnabend Gallery at 420 West Broadway. It was older than the Lehmann Maupin, and less spacious, yet somehow more sympathetic. Surprisingly, G&G's pictures were integral to each of the galleries, which complemented rather than competed with each other. Yet again there was the initial impact of their size and colour, but this time they had a new grandeur – 'They have grown,' Illeana Sonnabend told me later – and I found a fulfilment of all G&G had been striving for after so many controversial years. In spite of the pictures' controversial titles – Blood on Piss, Spit on Shit – apparently intended to shock, they instead succeeded in de-shocking, the words quickly accepted and absorbed until the shock was replaced by calm reassurance. There was a new confidence in G&G's knowledge that they were breaking new ground, crossing frontiers yet again, with their remarkable use of microscopic magnification. This was most apparent in the large, impressive *Blood Tears Spunk Piss*, in which the naked figures of G&G – George between the 'blood' and 'tears' of the title, with a white outline of Gilbert behind him, reversed on the other side with Gilbert, and George's white arms draped over his shoulders – were interspersed with the microscopic enlargements which had the beauty of delicate tracery. The tears, in black and white, were fern-like; the spunk was blacker, with sinister shapes; the piss a colourful yellow with black-and-white patterns. I returned to this particular picture, created in 1996, throughout my stay, and dare to consider it G&G's definitive picture to date – their equivalent of Picasso's *Les Demoiselles d'Avignon* (1906–7) – and believe it may come to be seen as another turning point in the history of twentieth-century art.

I had still to learn that while most people in New York galleries were clean-cut, their relationships could be complicated. At the Sonnabend we had been greeted by a volatile Portuguese, Antonio Homen, who had been dining with G&G the night before. When he was taken to Illeana's gallery in Paris twenty years earlier, he had fallen in love with her, leaving his wealthy Greek wife and pursuing her with red roses until she adopted him: 'I had found my son'. Leo Castelli, Illeana's husband, encouraged Antonio to join their business, and though she had doubts Antonio is now her business partner, while Castelli, no longer her husband, has the gallery below.

Illeanna, now in her mid-eighties, rises late, but she joined us for lunch at the Mezzogiorno nearby at 195 Spring Street, which seemed to be everyone's favourite Italian restaurant. I liked her instantly. It would have been hard not to. She has such serenity that it was easy to understand why G&G – who owed her so much – Antonio and Leo Castelli all loved her.

I was unknown to them all, and was introduced by Gilbert & George, but then the gallery-owner Leslie Waddington came over from another table to tell me that his wife always carried a newspaper cutting of mine which said that there was one great advantage to growing old: 'At last you lose the sex urge; it's like being *unchained from a lunatic.'* There was much laughter, and the company looked at me with new interest. Waddington, whom I had not met before, rejoined his wife, who waved the cutting at me from their table.

Illeana Sonnabend sat opposite me, observing all that went on, including a formidable lady from the Old Pecos Trail, Santa Fe, who told me to fax her everything about me so she could invite me to a 'cute little bistro' she and her husband had discovered in London off St James's – Le Caprice. Possibly noticing my look of incredulity, she turned to Illeana and gushed, 'I just hope I look as good as . . .' but even she was not brazen enough to complete the sentence. Illeana leant forward reassuringly: 'But you're doing very nicely, my dear!' and gave me a conspiratorial smile. Enchanted by such a lovely putdown, I told George about it later, but he was not amused: 'That woman's husband has just bought *Lavatory.'*

'The lavatory?' I cried before I could stop myself, remembering the picture of George full frontal, his trousers around his ankles, with Gilbert's back to us as he drops his trousers, in a public lavatory, 'I thought *Lavatory* would be the last to go!'

'Which shows how little you know,' said George scathingly, though he admitted his own surprise that the most 'difficult' pictures were selling the best.

Lunch at Mezzogiorno was plainly a ritual of table-hopping and greetings. At one moment Leo Castelli, the man most responsible for promoting Pop Art in America, came in, a sprightly figure in his nineties, kissed his former wife Illeana, and joined his companion, an attractive young lady in her early thirties who, it was whispered, hoped to be the next Mrs Castelli. Antonio beamed. Everyone was happy. It was all pleasantly incestuous.

Anxious to avoid the hanging-about I had endured in Shanghai, I left to explore New York on my own. I followed the tourist track to the Museum of Modern Art, largely to see *Painting* (1946), the first Francis Bacon to be sold to a museum. It had been bought in 1948 for £350 by the director Alfred Barr, who recognised Bacon's genius with his usual perception – he was also instrumental in his championship of Dalí.

I joined G&G for the two openings that evening. The audience reaction was wonder rather than outrage.

'Even if you hate them you can't ignore them,' said a man with a child in a pram.

'What is spunk?' asked a young black man with ringlets from California.

'Cum,' explained George.

'What is mooning?' asked a young Frenchman. When George replied it was 'baring your arse,' the Frenchman blinked: 'I think that's illegal in France.'

The surge of goodwill was so startling that even Gilbert was bemused: 'Fantastic! We show two naked men and get away with it. Middle-aged women see our bumholes and go away happy.'

The honesty with which G&G presented everyday functions was appreciated. Are the words 'piss' and 'shit' any more offensive than 'urine' or 'excrement'?

Familiar figures appeared – the ubiquitous Anthony d'Offay, smiling nervously as G&G virtually ignored him; those bizarre groupies Eva and Adele from Berlin, dressed identically in red PVC, one of them bald, presumably a man. Gilbert whispered with a hiss, 'George *loves* them!' I found it hard to understand why – their self-ingratiating smirks curdled the atmosphere.

One of the most sympathetic of G&G's aficionados was a smartly-dressed young Greek-American from London, Alexander Roussos, who had flown in with the catalogues, which he had published as a personal tribute. He told me that the only complaint came from US Customs, where the officials told him that the CD-roms which accompanied the catalogues should have stated 'Printed in the UK'. He had not been convinced: 'I'm sure it was the images which upset them, but they let the CDs and catalogues through.' Roussos was one of several admirers who had flown to New York especially for the exhibition. Dazed in the Sonnabend, he told me, 'I feel humble, wiser. They degrade themselves to do all this for us. I'd like to buy all the pictures.' He did buy *Spunk on Blood* before flying back to London the next morning. Subsequently I met him there, hoping to find out why G&G meant so much to him. Why, like so many, was he obsessed, I asked?

'I am *not* obsessed, just passionate. I have no obsession, so far, but they're the most extraordinary people I've met.' That included Francis Bacon, whom he had once told in the Colony Room that when he was fourteen on a Greek island he had had a wet dream about Bacon's painting *The Wrestlers*. Bacon took this as the supreme compliment. 'In fifty years' time,' he continued, 'students will think what a brilliant old man Bacon was, but of G&G what brilliant contemporary masters. Their imagery will never age – it will never look dated. They're devoting their daily hours to art; their commitment is amazing. *Bum Holes*, with both of them showing their bumholes – I think it is the greatest self-portrait of the twentieth century. Never been done before. A lot of men feel shocked because they feel the same vulnerability. I wouldn't want my bumhole seen by wankers – would you do it? The pictures show men: why not? That is their world. Only show what they feel themselves from a male point of view, yet the more you know them the *less* you think they're homosexual pictures.' Alexander met G&G for the first time in 1985 at their retrospective at the Guggenheim in New York. 'It was just like a church – a pilgrimage in a modern church – Antonio Homen introduced us. I was a young chicken then, and very shy.'

In London he had met them again at the bedside of their closest friend, David Robilliard, who was dying of AIDS. Unreserved tolerance is one of their rules, but the love they showed towards Robilliard was revelatory, and is his finest epitaph. G&G had published Robilliard's first book, *Inevitable*, in 1984, and posthumously, *Life Isn't Good, It's Excellent*, in 1993, to coincide with Robilliard's memorial retrospective exhibition at the Stedelijk Museum of Modern Art, Amsterdam.

'They push him, they push him,' Stainton Forrest told me, 'and get him off the crowd. Gilbert & George helped him – so sad the moment he was uplifted he was cut off.' Robilliard's verse and drawings had a mordant wit which could have won him a cult following had he lived. Even so, he has become a minor cult in New York, where an exhibition of his work in 1990 was accompanied by this moving tribute from G&G:

OUR DAVID

David Robilliard was the sweetest, kindest, most infuriating, artistic, foul-mouthed, wittiest, sexiest, charming, handsomest, thoughtful, unhappy, loving and friendly person we ever met. Over the nine years of our friendship David came closer to us than any other person. He will live forever in our hearts and minds.

Starting with pockets filled with disorganised writings and sketches he went on to produce highly original poetry, drawings and paintings. His truthfulness, sadness, desperation and love of people gave his work a brilliance and beauty that stands out a mile.

Roussos hopes the CD-rom for The Fundamental Pictures catalogue will reach millions of G&G admirers throughout the world by the 'Web' and the 'Net', words which I do not understand.

'Do you own any oil tankers?' I asked, thinking of the cost involved.

'Only a couple of rusty ones,' he smiled disarmingly. When he told me that he hoped to see G&G at least twice a week – 'Otherwise I'm not happy' – I wondered what they thought of that, knowing how jealously they guard their time.

'I guess they suffer me.'

Roussos knows them better than most: 'I know when they're in a bad mood, but they're very good at hiding it. I don't think I could ever fall out with them. There is a lot of sadness there, they sacrificed so much. Incredibly genuine. I'd do anything for them – very privileged.'

During the evening someone brought G&G a message of congratulations from their friend in London Lorcan O'Neill, who quoted a passage from a lecture, 'Friends of my Youth', delivered by W.B. Yeats in 1910, which is apposite to G&G today:

> To achieve anything in any art, to stand alone perhaps for many years, to go a path no other man has gone, to accept one's own thought when the thought of others has the authority of the world behind it, that it should seem but a little thing to give one's life as well as one's words which are much nearer one's soul, to the criticism of the world.

There is a ritual to these occasions, which G&G enjoy – or at least accept in the course of duty. In New York there was much to enjoy: dinner around the corner, with SoHo whooping it up on the Saturday night and the American ability to strike up instant friendships with strangers, followed by a lively party at Spy, which resembled a Victorian theatre where they might have presented vaudeville, though in this case it was high-performance 'drag'. 'This is the party that everyone wants to be at,' Alexander Roussos told me in the uproar. 'There are three parties tonight, but this is the one.'

I noticed how young everyone looked.

For the next couple of days, if ever I dared to wander out on my own, I would return to find a stack of messages from G&G, and would set out in pursuit of them by yellow cab: 'Daniel Dear, you are invited for lunch at Bill Erlich's [he proved to be a collector]. Love G&G'; or, more simply, 'Mrs Goetz' – a penthouse with a window the length of a G&G picture, overlooking a stunning view of Central Park with the lights cascading in the skyline beyond. The Rosenblum party was on again, in a comfortably Bohemian house off Washington Square, where we were served drinks and a square cake dotted with blobs of chocolate representing shit. There was a work by G&G in the dining room, and two separate portraits of themselves by someone, though Gilbert protested grumpily that they were hard to recognise.

There had been a frisson at the double opening when the venerable critic Hilton Kramer of the New York *Observer* honoured the galleries with a personal viewing, and some assumed he had come to 'praise'. Already, Robert Rosenblum had done G&G proud in the catalogue: indeed, he went so far that for one irreverent and private moment I wondered if you needed either a sense of humour to appreciate such criticism, or none whatsoever. Twenty-five years earlier, Rosenblum hailed *The Singing Sculpture* as a 'spectacular debut that seemed to arrive from a distant planet'. Now he found a new dimension: 'Brilliantly transforming the visible world into emblems of the spirit, Gilbert & George create from these microscopic facts an unprecedented heraldry that, in a wild mutation of the Stations of the Cross, fuses body and soul, life and death. Once again, they have crossed a new threshold, opening unfamiliar gates of eternity.' In this Rosenblum echoed David Sylvester, who was so overwhelmed by The Naked Shit Pictures at the South London Gallery that he compared the effect to a chapel, and claimed that one picture 'paraphrases Masaccio's *Expulsion from Eden*'.

Talking to Antonio Homen in the Sonnabend, I discovered that he felt the same: 'I see a great classical tradition, a medieval feeling.'

I looked at G&G, who sat opposite, with a new respect, as the religious artists of our time. They were unimpressed. 'Go and see *Piss* and *Lavatory* in the next room,' Gilbert told me scornfully, 'and find the Masaccio in them.' I returned baffled, shaking my head. He laughed: 'They're crazy!'

'Does the appreciative taxi-driver know Masaccio?' asked George. 'Even I don't know some of the painters they refer to.'

When I admitted that one picture (with themselves in the nude) made me think of Blake's *Adam and Eve*, George brought me crashing

down to earth: '*Adam and Steve*, you mean!' We laughed, and I felt
relieved that G&G do indeed have more humour than the critics
who read so much into their work.

Yet there is an element of Blake's biblical illustrations – and his
romanticism – which appealed to those who came to G&G's New
York shows. On Sunday we walked through the lovely, empty
streets, past the burlesque theatre, to the bastions of the financial
district to have brunch with G&G's old friends Carter Ratcliff and
his wife Phyllis in their spacious apartment, with glistening views
of the glass canyons opposite. I asked how it was possible, when
so many people apparently considered that G&G's work was vile,
that it was now being hailed as religious and compared to the
Stations of the Cross. Ratcliff referred me to the outrage over Andrés
Serrano's *Piss Christ* a few years earlier, which showed a crucifix in
a glass of urine, and to the Robert Mapplethorpe exhibition of
well-hung naked black men which ended with a gallery curator on
trial. He was acquitted, but the right-wing protesters had a field
day: 'They were totally opportunistic. It was election year, but their
anger was so excessive that it wore itself out.' Today there is a new
climate of tolerance, which has embraced G&G – a new morality.
Carter Ratcliff says there is no question of 'camp' in G&G's world
without women: 'They're not interested in such ambiguity. G&G
insist on honesty, and make their own rules and stick to them.
People have begun to appreciate that.'

Far from praising them, Hilton Kramer's review in the New York
Observer was venomous: 'Odious Gilbert & George Now Stinking Up
SoHo.' Kramer started, deceptive with sarcasm:

> It was a sad day when Andy Warhol gave up illustrating
> fashionable shoes for the advertising account of I. Miller
> in order to set up as a real artist, so to speak. Just think
> of all that we might have been spared if Andy had been
> content to soldier on in the fashionable shoe trade! It's
> enough to make us weep at the very thought. For one

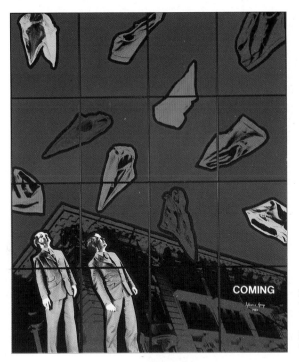

LEFT Coming (1983, 241 x 201cm).

BELOW Shitted (1983, 241 x 201cm).

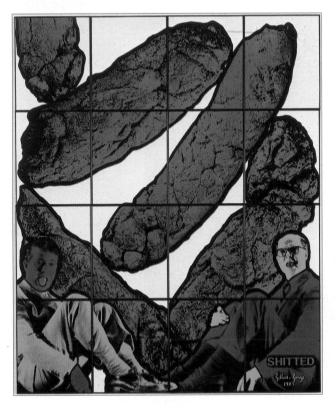

LEFT *Death* (from *Death, Hope, Life, Fear*), (1984, Collection Tate Gallery, London, 422 x 250cm).

BELOW *Hope* (from *Death, Hope, Life, Fear*), (1984, Collection Tate Gallery, London, 250 x 422cm).

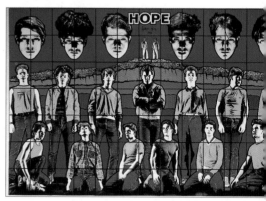

LEFT *Life* (from *Death, Hope, Life, Fear*), (1984, Collection Tate Gallery, London, 422 x 250cm).

ABOVE *Fear* (from *Death, Hope, Life, Fear*), (1984, Collection Tate Gallery, London, 250 x 422cm).

LEFT *We* (1983,
241 x 201cm).

BELOW *The Wall* (1986,
242 x 354cm).

ABOVE *Flow* (1987, 253 x 284cm).

RIGHT *Here* (1987, Collection Metropolitan Museum of Art, New York, 302 x 351cm).

BELOW *Tears* (1987, 241 x 201cm).

LEFT *One World* (1988, 226 x 254cm).

BELOW *Shag* (1988, 241 x 151cm).

Coloured People (1989, 241 x 175cm).

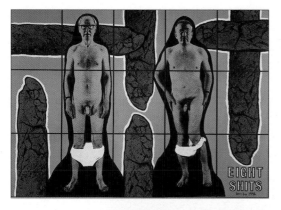

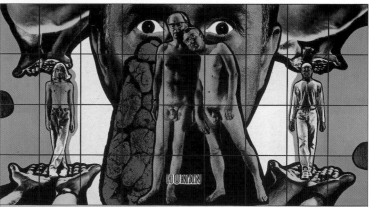

TOP *Eight Shits* (1994, 253 x 359cm).

ABOVE *Human* (1994, 338 x 639cm).

LEFT *Ill World* (1994, 253 x 426cm)

BELOW *Naked Eye* (1994, 253 x 639cm).

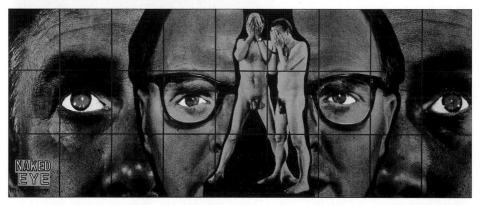

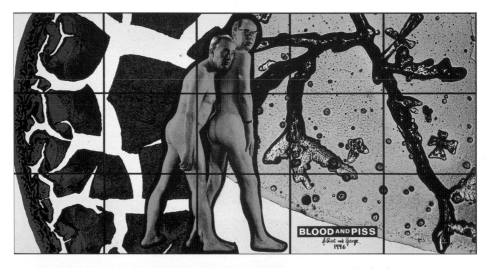

ABOVE *Blood and Piss* (1996, 190 x 377cm).

LEFT *Lavatory* (1996, 226 x 254cm).

BELOW *Piss on Us* (1996, 338 x 426cm).

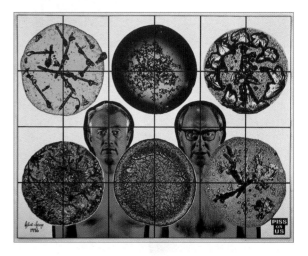

of the odious things we would very likely have been spared is the British team of Gilbert & George.

After referring to the Living Sculptures, Kramer was pleased to add that 'Mercifully, they never quite caught on here to anything like the extent they have in Europe. The Germans have been particularly avid fans, and even in Moscow and China they are said to have enjoyed a great success.' It did not occur to him that they did so because they were unlike anything the Russians or Chinese had seen before. He went on to place G&G – as so many of their detractors do – in too narrow a context:

> In this country the outré art of Gilbert & George has so far met with little in the way of public acclaim. There are curators and critics who adore it, of course, and there is a fringe constituency in the gay world that takes a keen interest in some of its 'transgressive' subject matter – the male anus, for example . . .
>
> That there are now signs that this is likely to change, owing to the sensational nature of the most recent work of Gilbert & George, is bad news for an art scene already beleaguered by a collapse of aesthetic standards. It is even worse news for what little remains of the tattered fabric of respectable public taste . . . they have certainly outdone all their previous attempts to befoul the art scene with pictures designed to disgust.
>
> When it comes to producing art that is really disgusting, it has to be acknowledged that Gilbert & George have succeeded in outdistancing most of the competition by concentrating on what – for the moment, anyway – may be the ultimate in disgusting subjects for art: shit. I regret having to use the word in this article, but there is no avoiding it in writing about the recent work of Gilbert & George. They have made both the word and

what it literally stands for central to their current enter-
prise. They have done for shit what Andy Warhol did
for the Campbell's soup can.

This comparison to one of the most famous icons of the twentieth century could well be taken as a compliment, and G&G
were gratified, though Alexander Roussos was indignant –
'I'm sure Hilton Kramer has a shit every day and has a good
look.'

Back in London, Roger Kimball was just as damning in the *Spectator*, describing G&G as 'an unusually malignant boil or pustule
on the countenance of contemporary art':

> It is part of Gilbert & George's act to pose as moralists
> whose art is wrestling with deep existential and religious
> questions. 'We believe our art can form morality in our
> time,' George tells us in one typical statement. [Though
> a new quote to me.] 'Our art is based on human life.
> All the important subjects of existence are involved,' Gil-
> bert says in another. They act like drunken pornographers
> but tell us that they are engaged in a holy mission. It's
> what Marxists used to call increasing the contradictions.
>
> It is a sign of the degraded times we live in that this
> sort of thing has been a wild commercial success. In
> 1986, Gilbert & George won the Turner Prize. In the last
> several years journalists regularly describe them
> as England's most famous and richest contemporary
> artists.

Gilbert told me that so much time and effort are involved in creating
their work that they are not the artists to make big fortunes, but
there is the added fact that their pictures are so big that few private
collectors have the space to hang them. Alexander Roussos hopes
to buy a large London house which he will fill with G&G pictures,
but he admits that it will be 'very difficult to live with – a G&G

picture takes a lot out of you'. Rachel Lehmann agrees that if you have a G&G picture on the wall you don't need, or simply cannot have, anything else. Owning a G&G is vastly different, literally, from owning a Matthew Smith, a Sickert or a Lucian Freud. Roussos bought *Spunk on Blood* in New York because he found it 'totally fundamental', and said that the establishment do not like two men to have so much power.

G&G's own view is ambivalent. When asked by the Tate Gallery to attend the Turner prize-giving, they said they would only go if they had won. Appalled, the organisers said they could not possibly tell them this in advance, but G&G were adamant in their refusal, and in the end they got their way. The Tate, however inadvertently, had their revenge in 1997 when a grand party was given to mark the gallery's centenary and to raise funds. Their supporter Jill Ritblat invited them to join her table, but they felt they had to refuse because not a single G&G picture would be on view, and they would find this too embarrassing. One begins to understand why G&G suspect that the establishment is against them.

Roger Kimball continued his *Spectator* attack by condemning the way that important critics celebrated G&G's 'narcissistic nihilism', quoting Richard Dorment's invocation of the Isenheim altarpiece; John McEwen's belief in their self-sacrifice for a higher cause, which is 'purposely moral and indeed Christian'; and David Sylvester's comment that 'these pictures have a plenitude, as if they were Renaissance pictures of male nudes in action'. Kimball dismissed this as 'harmless journalistic persiflage, but merely what one suspects of critics these days. The preposterous praise critics have lavished upon Gilbert & George is a sign of deep cultural malaise.' After visiting the Lehmann Maupin Gallery, Kimball wrote, his companion had remarked, 'Think of how much had to happen in our culture for Gilbert & George to be accepted as art and embraced as "spiritual".'

G&G are touchingly sensitive when it comes to criticism, and naïvely flattered when an interviewer praises them to their face. Of one they told me proudly, 'She said we were the most interesting artists she had ever talked to. You know how difficult most artists can be!' But in the case of Roger Kimball they were mischievously pleased: 'We loved that *Spectator* piece – the best! Kimball realised that we've won!'

That I loved New York more open-heartedly than I could have imagined I would was due to the steadfast loyalty of Gilbert & George, and my knowledge that I could rely on them to accept my bad behaviour as well as my good. As they said of themselves some years ago, one of their regrets was discovering bad behaviour so late. They are remarkably tolerant, except when they feel they have been betrayed or taken advantage of, and then the relationship ends abruptly.

I explored the city on my own in the late afternoons, following our lengthy lunches: one afternoon I took the Staten Island ferry from Manhattan, and then a taxi journey along the waterfront to the Plaza Hotel, which had been recommended by a woman in my village in Devon as 'one of the sights not to be missed', along with the Empire State Building and the Tavern on the Green. 'I don't know about you never being a normal man,' said Antonio, referring to the title of my autobiography, *Never a Normal Man*, 'but if you go to *those* places you'll end up a very boring one!' Yet, perversely, I rather liked them. When an attractively dressed woman sat beside me at the bar of the Plaza Hotel and showed me a necklace she had bought for her niece's birthday, I offered her a drink, which she accepted graciously. Though I had no ulterior motive, I felt surprisingly miffed when a man sat down on her other side and started to flirt with her. To regain my priority I offered her a second drink, and was startled when the ill-tempered barman said 'NO!' most decisively. Apparently she was a hooker, and he disapproved of her presence.

The next morning, while G&G endured more of their interminable interviews, I walked for a couple of hours in Central Park, amazed by the peacefulness and spaciousness and by a memorial garden to John Lennon, and a British stockade built during the War of Independence. The celebrated Tavern on the Green was surrounded by tables in the open air, with a statue of King Kong. The main building was a covered pavilion, lit by night with glass chandeliers like a fairy grotto. At midday it was quiet, and I sat outside, delighted to rest, and so pleased to find simple food on the menu after the messed-up Italian dishes of SoHo that I acted on extravagant impulse and ordered half a dozen oysters and a glass of champagne. I felt so happy that I was not crushed by the indifference of the Oriental waiter, who clearly did not give a damn.

At night I sought out bars in the Bowery. Most of them seemed to have turned into tea-gardens, finding an exception in a long, rough bar occupied by some 'good old boys', one of whom wore a cowboy hat, spat prodigiously, and seemed to like me. As I was about to leave, he surprised me by saying, 'You're a writer fellow, did you say? A couple of them used to come here once – heard of Tennessee Williams or Truman Capote?' The place must have changed.

On our last day I bought three bottles of champagne as my sole contribution to lunch, and asked the waiter to be sure that everyone knew they came from me, but nobody did.

Afterwards I went to the Metropolitan Museum to see an exhibition of Byzantine art, but it proved too much to absorb, like the British Museum, and a thunderstorm scattered the taxis which made me late for my appointment with an American publisher of the old school who was so charming that he forgave me. Then, filled with dry martinis (gin, not vodka), I returned to photograph the Rosenblums at their home, leaving my notebook by mistake. Robert Rosenblum later expressed it to my home in England, with such kindness that I felt guilty for having previously mocked his lavish praise of G&G, if only to myself. A stretch limo from the Lehmann Maupin Gallery picked me up from the hotel and whisked me to Kennedy Airport, where I was hurried to the VIP lounge for caviar and champagne. I found that I had been upgraded to a de luxe first class with a comfortable armchair, and woke invigorated as we landed at Heathrow.

I had only been in New York a few days, but on such occasions it is possible to learn more than you might do in six months if pointing in the wrong direction. My luck was in learning more about G&G, and in witnessing their most significant exhibition to date.

CHAPTER THIRTEEN

WITH GILBERT & GEORGE IN STOCKHOLM

'It's a bit out of the way, isn't it?' said Barry Flanagan cautiously when I told him I was going to Stockholm with G&G in August 1997. I moaned inwardly, for I was dreading my visit, which I considered a duty rather than a pleasure. Everyone I asked knew where Sweden was, but no one had gone there, or wanted to. As for Stockholm, it suffered from its reputation as the most expensive, dullest city on earth.

As if to provide me with an alibi for not going, I had an attack of gout the weekend before I was due to leave, the first twinge for thirty years. Fortunately I still had the Zyloric tablets I used then, but when I hobbled to the doctor on the Monday morning he shook his head, saying they could only have made the gout worse at this stage, and gave me some new ones which he vowed were miraculous.

So I set off on the Tuesday morning wearing my red-and-black bedroom slippers, which looked the height of chic and were so comfortable that I wondered why anyone ever bothered to squeeze their feet into tight leather. Once in the train I was immediately galvanised, my blasé indifference replaced by enthusiasm for the vital change of scene which is the be all and end all of travel. And this was only the train from Tiverton to Reading. From there I would take the bus to Heathrow, where even my appetite was restored as I tucked into breakfast.

The prospect of the Swedish reaction to G&G was enticing: would these people, who vaunt their broad-mindedness, be able to take them in their liberal stride? Or would the shit and nakedness prove too much?

I have always been allergic to airports and aeroplanes, and the stewardess on the flight to Stockholm was concentration-camp guard material. To make matters worse, she was plump, with a pudding-basin haircut, and looked much as I might have done in drag thirty years ago, far from a Nordic beauty. I took the bus from the airport to the city centre, which was half an hour's drive through flat countryside, not the swirling rivers and pine forests of expectation, arriving at the Esplanade Hotel in time to join Gilbert & George as they set out for the evening parties. They were gleeful.

'The Swedish people are able to see our work for the first time,' Gilbert enthused, 'in our big public show here.' They had seen it hung that afternoon. 'Until now Sweden only looked to America; now they realise that England exists.'

A stretch limo which could comfortably have taken ten people drove us to the first party in a posh penthouse, given by an art dealer with curly grey hair and a smile worthy of Harpo Marx. The first picture he had ever bought was a G&G, the winsome boy surrounded by blossom called *Lone* (1988), so he greeted us enthusiastically. We continued into the crowded rooms, served champagne and wine by waiters, and he was equally delighted to see us again, and asked to be introduced. Doubly welcomed, I spoke to his boyfriend, a younger version of himself, to whom he was 'legally' married, not uncommon in Sweden.

Everyone at the party appeared to be gay in every sense, including a handsome young man who kept glancing at me – presumably he was drunk, or was prone to geriatrics. The host bought his pictures in America, then got rid of them as soon as he was bored by them – presumably making a handsome profit in the process. When I admired a remarkable Picasso of a man, with the distortion of half a moustache, as fine as any of the portraits I had seen of women in a similar style, our host's 'husband' told me that it had belonged to his former lover, and had been left to him in his will. When the man died, his estate seized it instead, but it was bought by our host, presumably as a wedding gift.

Seldom have I moved among such very rich people, and I was reminded that Sweden had a good war due to her neutrality while her neighbours were invaded, building the foundations for the present prosperity.

The second party that evening was an informal dinner held in the open air on the spacious upstairs terrace of a house which might have been designed yesterday, but was in fact built thirty years ago by the Stockholm city architect, who divorced soon afterwards and had to sell. It stands in open country, with a glimpse of a surrounding canal, and was the last private house to be built in the royal park – there will be no more.

Millionaires look different, because we invest them with the knowledge of their awesome wealth, but billionaires seem much like the rest of us. This was certainly so in the case of Robert Weil, who might have been a guest rather than the host as he dispensed with servants and prepared us all a large dish of pasta. Weil sold his business empire and several Swedish banks a few years ago when he was forty-seven, in order to collect art for the love of it. To this end he is the partner of David Neuman, the director of Magasin 3 where the G&G exhibition was being held. Without him, our visit to Stockholm could have been deadly. Instead it was unexpectedly rewarding, due to his generous hospitality, in which I was included throughout as a friend of G&G. Famous for his ability to raise funds, Weil organised the exhibition, encouraged by his American wife, Amy. Anders Kold, a Dane who worked

briefly for the d'Offay Gallery and who now curates his own exhibitions in the Aarhus Kunstmuseum in Jutland, was the origina-
tor, flying especially to Stockholm to meet Neuman who took to
the idea at once, and a week later it was approved by G&G: 'You
know how quickly they work; I was just the go-between.' They
invited Neuman to the Neal Street restaurant in Covent Garden for
dinner, an evening described by Neuman in one of the least arty
prologues I have known in a catalogue. He described how, at
12.55 a.m., on 18 May 1997, the head waiter approached their
table and whispered in Gilbert's ear that some fans were waiting
outside – it was almost as if G&G had planned their arrival. When
they did leave they found seventy-five young people waiting for
them: 'G&G sign autographs and pose for photos,' then the four
of them continued at a brisk pace, with Gilbert as navigator. 'I
think he's pimping for us,' laughed George, referring to the head
waiter.

'Hello, Gilbert! Hello, George!' called someone from a second-
floor balcony.

George: 'Hello! Who's there?'

'It's John.'

George: 'Hello, John!'

Gilbert: 'Hello, John!'

George: 'These are our friends, Amy and David from Stockholm.'

John: 'Hello, Amy! Hello, David!'

David: 'Hello, John!'

Amy: 'Hello, John.'

George: 'Are you living here now?'

John: 'Yes, I'm living here now.'

George: 'Lovely!'

After these bland pleasantries they walked on. 'That was John,'
George explained superfluously. 'He used to live in our street before
he was robbed, kidnapped and tied up. He escaped and was running
through London naked. The kidnappers had taken all his clothes,

it was horrible. No one helped him, they thought he was a crazy person.'

Amy and David: 'Really?!'

George: 'Yes, really.'

They continued walking.

David Neuman proved one of the most impressive curators I have seen at work, largely because he seemed to do so little, with none of the fuss of a vast team, but with an efficient assistant called Evalina. Born in Sweden, he moved to New York in 1979 when he was twenty-five, studying psychology at New York University. He grew up with four uncles and a grandfather who were famous dealers in art and antiques, and opened his own small gallery in New York in 1983, and Magasin 3 in Stockholm in 1988, with Robert Weil as the entrepreneur. The gallery's previous one-person shows included such British artists as Richard Long, which was particularly successful, and Antony Gormley, but he said the G&G was the most important: 'I admire the way they decided to remain in England, unlike other artists who gravitated to the States. It's great to introduce them to Sweden, one of the small group of influential post-war artists, changing the whole thing. Without them the contemporary scene would look very different.'

I wondered what difference it made for the Swedish public to have the chance to meet G&G personally.

'It's very important for those truly interested in art to see the artists for themselves, because Gilbert & George are the objects, as in The Singing Sculpture. G&G are the ambassadors of British art.'

At first such statements may sound presumptuous, but I have witnessed the effect G&G have on strangers, who are flattered by their attention. Few other artists appear as if they are quite so much a part of the show – particularly relevant in the case of G&G.

One thing puzzled me about the Stockholm show: few of the pictures were for sale, and money seemed irrelevant. What did anyone gain from it, apart from prestige? 'Robert Weil may add a G&G or two to his collection,' said David. 'But he'll pay for it.'

'That sounds like philanthropy!' I exclaimed.

'Exactly!'

Swedish dealers can afford to be philanthropists too, which makes them unique.

The constantly smiling Neuman has his endearing lapses, too. Over dinner he picked up a magnificent decanter to show the Minister for Justice (or some equivalent notability) the silver hall-mark on the base. Unfortunately it was half full of red wine, and splattered all over the Minister's suit. It made the evening.

I was tired after my first day and was driven back through the park, waking in the stretch limo. The following morning, refreshed, I joined G&G for breakfast, which was becoming a pattern, though the food differs in every city: after the 'homo-fries', as George called them, in New York, there was a tepid boiled egg, cheese, ham and excellent jam in Stockholm. I forgot to ask G&G what they had had in Tokyo, where they had been a few weeks earlier. Apart from the flight, I would have found the trip hellish, for they were interviewed from morning to night, and told me that they saw nothing except from taxis – 'Tokyo has the worst traffic conges-tion in the world'. They were even interviewed in the car back to the airport by MTV, but they were exuberant nevertheless.

'The opening was *unbelievable!*' a smiling Gilbert told me, 'because we're *so* well known there!'

George agreed: 'We signed catalogues for five hours.'

One middle-aged Japanese woman told them she had gone to New York in 1971, and had seen *The Singing Sculpture*: 'It was my first sight of modern art, so I had to be here today.'

However, there was one problem: the Japanese could take the shit, but not the nakedness – *Shitted* (1983) was their favourite picture, and was reproduced in every newspaper, but frontal naked-ness is not yet allowed. This applied to the Sezon Museum in the centre of Tokyo, but the director of a more recently established museum on the outskirts of the city, owned by Toyota, wanted to stage an exhibition containing nakedness as well as shit. He astonished G&G by going to the Mayor with the catalogue and asking permission to buy one of the pictures, which would be paid for by the city funds.

'Think of it,' said George. 'The Tate Gallery would be horrified at the thought of buying a Naked Shit Picture.'

The Japanese have a tradition of erotic literature and drawings which has been confined to an elite until now, the homosexual aspect well-known but only discussed in private. Now the attitude seems to be changing.

While their visit to Japan was fresh in their minds, G&G told me eagerly of two comments translated by their young, modern, highly professional interpreter, Junko. She told them that one interviewer had seen them on television ten years earlier and had written them a love letter; and another male interviewer admitted, 'I'm very jealous.'

'Why?'

'Because I can't shit like you.'

G&G burst into laughter.

David Neuman picked us up in his car and drove to the Magasin 3, a large warehouse with the vital space required to hang G&G's pictures. On one side it overlooked the port, where a passenger ship from Lithuania was docking imperceptibly, though it seemed to have a few passengers. Evalina told me that smuggling was rife, with cigarettes costing £4 a packet in Stockholm.

Assembled from various exhibitions, such as The New Democratic Pictures of 1991, several of those on display were new to me, except in reproduction: *Naked Dream*, *Open Leg* and *Headache* (all 1991), a violent, aggressive work, in rippling reds with G&G suspended upside down, their expressions distorted by unusual anger. It covered the end wall of the largest and most spectacular room, which also featured the urban landscape *Kick City* (1991) and *Beached* (1992). *Teething* (1991) showed two mouths with green teeth and the head (open-mouthed) of a young man with green hair. On either side below were black-and-white scenes of a street market with people walking through it, giving the picture an extra vitality.

This was a formidable exhibition, and only the narrow-minded could fail to be impressed. But how would the Swedes, with their vaunted liberalism, cope with the explicit *Bum Holes* (1994), *Human Shits* (1994) and other pictures of flying turds and G&G stark, bollock naked? In the event it was almost disappointing to see that the Swedish reputation for sexual tolerance was justified. They accepted everything, without a hint of 'Look at us, how broad-minded we are!'

On the surface at least, the Swedes appear depressingly sane, although they do have one of the highest suicide rates in the world, partly due to their affluence, with so little to kick against, and to those infernal winter days which darken into early night – the land of the midday moon – sex in the morning, death in the afternoon. They have a royal family whose lives are devoid of scandal, are uninhibited by religion, remote from the woes of the outside world, were among the first in Europe to practise free love, and became notorious as unshockable. My father loved the Scandinavians, but asked in his book *A Mirror for Narcissus*: 'Is it because by robbing life of nearly all its risks they have also robbed it of its adventures? Made it too dull to go on with? Or that where life has been made so easy even the most ordinary trouble assumes extraordinary, even fatal proportions.' Overlooking the gloomy August Strindberg, he concluded, 'almost free from tragedy, they have seldom produced an artist'.

Consequently, G&G's exhibition struck Sweden like a meteor in the surrounding calm. Its impact was made all the more evident by the contrast between Stockholm and London, where there might be fifty shows at any given moment, ranging from displays of soiled disposable nappies to pickled pigs. In Stockholm, G&G were both the aberration and the norm, their titles *Piss, Shit, Bum Holes* losing their shock value in moments. As respectably-behaved ambassadors they were fêted, and I tagged along. Few hosts could have been kinder than David Neuman, both in his generosity and in his thoughtfulness in choosing the most interesting restaurants, where the food was exceptional, with not a smorgasbord or an aquavit in sight. Instead I enjoyed soused and smoked herrings, the best I had had since, surprisingly, Amsterdam airport, and the vaunted national dish of *pytt i panna* (titbits in a pan of potatoes and steak with a raw egg), the Swedish equivalent of the American corned-beef hash, though not quite so terrific. One restaurant, the equivalent of New York's Tavern on the Green, was near the Natural History Museum, which was built dramatically like a Viking fortress, with spectacular cycloramas of stuffed wild animals against painted backgrounds of woodland and wild seas.

My gout was fading, allowing me to wear shoes again, though I kept the left one loosely tied. Then, one afternoon, wham! The stairs were dark and I fell headlong down them – and I had only had one beer for lunch. I seized the last split-second to ride with the fall, my camera hitting the wooden floor like a bullet. I lay there dazed until I was helped to my feet. Miraculously, both the camera and I survived. My only injury was a bruised knee, when it could easily have been broken – a lucky escape.

While G&G returned to Magasin 3 for more interviews, I explored the old town of Stockholm, which I found disappointing. The Royal Palace was like a municipal building, the cobbled streets strangely charmless – they might have been better if they were more twee – and a cup of coffee cost more than £4.

Still shaken by my fall, I walked back to the Esplanade Hotel to lie down, but I ran into Anders Kold in the foyer. As the Esplanade had no bar, we went next door to the Diplomat. Anders had flown in especially for the exhibition. He talked of G&G excitedly, and said he believed The Fundamental Pictures show in New York had given them new confidence: 'But people still have to understand their role as world important artists. How many artists do their best work *after* they are fifty? Now they are at the peak. Future microscopic work will become more and more essential, not relying on the world, but throwing themselves into the future; not wanting to know about tomorrow, but just bumping into it!' Anders had struck me as unfriendly before, but now he was carried away with his enthusiasm. G&G had needed to sell their pictures in the difficult recent years of the art market, he said, but 'In twenty years from now they will be one of the handful of artists who encompass the world in our time. One of their historic roles is as a bridge – the most generous artists, who never let the viewer down. They genuinely absorb the response, and use it.'

Apart from G&G themselves and the gallery's curator, one man is consistently responsible for their exhibitions – yet he remains virtually invisible, his job needing to be accomplished before the public descend. I have seen Raymond O'Daly at work in Moscow, China, New York and now Stockholm, but few of those who attend G&G's exhibitions know his name, though he is credited in the catalogues as a 'technical assistant'. The one aspect of an exhibition which people take for granted is the hanging, as if the pictures appear on the walls automatically, but in fact the hanging is complicated, an art in itself, and Raymond O'Daly is the master hangman. He is a burly, ever-smiling gentle giant of thirty-six who looks as if he might have been a boxer, though in fact his sport was ice hockey.

He arrived in Stockholm several days before the opening, as usual, which must be a lonely and sometimes a daunting experience. Often he is told there has been a change of plan – that the gallery has not yet been cleared of the previous exhibition, for example, which can mean he and his team have to work through the night if the show is to open on time. Yet I have never seen him ruffled.

In thirteen years O'Daly has hung fifty G&G shows, consisting of tens of thousands of panels. That these can be packed and transported in separate chests is a great advantage, but reassembling them is an extremely complex task. O'Daly describes himself guardedly as G&G's assistant in installations, and he sees little of them between the shows until he collects their detailed maquettes for reference.

Though he is not involved in choosing the look of the exhibition or making the selection of pictures, he can make slight changes for reasons of space or light, and then the maquettes are vital: 'Otherwise, trying to get everything in their right places could take weeks.' As I first realised in Moscow, mounting a G&G exhibition is like a military operation. In Tokyo O'Daly had only one day off, which he spent sleeping.

G&G are fully aware of his value to them, and the galleries pay him to hang their shows. He met them in 1984 after he left Goldsmith's College, where he studied performance art: 'I spent four weeks unemployed until a job as a technician at the d'Offay Gallery came up. On the third day I was asked to visit G&G at Fournier Street – an event, never having seen anything like it.' They took to him immediately, and he is now one of their most trusted disciples and friends.

I had encountered so much devotion to G&G and so few of those who knew them prepared to make the slightest criticism, that I began to long for someone to say something really nasty about them. I asked O'Daly if he had ever known them to be unpleasant. 'NEVER!' he grinned at such absurdity. 'They get nervous before it's hung, can't wait for the job to be completed, and I have to try to get them out of the way so I can get it done, but once it is they're very calm and leave me alone to recover.' O'Daly's life seems to be divided between work and recovering from the stresses of hanging major exhibitions, but he says: 'It's hard work, because they set such high standards. As you can see, in their work they are extreme perfectionists, and my job is to make it look as perfect as possible, so the hanging is not noticeable. It's tough to start with – a blank wall, cases everywhere. Once or twice they've complained [I suspect this is Gilbert in particular] that it's too light or too low, then it's "Take this or that one down," and one's heart sinks and you work through the night. This doesn't happen often, but it does happen. They only lose their temper when people are not doing their best for them, like light pouring in, which would damage the work, and then they just sit – very determined, very powerful, in *silence!*' It sounds terrifying. 'But once it's done, everything is back to normal. They don't hold grudges.'

Has he met with hostility towards their work?

'One of the surprising things about their new work – and I was apprehensive: taking off one's clothes is such an enormous step, and I was very nervous about the reception – was that most people accepted it without question! Families take their children, who love it; the only coyness comes from the parents. Now they're rediscovering, re-examining. The Naked Shit Pictures are more *specific*, not necessarily better, but different. One of the great things is that they keep you hanging on – what are they going to do next? A lot of artists stop trying after they're twenty-five, and stick in the same groove until they become boring, but G&G are always surprising, they even surprise themselves. I was nervous about the reaction to The Naked Shit Pictures, and surprised how the critics turned in their favour.'

Modestly, O'Daly declares: 'I'm clear where I stand with G&G. There's friendship, but I'm the worker and they're the boss, and I think and hope they appreciate that. It would be too easy to confuse the relationship – it's important to see one's role, and not to cross it. They leave themselves so open. People knock on the door, and they hate turning them away. They attract a lot of hangers-on. Artists need support, but it draws a lot of energy. They're private people when they're allowed to be. I love them. Very warm people – the happiest, most miserable people in the world!'

Raymond O'Daly's sympathy for Gilbert & George is enhanced by the similarity of his own early work at Goldsmith's to theirs, though he was not influenced by them, and as soon as he started working for them, he stopped. 'I was unhappy anyhow with what I was doing, and I had a family – the dreaded *pram in the hall*. But I'm very happy the way things are going, though I might start again.'

G&G have the intuition to surround themselves with the right people: Illeana Sonnabend in New York; Stainton Forrest at

Fournier Street; O'Daly the hangman. Conversely, they are now discouraging the large entourage that descended in force on Moscow and Beijing. 'We don't invite anyone,' Gilbert told me about the 1997–98 Paris exhibition. He shrugged: 'If they want to come, that is up to them.' I had the impression of a slight disillusionment at having had to play the piper too often. When they play, their generosity is as unreserved as Francis Bacon's. But, like Bacon, they need to conserve their energy for their work, and for special occasions.

Next evening I was collected by David Neuman and G&G and driven to the Cinema Sture for a private showing for three hundred invited guests of the *South Bank Show* about Gilbert & George, which was well-received by an appreciative audience. From there it was a short walk to the spacious apartment of the Neumans, who hosted a dinner party at which I consumed too much Brie. I hadn't quite recovered from my fall, so I took a taxi back to the hotel at 11.30 for an early night, but the cheese had done for me, and I suffered a succession of nightmares, ending up with myself as one of the last two men on earth – the other being a satanic stranger.

I met Massimo Martino at breakfast, while G&G were with the indefatigable TV crew upstairs, and was comforted to learn he had suffered from the Brie as well. Increasingly, I find that breakfast is the perfect time for research: the mind is clear, like the cream at the top of the milk, and there is the rare chance to be alone. Though we had met in Moscow I knew little about Massimo, assuming he was a collector rather than a dealer.

'I started in 1967,' he explained, 'and worked with the Galleria Galatea, who brought Francis Bacon's work to Turin.' Then in the 1980s Anthony d'Offay showed him the first G&G catalogues, and he spent 'enormous sums' on eight of their pictures, though it was not until 1993 that he started to collect them seriously – 'for my office and my home'.

'How many G&Gs do you have today?' I asked him.

He looked around almost sheepishly. 'I would not like to say this in front of them, but I own sixty of their pictures.'

Sixty! When I mentioned Anders Kold's outrage that anyone should own so many of G&G's works – though I was careful not to mention him by name – Rachel Lehmann, who had flown in from New York and joined us for breakfast, was highly amused: 'I certainly hope that I have some commercial interest in being here! What would the art market do without collectors who collect so passionately as Massimo?'

But he was less amused: 'I paid the best prices when I bought them, and no one else did. If you make with the money you must play with the money. If anyone thinks I have too many pictures by Gilbert & George, let him buy some of them, and I'd be delighted. If he could visit me it would be a pleasure to discuss selling, and he could have the pleasure of the picture.'

Meanwhile, Massimo continues to collect, in order to have one G&G picture from every year. He is contemptuous of those who collect simply in order to buy the signature. Like the philanthropy of Robert Weil and David Neuman in Stockholm, his collecting seems disturbingly altruistic.

G&G themselves have told me: 'We don't want dealers buying our work to speculate.' Perhaps they meant that they do not want to know that dealers are speculating, for otherwise they would be being remarkably naive – that is what dealers do!

When I asked Rachel Lehmann if the new Guggenheim Museum in Bilbao had bought G&G's *Blood Tears Spunk Piss* (1996), she looked irritated: 'They bought an earlier picture owned by another gallery instead. They could still buy the other, but they need to raise the funds.'

'But why do they need funds?' I persisted. 'Surely, if they're the Guggenheim, they don't *need* funds!'

'You don't understand how it works,' she sighed.

What a curiously cloak-and-dagger business the art world is! The

Swedish philanthropists I could just understand, but the idea of Massimo buying sixty pictures by G&G (and, he told me, a similar number by Francis Bacon) for his home and office (their rooms must be huge!) was almost inconceivable. How did he make a living?

G&G, still in the clutches of Swedish television, were taken to the National Museum of Arts, with myself and Massimo following. It's an impressive edifice, with a tremendous staircase with two urns at the top filled, engagingly, with grasses and wildflowers by a young woman who turned out to be a painter herself, and who had gathered them that morning. They made a welcome change from the usual stiff 'arrangement'. Vast, neo-romantic, allegorical murals decorated the walls. It was all very Nordic, and I could imagine that the artist had played the role of the grand old man of Swedish brushes at the turn of the century, and had been taken very, very seriously – not least by himself.

'Every time we go into a museum,' Gilbert whispered to me, 'we realise they are more and more boring!'

They perked up when they were shown some highly erotic nineteenth-century drawings and a picture by Carl Hill of two naked boys arm in arm, which looked very modern although it was dated 1848. Otherwise the museum's pictures were everything I dislike: a lush Boucher of the Triumph of Venus, various half-draped beauties breaking from the waves, and an inferior Oudry of a lion. The collection was redeemed, as they so often are, by a number of Impressionists which I discovered as I wandered on my own through the labyrinthine corridors: a Manet of a boy peeling a pear; a lively Toulouse-Lautrec of a rope dancer against a green background; a small painting of branches and leaves by Van Gogh; and three Russian dancers by Degas. Every artist should be allowed an off-day, and Monet and Sisley certainly had theirs here.

All, though, could be forgiven for the tiny Rembrandt self-portrait, the man looking back with a wry sceptism at the artist –

himself. Otherwise the greatest surprise was a superb seascape by August Strindberg, clearly almost as fine a painter as he was a dramatist. The Swedes must have been proud of him, yet it was tucked away.

Eventually released, G&G hurried down the staircase but were steered into the current exhibition, which was devoted to the work of Fabergé, including several eggs. G&G took one unsmiling stare from the doorway, and marched out again.

When I told them about my disappointment with the old centre of Stockholm – though a summer's day with people drinking in the open air would no doubt have enhanced it – Gilbert & George surprised me by saying that 'after India no city stands comparison'. They had gone there for Christmas in 1993 with James Birch and Kate Bernard, Jeffrey Bernard's niece. 'The most extraordinary journey,' said George. 'Nothing like it. India has something so powerful – the light and visions, like Chaucer come to life. Boys lifting up their skirts to show they're castrated; dog boys walking on all fours; and beggars, with a population of four million living on the streets.' Stockholm could hardly be a greater contrast.

We had a final lunch, probably the best of the visit, in the crowded covered market which goes back several hundred years, the happy juxtaposition of food stalls and small restaurants making me wonder why the Swedes are so slim. David Neuman had ordered in advance: red caviar, herrings, and langoustines, followed by thick slices of Swedish smoked salmon, close to gravadlax and as good as I have eaten.

The triumphant opening, with quantities of wine, took place in the early evening at Magasin 3, followed by a party on board the ancient M/S Östanå, which cruised the canals and rivers, though the waterfront was invisible in the darkness.

Every artist, it is said, grows to hate his dealer. Francis Bacon startled an elderly stage-doorman one lunchtime at the Coach and Horses, breezing in to announce that he suspected he was being cheated by the Marlborough Gallery. He may not have believed it, but felt it was time that he did. Inevitably, there comes resentment.

When Anthony d'Offay had arrived in New York for The Fundamental Pictures openings, I noticed that G&G virtually ignored him; but now, after the Stockholm opening, they ate together on board the boat. It was in Stockholm that Gilbert raised the vexed question of money: 'A lot of art is only admired because of the financial value given it. We want to go outside that. We are very controversial, but if you want to make money you don't do it with shit. d'Offay have all the money but are still jealous of our power over the viewers. We have a following which has nothing to do with money.' He conceded: 'They're very efficient at the d'Offay Gallery, better than anywhere else.'

'Awful if they didn't have any saving graces!' said George. 'But even in the planning of the exhibitions we're involved in, nearly all the preparations here were made by ourselves.'

G&G went to d'Offay with their magazine sculpture *George the Cunt & Gilbert the Shit* in 1969, when they were totally unknown and he was dealing in early twentieth-century painters like Bomberg, the Vorticists and Wyndham Lewis. Unable to exhibit the magazine sculpture for obvious reasons – fear of the police – he asked G&G to keep in touch, and they began to see a lot of each other, becoming close friends. George said, 'For five years we met at least twice a week and went to clubs.' In those days d'Offay was surprisingly trendy – much more so than he appears now. Or at least he tried to be, appearing one evening for dinner with a shoulderbag and a bright yellow suit which was so disastrous that he ended up 'rolling on the floor furiously trying to fuck it up'.

After opening his own contemporary gallery in 1980, d'Offay sought out the most important artists, travelling the world continually with this aim. Has there been a falling out?

'The trouble is he wants to be the artist,' says George. 'Let him be the best in the world at his job, but not compete with artists.'

This reveals a conflict, for how can d'Offay be in competition with G&G when he is promoting them?

'He has one problem: he wants to stick his fingers in everything.'

'Is it a happy relationship?' I asked.

'Certainly not,' said George decisively. 'Very vexed!'

They complained that d'Offay has too many artists to look after, possibly as many as fifty, which suggests that they may feel slightly left out, and are jealous. I would say that there is jealousy on both sides, and that this is the norm between artists and their dealers. Ironically, the situation is exacerbated because d'Offay's promotion of his artists is so successful. And even though G&G might bitch about him, one thing is irrefutable: would any other gallery have donated its profits from an exhibition to charities, as d'Offay did with G&G's For AIDS show in 1989? That loyalty and altruism towards the artists is astonishing, and helps to put the 'love-hate' relationship in perspective.

I flew back to London the next day with G&G and Raymond O'Daly. We took a taxi from Heathrow in the late afternoon, and the traffic jams and crowded streets were the first intimation of the vast crowds arriving for Princess Diana's funeral the following day. G&G dropped me off at my hotel in Shaftesbury Avenue, where there was a message for me to ring the *Daily Mail*.

'It's about Jeffrey Bernard,' the secretary told me.

'Yes. I'm having lunch with him tomorrow.'

She gave a gasp of dismay: 'I'm afraid you're not. He died last night.'

Jeffrey had been in very poor health, and I had posted a profile on him in advance to serve as an obituary.

'We would publish it tomorrow,' said the secretary, 'except for Diana's funeral.'

I have never seen London looking lovelier than it did the next morning. I walked down to Carlton House Terrace and joined the crowds in the Mall waiting for the funeral procession to pass. The people there were not as outwardly emotional as those picked out by the television cameras, but seemed to have been drawn there, like myself, because this was a historic occasion. I had seen my first royal funeral – George V's – from the Savage Club balcony over sixty years earlier. Now I saw the two young Princes, William's eyes cast to the ground as he walked past in line with his brother, father and grandfather.

The crowds disappeared, and I arrived at the French House, which had opened especially at eleven instead of their usual twelve o'clock, in time to watch the service in Westminster Abbey.

And then I went home.

CHAPTER FOURTEEN

WITH GILBERT & GEORGE
IN BARNSTAPLE

O f all the towns I have been in with Gilbert & George, Barnstaple in North Devon was the most unlikely.

In the summer of 1997, with remarkable unselfishness, considering the demands of their exhibitions that year, they made the arduous train journey from Paddington – where they noticed the painter Terry Frost glaring at them from the opposite platform as they signed autographs for young fans. After changing at Exeter they took the uncomfortable little train north-west to Barnstaple, through the beautifully unspoilt Devonshire countryside. They said they did not want me to meet them at the station, so while they checked in at the Imperial Hotel I waited for them on the terrace of the Commodore Hotel in Instow, across the estuary from the village of Appledore, where I live.

It was a perfect evening for their arrival, but if – as I have been told – I am the guest from hell, I am even worse when it comes to entertaining myself, for I have a knack of getting things wrong as if I were jinxed. With the host's proprietorial paranoia when G&G failed to show up, I hurried back and forth to the phone to check that they had arrived. I waited for their arrival with increasing impatience, surrounded by a Saturday wedding party. This was a posh affair, and probably cost a fortune, with the ladies having gone to a lot of trouble to look their ugliest with precarious, swooping hats, while their men perversely removed their jackets and ties as if in a gesture of defiance. They did not laugh, but brayed, and it was hard to tell if they were really having a good time or were only pretending to.

It was hot, the climax of a sizzling few days, and I had chosen the Commodore for its spectacular view of the sunset, though I began to fear that the molten ball would slip into the sea before G&G arrived. Damn them for being late and missing it! It occurred to me also that their taxi might drop them off in the road, so they would have to walk across the lawn in full view of the crowded terrace. Would the wedding guests giggle at their identical suits and robotic stride? In the event, I need not have worried: they were so smart in their full fig and ties that everyone probably assumed they were honoured guests – though hardly local: possibly from the colonies, or Germany.

G&G arrived just as the sunset indulged in its final blaze. It was so dramatic that they took photographs, which looked as if they had been taken in the West Indies when they were developed. Later, we moved to a pleasant, modest nearby hotel where I had been told that the food was outstanding. It might have been, but the woman who usually cooked it, and who ran the restaurant too, was celebrating a wedding anniversary somewhere else with her husband, who usually ran the bar, and who I had been promised would be 'a joy to meet'. Instead, their teenage daughter was deputising, and she did her best. Oh dear! Jinxed again. After the inevitable disappointment of the meal, served by sweet but inexperienced local girls, I steered G&G to the bar – which was indeed sympathetic – in the hope of salvage. I could not remember the taxi ride home, while they returned to Barnstaple.

Like all alcoholics, I dread the recriminations of the morning after: the knowing 'And how are you this morning? Feeling all right, are we?' – and the recollection of one's bad behaviour retrieved fleetingly with torn images: 'No need to worry. They were awfully decent about it.'

There is none of that with G&G, probably because they have plumbed these depths themselves. Instead they turned up immaculate the next morning and we got down to work as they told me the background of their early years, the main point of their visit. When I commented on their seemingly inexhaustible reserves of stamina they conceded that they felt 'a little bit tired – all the time – but never exhausted'. Once, when we were alone, Gilbert told me that George sometimes goes for a three-hour walk in London from Fournier Street to Hampstead and back, walking at tremendous speed – as he would have to do to cover such a distance in that time. 'That's why George is so fit!' exclaimed Gilbert admiringly. Due to a bad back he said he could not always join him, but I wondered if he would have done without it.

Surprisingly, George revealed that he had come to Appledore thirty years earlier to help the father of his ward at Oxford launch a boat. This did not prove a successful venture, as they found themselves sailing in circles in the estuary, their ropes and anchor snared, and had to turn back once they were freed. George remembered a verse framed outside the Seamen's Mission, but though the building was still there, the prayer had gone.

Suspecting that I wanted to hold a party in their honour, G&G had warned me that they had no wish to meet anyone in the village. I should have respected this, but I knew all along that I would not be able to resist showing them off, and they yielded gracefully, first in the Royal, then at the Champion of Wales, where various friends were looking forward to meeting them, impressed and curious after the recent *South Bank Show* films on television. As always, I was intrigued by G&G's chameleonic adaptability. Self-contained yet also shy, they feel their way in strange surroundings, and do not like to commit themselves easily to strangers. They are on parade so often that they must be consistently on their guard, though they deny this, deflating invitations from strangers to visit and even stay with them with a warm 'We'd love to,' though they have no intention of going. This leaves everyone happier than before they met them.

In the Champ they were ill at ease to start with – they are more at home in restaurants than pubs – but they relaxed as they felt the genuine interest in them.

This was exemplified by my closest friend in the village, Lance Oliver, a wild young artist who refuses to paint but who possesses the best 'eye' of anyone I know, and who helped me immeasurably when I was an art critic. His daughter was a fan of G&G, but he was unsure until he met them: 'I couldn't get over how well they seem to fit in with everybody, and that Appledore types didn't bat an eyelid. Very strange! They didn't try to monopolise talk, not even their own art work, let alone anybody else's. My overall impression of them is of a very generous and amusing couple.' With his usual candour, Lance asked what would happen to one of them if the other 'buggered off'.

'That will never happen,' George told him.

'But if something should happen to one of you?'

'We'll go together.'

Lance even referred to an incident which I had told him about in confidence: a nightmare occasion a few years earlier when George was visiting the West Country, presumably to see his family. One afternoon he was walking along a Torquay cliff-path when it started to rain, and he sheltered in a public lavatory. He returned to his hotel, and a couple of hours later the police arrived to check on any single male guests. It transpired that a child had been raped on the cliff-tops around the time George had been there: 'I spent a terrifying couple of hours, which was resolved when a fifteen-year-old tourist confessed to the whole thing.' George was able to leave after profuse apologies from the police, but 'It was a very nasty moment.'

In today's climate, almost any dealings with children – which should be so innocent – are fraught with risk. Gilbert admitted that they would have liked to use more children as models, 'but for a while that became very dangerous. People came close to saying we were going to molest them.'

George: 'You can ask children if you know the parents, then they're delighted to bring their little Johnny round to be a model.'

Wolf Jahn asked them what their interest was in the children.

'Innocence.'

We moved on to my home on the estuary, where we had a spontaneous party – though I had organised a whole salmon from Chris Sylvester, the fishmonger who lives in the cottage next door, prepared by his girlfriend Karen. It was one of the most cheerful parties I have ever given, due to the high spirits of Gilbert & George, who completed the day with that delightful, silly ditty with which they ended their *South Bank Show*, complete with robotic gestures:

> 'My mommy is a baker,
> Yum yummy, yum yummy.
> My daddy is a dentist,
> Uh uh uh, uh uh uh.
> My sister is a show-off,
> Hokey-pokey, hokey, pokey.
> My brother is a cowboy,
> Look this way, look that way,
> Bang bang!'

Pointless and hilarious.

Gilbert & George returned glowingly to the Imperial Hotel in Barnstaple, leaving everybody in Appledore happy and impressed.

The next morning they stopped their taxi at Chris Sylvester's fish shop to thank him for the salmon. George described what happened next. The estuary was at high tide, shafts of sunlight penetrated the early mist, and the entire scene was elegiac as they walked past the church, where the graveyard was bright with spring flowers. A beautiful girl and a handsome young man sat on the wall with their baby, such a heart-warming sight that George raised his Panama hat, smiled and said 'Good morning!'

The young man turned on them viciously: 'Fuck off, you weird-looking twats!'

George added: '*That's* why I left the West Country.'

I spoke to my friends about the incident, and they were outraged. 'They weren't locals,' said Lance. When I told George this, he laughed – 'Oh yes they were!'

After the happiness and innocence of the day before, this was a sad let-down. It is possible that George was mistaken, and that the young man – George said his girlfriend had flinched from his rudeness – was not local. Certainly I heard no word of who he might have been. Indeed, the more I think about the incident, the more surprised I am. Possibly the young man just happened to be in a vile temper. Or was it George's smart Panama hat, which he bought at Eastbourne several years earlier to protect his bald head from the sun – 'Would sir consider a Panama?' he was asked. Or was it the identical suits? In Barnstaple I had noticed that people looked back at us as we passed, and there is no denying that G&G looked conspicuous. It would be surprising if their appearance did not attract attention. Ironically, or perhaps significantly, when they walked down Fournier Street for the *South Bank Show*, their faces and hands painted bright red, they were ignored by the surrounding crowd of men leaving a mosque. Presumably they had higher things on their minds, and knew that appearances should not be held against anyone.

Yet, George's hurt made me realise how sensitive and vulnerable he is.

CHAPTER FIFTEEN

WITH GILBERT & GEORGE IN PARIS

I t was in Paris, of all places, that I lost my *panache*. I also lost the chance of close encounters with Gilbert & George. Apart from the fact of their being mobbed by a growing entourage, this was partly due to breakfast, a meal the French tend to despise, while recognising that it is the one in which the British excel. Breakfast times in the elegant dining-room of the SoHo Grand in New York, or the small but sympathetic room in the Esplanade in Stockholm, were happy occasions, and extremely useful opportunities to talk to G&G *tête-à-tête*, but breakfast in a Paris hotel is a hole-and-corner affair in the corner of the foyer, where it is difficult to talk. In any case, we were staying in different hotels. This was due to G&G's travel agent, whom I knew only as a thin, sanctimonious voice on the answerphone who terminated an interminable message with a smarmy 'Thank you.' He proved the most incompetent agent I have ever come across.

Generous as ever, G&G had invited me to Paris as their guest, but when I rang the agent a girl assistant told me that a second-class return on the Shuttle cost £275. I checked with Eurostar, who were

highly amused: 'They're mad! It's £89 return.' I gave the agent the
name of two hotels – the Saint-Germain-des-Prés, which I had liked
on my visit to see the Bacon exhibition at the Pompidou earlier in
the year, and the Hôtel Chambellas, where G&G were staying. He
protested that neither hotel was in his 'special list', as if they were
so far beneath him that I demeaned him by such a request. I
suggested he should phone them anyway, and he came back triumphantly to say they were full. This was true, though if I had rung
them myself a few weeks earlier there would have been no problem.
Now it was Paris's busiest time in the year, with the *pret à porter*
fashion week and a further invasion of twenty thousand race-goers
arriving for the Prix de l'Arc de Triomphe at Longchamp. Such
crowds added to the excitement of the city, but made the quest for
somewhere to sleep a nightmare. The agent promised to get back
to me, but I never heard from him again, though I left a message
on his machine when I returned to Devon, asking him to invoice
me, for it seemed unfair to impose further on G&G.

Guilt was involved, as it usually is with me. More even than
before, G&G already had too many demands on their time, without
having to worry about my hotel. Alexander Roussos confirmed that
the hotel situation in Paris was a nightmare – 'This is the most
crowded week of the year' – and told me he had abandoned the
attempt to find somewhere to stay on Saturday night, as I did too.
But then G&G, with their usual acerbity, told me they had looked
into several hotels near their own, and were told there were rooms
available. I found this hard to believe, for I had tried at least twenty
hotels all over Paris, and had invariably been met by the satisfied
cry of 'Complet!'

Meanwhile, with his characteristic efficiency, Noel Botham of
the French House in Soho had phoned a contact in Paris, and he
had booked me into the pleasant Élysées Mermoz near the Champs
Élysées (though he had been unable to get me a room there for
the Saturday night). Fortunately I had written to G&G saying I
would meet them at their hotel, to be on the safe side, and I received

a letter from Margot Heller of the d'Offay Gallery confirming that she had told them I would be arriving soon after 12.30 on Sunday, and that I had invited them to lunch. In retrospect, I realise this was presumptuous of me at a time when they must have been so preoccupied with cameras and journalists, but I didn't think of that at the time.

When I arrived at G&G's hotel there was no sign of them, nor was there any message. As Margot had warned me about their heavy schedule of interviews, I assumed they must be held up in a television studio somewhere, and left a message for them to join me at a delightful bistro I had found around the corner from the hotel. I ate alone, which always feels like failure, though the place was small, crowded and happy.

When I checked into my hotel there were no messages, so I went out to have a glass of champagne at the Ritz, which I found as common as muck, with a lady harpist playing in an inside garden; admittedly rather well – you have to be gracious to play the harp. Impulsively I asked at reception if Michael Cole was staying there, having spoken to him at the recent launch party in Harrods for Punch, which had been revived by Mohammed al-Fayed. They had never heard of him, and when I explained that he was al-Fayed's spokesman, they shook their heads – 'Who?'

'He owns the joint!' I said incredulously.

Lured by the description I had read in the Daily Telegraph of Harry's New York Bar in the nearby rue Daunou as 'the quintessential American-in-Paris watering hole that calls itself Europe's oldest cocktail bar', I moved on, and found it sympathetic, evidently popular with journalists. But when I mentioned the unfortunate Henri Paul, the driver who was killed with Princess Diana and Dodi Fayed, the previously friendly barman told me abruptly that Paul never drank there. Understandably, he must have thought I was yet another investigator, though a few minutes later a Scottish journalist told me, 'That's nonsense! Henri was a regular, drank here all the time.'

Hating to be alone, I continued by taxi to Saint-Germain-des-Prés to indulge in an extravagant *Coupe de Dom Perignon* at the Café Flore, in the hope that the claim would be proven that if you waited there long enough you were bound to meet someone you knew. Indeed, that had been the case three years earlier when I sat there drinking gently after the Francis Bacon private view, and was joined by the American artist Peter Beard, who recognised me, and later by Norman Rosenthal, Exhibitions Secretary of the Royal Academy of Arts. This time, though, I knew nobody, and though I smiled wistfully, no one showed the slightest interest in me. Everybody seemed busily in love.

Finally I moved on to Fouquet's in the Champs Élysées, where I hoped to meet up with Gilbert & George. I was joined there by Margot Heller and her friend Michael, and was thankful for their company as we sat on the terrace and talked while evening drew in. But by the time they took me to the restaurant where the others were waiting, I was worn out, and I returned to my hotel though I had caught up with Gilbert & George at last. They were as friendly as ever, in spite of the day's confusion and frustration.

Paris herself, as ever, was radiant. Once I asked George Melly why we fall in love with the city every time we return. It sounds a fatuous question, but George gave an instant explanation: we first came to Paris just after the war, when London was sour and fatigued. We tasted new foods, and drank good wine, and enjoyed sex without a twinge of British guilt. Now, nearly fifty years later, Paris still looks much the same, the marvellous buildings more tempered by time, so we are not just returning to the city we fell in love with, but are returning to our youth. It is not Paris which changes, but ourselves.

On one of my first visits, fifty years earlier, I woke in a brass bed with bolsters to be served breakfast on a tray: croissants and the most delicious, darkest coffee I have tasted before or since, with accompanying confiture and a small jug of hot milk. Outside, the street market was coming to life. To make it perfect, I was not alone – though today I would dread finding a body in bed beside me. The French maid who brought the breakfast showed no surprise, even though the body was black – he was from Martinique.

Breakfast in Paris hotels may no longer be the pleasure it was, but I was relieved, as always, to find how familiar the city itself was when I left the hotel at 7.30 a.m. and walked down the rue Jean Mermoz, which was starting to do business. The butcher's shop next door to the hotel was glowing with fresh red meat, which reminded me with a twinge of shame that not a single butcher is left in Soho. On the corner the boulangerie was already busy serving a cascade of customers, many of them running in from their parked and still-running vehicles, while local women bustled in with trays of home-made pastries covered with a white cloth. Everyone was smiling.

At the top of the Faubourg-Saint-Honoré, which gave no hint at this point of the fashionable chic higher up, the road divided, creating a small island in the centre where a man slept above a hot-air grid next to a kiosk where I bought an English newspaper. It was now eight o'clock, and two café bars were open, with men drinking beer. I ordered a large coffee and *oeufs et jambon*, with the eggs running over the thinly sliced, lightly cooked ham, unique to France, as I realised when I tried to emulate them back home. On my second morning I went to the opposite bar, where they were identical, with the advantage of a family dog.

In every place the French made me welcome, pleased to please. I thought yet again that the British are insane in their antipathy towards the Parisians, accusing them of being venal because they give excellent service and expect to be paid for it. Instead I have always found an instinctive friendliness: beer and eggs and bacon at eight – how civilised. Those two breakfasts were among the most satisfying moments of my stay.

One of the more disappointing was lunch later that day with

G&G outside the canteen of the Musée d'art moderne de la Ville de Paris, where their exhibition was being held. It proved that a canteen is a canteen is a canteen the world over, even in Paris. After an interminable delay, the harassed waiter deposited a plate of salade niçoise on my table. It was not helped by the absence of any dressing, when it should have been drenched in olive oil. Apparently the new cuisine dictates that oil and vinegar are unacceptable, and that lettuce is healthier if it tastes of the soil it came from – as this did.

Referring to this book, George turned to me at one point to assure me kindly that he did not mind what opinions I expressed: 'We only care about the facts. I don't mind about opinions.'

A moment later, Gilbert whispered gleefully: 'Oh yes he does mind!' and wiped away invisible tears.

All of 1997 had been leading up to this retrospective. The shows in New York, Tokyo and Stockholm reached their culmination in Paris at the beginning of October. With their usual prescience, G&G had been ecstatic from the outset, realising that an exhibition on this scale and in such a setting would be the fulfilment of everything they had been working towards. There was one hiccup: the charming young directress, Suzanne Pagé, had been anxious to exhibit G&G ever since she had seen the reaction to their work in London a few years earlier, noticing their special appeal to the young. But she had to tell them, 'Unfortunately I cannot give you the ground floor of the main gallery, which is reserved for dead artists.'

Without blinking – though he must have been dismayed – George suggested: 'If we were run over by a lorry, would that be all right?'

She laughed, and they were in – on the ground floor.

'The Germans always think they know better,' said Gilbert. 'They want to dominate; but we've only met with friendliness from the French.'

Seeing the exhibition with G&G on the morning before the opening, when the galleries were blessedly free of crowds, the wildest of the familiar superlatives were fully justified: 'Unbeliev-able, don't you think!' Gilbert exulted. 'We've never seen anything like it.' They looked like children who had just won the prize at a party.

As usual, Raymond O'Daly had melted into the background, though I saw him briefly later, looking stressed. Delighted with the close hanging, Gilbert said, 'We don't like a lot of white space around the pictures as most artists do. We like them close together, so that the whole room starts to speak.' After he had pointed this out, I could see what a crucial difference it made.

There was the special excitement of work I had not seen before, some of it not even in reproduction. The early black-and-white pictures of the East End were overwhelming in their scale, yet their strength lay in the startling simplicity, which was so bold in the *Dead Boards* pictures (1976) that many of them were exactly that – bare wooden boards and nothing else. Depicting themselves in casual, sometimes hands-in-pockets positions rather than the later full-frontals, G&G seem caught rather than carefully posed, creating a mood of melancholy wistfulness which was curiously disturbing. I wondered if their description of themselves as 'deeply unhappy artists' might be true after all. The title of the work *Living with Madness* (1980) is calculated: 'Everyone identifies with it,' says George. The 'madman' was a passer-by in the street who gave permission for them to take his picture. They resent the allegations that they have taken advantage of hooligans in the East End: 'Not at all. Fantastic people!'

One of the most impressive sights that morning was the notorious picture *Queer* (1977), which I had assumed would be as provocative as its title. Instead, the word is scrawled in white chalk as if on a wall, with images of broken windows below, and full-length portraits of G&G and two desperate down-and-outs, their faces half averted. In mocking contrast, the foreground is a pristine landscape of the new London: a mix of modern skyscrapers and churches, including St Paul's.

By contrast, *Light Headed* (1991) is almost a conventional land-scape, or seascape. The title comes from the lighthouse at the end of the bay – unless it is a factory chimney! The picture was used for the cover of the Lugano catalogue in 1994 (Museo d'Arte Moderna della Citta di Lugano). A boat is near the water, and G&G's bright-yellow faces rest on their crimson hands.

That evening, as I watched the enraptured attention of the French crowds, it was an effort to remember that G&G's work was as alien to them as it had been in Moscow or Shanghai. The Parisians studied the coloured magazine sculpture of *George the Cunt & Gilbert the Shit*, displayed inside a glass case as if it were an ancient artefact, with respect rather than sensationalism.

Seeing such a magnificent progression revealing the variety and versatility of G&G's art, there was no hint of the charges of sensationalism that might be levelled at a single picture. Instead, the viewer was led forward through experiment and new technique until the fulfilment and final poignancy of the small last room, which took us right back to the beginning with the 1970 Charcoal on Paper Sculptures shown in the Bordeaux retrospective in 1986 but rarely seen since. With touching naivety, the paper is badly – perhaps deliberately – stained, and the portrayal of G&G beside a tree overlooking a river (George carries a stick) is infinitely forlorn. The text reads: *Forever we will search and give our thought to the picture we have in our mind. We are walking round now as sad as can be.* On either side of the door leading into this room at the Musée were two full-length primitive portraits of G&G with the delightful title *All My Life I Give You Nothing and Still You Ask for More*.

The contrast with *Street* (1983), which was used for the posters which now plastered Paris unnervingly, G&G's crimson faces screaming against a livid green background, suggested how their work had come full circle. I found myself experiencing something like a sense of loss. For G&G the total triumph of this retrospective was the start of a new beginning, probably venturing further into the microscopic world – but for me it was the end of the journey.

That night I was no longer a participant but an observer, as an estimated eight thousand Parisians descended on the Musée clutching their invitation cards. Going outside two and a half hours later to get some air, I saw several hundred people still queuing on the steps. Inside, G&G were hemmed in as they signed hundreds of catalogues. Understandably, for this was their night, they were relishing the kisses, the autograph hunters, the flashbulbs and the video screens perpetually displaying them screaming at each other while alternately sticking out their tongues. It was totally different from the 1994 Bacon retrospective at the Pompidou. That was adoration and respect. Here was the excitement of work entirely new.

When G&G greeted me as punctiliously as ever, I was embarrassed for the first time by their introductions: 'Daniel is a very famous writer in England!' – a debatable claim which meant absolutely nothing, and which was received with a blanket of suspicious stares which made me feel an impostor, separate from the idolatry surrounding them, unable to join in with the old exuberance.

There was a party afterwards, with a buffet and wine, delayed for an hour to deter potential gatecrashers. The razzmatazz and celebrations continued until I took myself off to the sympathetic Jazz Bar at Saint-Germain, where I sang Hoagy Carmichael's 'Georgia'.

The next morning I joined G&G at the British Embassy, where the Ambassador had invited us for drinks. It was an unexpectedly magnificent building, bought from Napoleon's sister Eugenie by the Duke of Wellington in 1815, when he was briefly Ambassador to Paris himself, until Napoleon returned from Elba and he prepared to face him. As we walked in the spacious grounds with English lawns in the heart of Paris, the Ambassador told me that by the time the Germans occupied Paris in 1940 the Embassy staff had all been evacuated, leaving behind an aged caretaker. When the soldiers knocked on the heavy, locked doors, this heroic man opened them only to say that they would not be admitted, and had to leave. Surprisingly, they obeyed. In August 1944 the occupying force departed, and there came another knock on the door. This time it was the British, who had returned. 'I've been expecting you,' said the caretaker. 'Would you like some tea?'

'I hope he was given an award,' I said.

'Funnily enough, that's exactly what Robin Cook [the Foreign Secretary] said at breakfast this morning. Yes, the man was given an MBE.'

I am surprised that his story is not better known.

I had never seen G&G as happy as they were that day. George confided: 'We were so excited we woke up every half-hour throughout the night to make sure it really happened.'

'Unbelievable,' echoed Gilbert, almost jumping for joy. 'Don't you think?'

The directress came straight from the museum with the news that young people were starting to queue for entry before the doors had even opened. Word was spreading that this exhibition was particularly for them, an event to go to and to be seen at.

Though I felt closer to G&G than ever, it was somehow like the end of a long love affair. They had to go to the Musée for more interviews, but I decided suddenly that it was time for me to go home. This meant I would miss the party being held in their honour by their Austrian dealer in Paris, Thaddeus Ropac – one banquet too far. I knew it was the end of my journey, and I needed to banish my sense of melancholy.

CHAPTER SIXTEEN

SENSATION?

The day before I took the Shuttle to Paris, I had seen Norman Rosenthal at the Royal Academy. The last time we met was at the Café Flore during the Francis Bacon exhibition at the Pompidou in June 1994. Outside his normal territory, Rosenthal was outgoing, friendly and humorous, his conversation vastly different from the snarled reaction I remembered from years earlier when I asked him why he had excluded Augustus John from the RA's major exhibition of twentieth-century British art.

Now, slouched behind his desk in his charmless office in the Academy, I remembered his other persona, which had earned him the title 'the Himmler of the arts', though he bore no physical resemblance to the severe, bespectacled Nazi whom Francis Bacon always claimed to find physically attractive.

It was understandable that Rosenthal was not in the most relaxed of moods, indeed it was kind of him to see me at all, for at the time he was being held responsible for perhaps the worst scandal to afflict the Academy this century, due to its current exhibition with the apt title of Sensation. Three Royal Academicians had resigned in protest, including the gentle Craigie Aitchison, who did so quietly, and the sculptor Ralph Brown, who called for Rosenthal's resignation and vowed in a letter to the President, Sir Philip Dowson, that he would 'exert every effort to get rid of him'. The eighty-year-old traditionalist figurative painter John Ward said of Sensation: 'I can't bear it. It is rubbish. Art should be about love, about generosity, about workmanship, about craft. My generation was more tolerant. [Judging by his own reaction, this is arguable.] These modernists are intolerant and they just want to stick their tongues out. They care nothing for people's feelings.' Ward had submitted to Rosenthal's power as the RA's Exhibitions Secretary for twenty years, but when Rosenthal declared in a television interview that he doubted if posterity would regard his work kindly, Ward announced his resignation.

The *cause-célèbre* which had most outraged public opinion was the inclusion in Sensation of Marcus Harvey's 1995 portrait of the moors murderer Myra Hindley, based on the infamous photograph which showed her with dyed blonde hair. The fury of the parents whose children had been killed by Hindley and her accomplice Ian Brady was understandable. The picture was composed of the handprints of small children, and at first it was assumed that dozens of tots had been rounded up to press the canvas and form the image – which would have been a difficult process. In fact a single template had been used, though this did not lessen the shock of Harvey's subject matter which was deliberately provocative. In the prevailing atmosphere of hysteria, I found the impact of the original (which had had to be removed for repairs after it was vandalised by two members of the public) impressive, due to its sheer scale and boldness.

More offensive to me were the sculptures by Dinos and Jake Chapman of childlike female mannequins with enlarged vaginas, anuses and penises instead of mouths and noses. There was also a painting of the Virgin Mary surrounded by pornographic photos of genitalia. Worst of all to my mind was the mattress with an erect cucumber and two oranges in the middle to represent the male organs. It was so silly, so utterly pointless that I have forgotten the name of the woman artist.

This was the revelation to me: that so much of Sensation was old hat. I had seen many of the exhibits before in the Saatchi Gallery, such as Damien Hirst's shark and Marc Quinn's head cast in his own frozen blood, and this was another grievance on the part of the critics, if not of the public.

Largely as a consequence of the controversy it attracted, the show was a triumph financially and for Rosenthal personally, and gave the shaky and debt-laden Academy the windfall it needed so desperately. But, I wondered, was this what Sir Joshua Reynolds had had in mind when he declared in 1780: 'The Art which we profess has beauty for its object; this it is our business to discover and to express; but the beauty of which we are in quest is general and intellectual; it is an idea that subsists only in the mind; the sight never beheld it, nor has the hand expressed it.'

No less an authority than Sir Ernst Gombrich, arguably the twentieth century's most eminent art historian, author of the classic The Story of Art, defended Sensation, pointing out that critics and Academicians should not 'abuse those who have different opinions'. At the same time he stated his belief that such avant-garde work would be forgotten in fifty years' time, relegated to museum storerooms.

This was the lesson of the exhibits in Sensation when the show was stripped of its crowd-pulling controversy: that they were ultimately of fleeting interest, many of them thrown together in a few minutes. It was all too easy, the subject more important than the execution. How ephemeral they seemed compared to the work of Gilbert & George, which appears so youthful and original by comparison. That was why I had come to see Norman Rosenthal: to ask if Sensation had ruled out G&G's chances of being shown in the RA's Sackler Gallery, as had been proposed a few years ago. He leant back in his swivel chair, and looked uncomfortable: 'I couldn't find the consensus among the members of the Royal Academy today,' he said.

Because of the content of The Naked Shit Pictures, and the recent fuss about the Myra Hindley painting, this could well be true. But does this mean G&G have been bypassed?

'Not at all, except that sons are never nice to their fathers, and they are among the fathers and mothers today – I leave it to you to decide which is which.' With a burst of enthusiasm, he declared: 'The Brits are coming. They're taking over, they're sweeping the world, and G&G are like two John the Baptists. Would you like to be baptised by St George or St Gilbert?'

As I found this question unanswerable, I asked Rosenthal how he saw G&G's role in the future.

'Nobody knows about the next century. I find them slightly dangerous, beautiful, sexy. They've made images which make you think. I think they're very useful. Feeling is important, compassion is important. They've created a language unmistakably their own, which gives them the incredible freedom to make the images they want. We are very glad they exist. The world would be poorer without them.'

28 October 1997

Gilbert & George phoned me at eight in the morning, still in a state of post-Paris euphoria: 'They estimate that seven or eight thousand came to the opening.'

'It's a totally amazing response,' says Gilbert. 'The most amazing thing they've ever done.'

George says the crowds are so big that the directress wants them to return.

Unexpectedly, Gilbert admitted that he did not find the Musée or its location wholly sympathetic, unlike the Pompidou. 'It has an identity crisis,' he adds mysteriously, but I know exactly what he means. This helps to explain my own antipathy to the monumental, almost Teutonic edifice across the Seine from the Eiffel Tower. I am relieved it is not just my current cussedness.

Switching subjects as they hand the phone back and forth, one to the other, George tells me as a complete non-sequitur that a total of 250 articles were published about them in Tokyo – 'Normally it's sixty.'

Gilbert admits that for once they're exhausted. Their stamina must have been stretched to the limit, yet still they find it impossible to say 'no'. The previous week had seen the publication of *The Words of Gilbert & George*, and it had received unusually widespread coverage, especially as it contains little that is new – but that is not the point of it. It featured in a two-page profile in the *Evening Standard*, with a pleasing photo of G&G sitting on swings in a playground, and they were the lead cover story in the *Guardian Weekend*, spread over seven pages. I congratulate Gilbert out of politeness, and he assures me, 'There's more, much more!' – a TV interview with Mariella Frostrup and another with Paul Ross (the brother of Jonathan), whom they like: 'Very sensitive,' says George. Their recent praise for William Hague has also been widely quoted: 'He's fantastic. It's wonderful to have three lower-class Conservative leaders in a row.'

I increasingly fear that the deluge of publicity, interviews and photographs about themselves, Fournier Street and their lives will eclipse their actual work. Isn't this the wrong way round?

29 October 1997. 5 a.m.

Something odd is happening to me, apart from the inevitable wear and tear. With Chris and Karen away on holiday, I am looking after their collie dog Heidi, who misses them painfully, while I seize the opportunity to give my body and mind a needed if undeserved rest. But it is not working out like that. In the first place, time seems out of joint, especially now that the clocks have gone back. Also, to escape the freezing cold and east wind which is making 'walkies' a punishment, I go to bed soon after eight, intending to read Tess of the d'Urbervilles, but I fall asleep instantly, missing the few decent television programmes after 9 o'clock, unless my video has decided to be co-operative.

This is no hardship, except for the added aggravation of having to get up to pee several times a night due to my prostate. But last night, presumably soon after midnight, I woke suddenly, as if struck by an internal explosion of noise and fire, yet with no preparatory dream or nightmare, so it was confusing to sort out the reality. The landscape I was in was bleakly Scandinavian, redolent of Munch, with an interminable flat coastline and deathless sea washed in sepia, down which Gilbert and I walked together with no other sign of life. Inland – and this was baffling – it seemed an alien, unrecognisable world, with the top of the picture sliced off as if by masking paper. I believe George was there, somewhere. All this without sound. At last I summoned the effort to brave the cold, turn on the gas cylinder, make myself a cup of hot lemon and water, and return thankfully to bed and to *Tess*, who gradually calmed me down. So much for sobriety and behaving well, which is more of an effort than behaving badly, and does not seem to work. I shall see how I feel at the end of the week, but suspect I shall go out to the pubs to see Lance, accompanied by Heidi, who enjoys pubs as much as I do, while providing the responsibility of getting her safely home again.

On 27 November our dear Daniel died, not knowing how much we loved him (though we told him often enough).

Gilbert & George
London, 1998

EXHIBITIONS OF GILBERT & GEORGE

GALLERY EXHIBITIONS

1968
Three Works/Three Works, Frank's Sandwich Bar, London
Snow Show, St Martin's School of Art, London
Bacon 32, Allied Services, London
Christmas Show, Robert Fraser Gallery, London

1969
Anniversary, Frank's Sandwich Bar, London
Shit and Cunt, Robert Fraser Gallery, London

1970
George by Gilbert & Gilbert by George, Fournier Street, London
The Pencil on Paper Descriptive Works, Konrad Fischer Gallery, Düsseldorf

Art Notes and Thoughts, Art & Project, Amsterdam
Frozen into the Nature for You Art, Françoise Lambert Gallery, Milan
The Pencil on Paper Descriptive Works, Folker Skulima Gallery, Berlin
Frozen into the Nature for You Art, Heiner Friedrich Gallery, Cologne
To be with Art is All We Ask, Nigel Greenwood Gallery, London

1971
There Were Two Young Men, Sperone Gallery, Turin
The General Jungle, Sonnabend Gallery, New York
The Ten Speeches, Nigel Greenwood Gallery, London
New Photo-Pieces, Art & Project, Amsterdam

1972
New Photo-Pieces, Konrad Fischer
Gallery, Düsseldorf
Three Sculptures on Video Tape, Gerry
Schum Video Gallery, Düsseldorf
The Bar, Anthony d'Offay Gallery,
London
The Evening before the Morning after,
Nigel Greenwood Gallery, London
*It Takes a Boy to Understand a Boy's Point
of View*, Situation Gallery, London
A New Sculpture, Sperone Gallery,
Rome

1973
Any Port in a Storm, Sonnabend
Gallery, Paris
New Decorative Works, Sperone
Gallery, Turin
Reclining Drunk, Nigel Greenwood
Gallery, London
Modern Rubbish, Sonnabend Gallery,
New York

1974
Drinking Sculptures, Art & Project/
MTL Gallery, Antwerp
Human Bondage, Konrad Fischer
Gallery, Düsseldorf
Dark Shadow, Art & Project,
Amsterdam; Nigel Greenwood
Gallery, London
Cherry Blossom, Sperone Gallery,
Rome

1975
Bloody Life, Sonnabend Gallery,
Paris; Sonnabend Gallery, Geneva;
Lucio Amelio Gallery, Naples
Post Card Sculptures, Sperone
Westwater Fischer, New York

Bad Thoughts, Gallery Spillemaekers,
Brussels
Dusty Corners, Art Agency, Tokyo

1976
Dead Boards, Sonnabend Gallery,
New York
Mental, Robert Self Gallery,
London; Robert Self Gallery,
Newcastle

1977
Red Morning, Sperone Fischer
Gallery, Basel
New Photo-Pieces, Art & Project,
Amsterdam; Konrad Fischer
Gallery, Düsseldorf

1978
New Photo-Pieces, Dartington Hall
Gallery, Dartington Hall;
Sonnabend Gallery, New York;
Art Agency, Tokyo

1980
Post Card Sculptures, Art & Project,
Amsterdam; Konrad Fischer
Gallery, Düsseldorf
New Photo-Pieces, Karen & Jean
Bernier Gallery, Athens;
Sonnabend Gallery, New York
Modern Fears, Anthony d'Offay
Gallery, London

1981
Photo-Pieces 1980–1981, Chantal
Crousel Gallery, Paris

1982
Crusade, Anthony d'Offay Gallery,
London

1983
Modern Faith, Sonnabend Gallery,
New York
Photo-Pieces 1980–1982, David
Bellman Gallery, Toronto
New Works, Crousel-Hussenot
Gallery, Paris

1984
The Believing World, Anthony
d'Offay Gallery, London
Hands Up, Gallery Schellmann &
Klüser, Munich
Lives, Gallery Pieroni, Rome

1985
New Moral Works, Sonnabend
Gallery, New York

1987
The 1986 Pictures, Sonnabend
Gallery, New York
New Pictures, Anthony d'Offay
Gallery, London
Gilbert & George Pictures, Aldrich
Museum of Contemporary Art,
Connecticut

1988
The 1988 Pictures, Ascan Crone
Gallery, Hamburg; Sonnabend
Gallery, New York

1989
The 1988 Pictures, Christian Stein
Gallery, Milan
For AIDS Exhibition, Anthony
d'Offay Gallery, London

1990
Gilbert & George, Hirschl and Adler
Modern, New York
Twenty-five Worlds by Gilbert & George,
Robert Miller Gallery, New York
The Cosmological Pictures, Sonnabend
Gallery, New York
Worlds & Windows, Anthony
d'Offay Gallery, London
*Eleven Worlds by Gilbert & George and
Antique Clocks*, Désiré Feuerle
Gallery, Cologne

1991
20th Anniversary Exhibition,
Sonnabend Gallery, New York

1992
New Democratic Pictures, Anthony
d'Offay Gallery, London

1994
Gilbert & George, Robert Miller
Gallery, New York
New Shit Pictures, Galerie Jablonka,
Cologne

1995
Gilbert & George, Galerie Nikolas
Sonne, Berlin
The Naked Shit Pictures, South
London Art Gallery, London

1997
The Fundamental Pictures, Sonnabend
Gallery, Lehmann Maupin, New
York

MUSEUM EXHIBITIONS

1971
The Paintings (with Us in the Nature), Whitechapel Art Gallery, London; Stedelijk Museum, Amsterdam; Kunstverein, Düsseldorf

1972
The Paintings (with Us in the Nature), Koninklijk Museum voor Schone Kunsten, Antwerp

1973
The Shrubberies & Singing Sculpture, National Gallery of New South Wales, John Kaldor Project, Sydney; National Gallery of Victoria, John Kaldor Project, Melbourne

1976
The General Jungle, Albright-Knox Art Gallery, Buffalo

1980
Photo-Pieces 1971–1980, Stedelijk van Abbemuseum, Eindhoven

1981
Photo-Pieces 1971-1980, Kunsthalle, Düsseldorf; Kunsthalle, Bern; Musée national d'art moderne, Centre Georges Pompidou, Paris; Whitechapel Art Gallery, London

1982
New Photo-Pieces, Gewad Gallery, Ghent

1984
Gilbert & George, Baltimore Museum of Art; Contemporary Arts Museum, Houston; Norton Gallery of Art, West Palm Beach, Florida

1985
Gilbert & George, Milwaukee Art Museum; Solomon R. Guggenheim Museum, New York

1986
Pictures 1982 to 1985, Musée d'art contemporain, Bordeaux
Charcoal on Paper Sculptures 1970 to 1974, Musée d'art contemporain, Bordeaux
The Paintings 1971, Fruitmarket Gallery, Edinburgh
Pictures 1982 to 1985, Kunsthalle, Basel

1987
Pictures 1982 to 1985, Palais des Beaux-Arts, Brussels; Palacio Velásquez, Madrid; Lenbachhaus, Munich; Hayward Gallery, London
Pictures, Aldrich Museum, Connecticut

1990
Pictures 1983–1988, Central House of the Artists, New Tretyakov Gallery, Moscow

1991
The Cosmological Pictures, Palac
Sztuki, Krakow; Palazzo delle
Esposizioni, Rome

1992
The Cosmological Pictures, Kunsthalle,
Zurich; Wiener Sezession, Vienna;
Ernst Muzeum, Budapest; Haags
Gemeentemuseum, The Hague;
Aarhus Kunstmuseum, Denmark;
Irish Museum of Modern Art,
Royal Hospital Kilmainham,
Dublin; Fundació Joan Miró,
Barcelona

1993
The Cosmological Pictures, Tate
Gallery, Liverpool;
Württembergischer Kunstverein,
Stuttgart
Gilbert & George: China Exhibition,
National Art Gallery, Beijing; The
Art Museum, Shanghai

1994
Gilbert & George, Museo d'Arte
Moderna della Citta di Lugano
Shitty Naked Human World,
Kunstmuseum, Wolfsburg

1996
Gilbert & George, Galleria d'Arte
Moderna, Bologna

1997
Gilbert & George: Art For All 1971–
1996, Sezon Museum of Art,
Tokyo
Gilbert & George, Magasin 3
Stockholm Konsthall, Stockholm
Gilbert & George, ARC Musée d'art
moderne de la Ville de Paris,
Paris

1998
The New Testamental Pictures, Galerie
Thaddeus Ropac, Paris/Salzburg
The Complete New Testamental Pictures,
Museo Capo di Monte, Naples.